THE ULTIMATE BACKCOUNTRY TRAVEL

Michael Lanza

Also available from Appalachian Mountain Club Books...

Trail Guides

Guide to Mount Desert Island and Acadia National Park
Hiking Guide to Mount Washington and the Presidential Range
Massachusetts and Rhode Island Trail Guide
North Carolina Hiking Trails
West Virginia Hiking Trails
White Mountain Guide

Paddling Guides

Classic Northeastern Whitewater Guide
Quiet Water Canoe Guide: Maine
Quiet Water Canoe Guide: Massachusetts/Connecticut/Rhode Island
Quiet Water Canoe Guide: New Hampshire/Vermont
Quiet Water Canoe Guide: New York
Sea Kayaking along the New England Coast
Sea Kayaking along the Mid-Atlantic Coast
Whitewater Handbook

Outdoor Skill Guides

Guide to Trail Building and Maintenance
Organizing Outdoor Volunteers
River Rescue
Watercolor Painting on the Trail

THE ULTIMATE GUIDE TO BACKCOUNTRY TRAVEL

Michael Lanza

APPALACHIAN MOUNTAIN CLUB BOOKS
BOSTON, MASSACHUSETTS

Cover Photographs: Michael Lanza
All photographs by the author unless otherwise noted
Cover Design: Ola Frank
Book Design: Carol Bast Tyler

© 1999 Michael Lanza. All rights reserved.

Distributed by The Globe Pequot Press, Inc., Old Saybrook, CT

Published by the Appalachian Mountain Club. No part of this publication may be reproduced or transmitted in any form or by any means, electronic or mechanical, including photocopying and recording, or by any information storage or retrieval system, except as may by expressly permitted by the 1976 Copyright Act or in writing from the publisher. Requests for permission should be addressed in writing to Appalachian Mountain Club Books, 5 Joy Street, Boston, MA 02108.

Library of Congress Cataloging-in-Publication Data

The paper used in this publication meets the minimum requirements of the American National Standard for Information Sciences—Permanence of Paper for Printed Library Materials, ANSI Z39.48–1984.∞

Due to changes in conditions,
use of the information in this book
is at the sole risk of the user.

Printed on recycled paper using soy-based inks.

Printed in the United States of America.

10 9 8 7 6 5 4 3 2 1   98 99 00 01 02 03

CONTENTS

Introduction ix
Acknowledgments xi

1. Trip Planning 1
Choosing a Route 3
Tips on choosing a Map and Guidebook 6
Avoiding the Masses 12
Play by the Rules 13
Getting in Shape 15
Keep Your Gear Organized and Make Sure It Works 17
Need This, Don't Need That .19
Traveling with Your Gear 21
What if Something Goes Wrong? 23
Be Flexible 24
Resources 25

2. Gear 27
Packs 29
Tips on Buying Gear 30
Boots 38
Tents 44
Sleeping Bags 51
Sleeping Pads 57

    Stoves and Cookware 58
    Other Essential and "Luxury" Gear 64

3. Clothing 67
    Dress for Success 69
    Layering 70
    Synthetics and Wool versus Cotton 73
    Technical Outerwear 75
    Buying Outdoor Clothing 80
    Care of Technical Clothing 81
    Clothing Ethics 83
    Deciding on Your Wardrobe 83
    Regional Climate and Clothing .84

4. Water 87
    How Much to Drink and When 88
    How Much Water to Carry 90
    Treat It Right 92
    Water Bottles or Hydration Systems? 96
    Children and Water 97

5. Food 99
    Lugging the Chuck Wagon 100
    Chow Time 102
    The Menu 103
    Backcountry Cuisine 103
    Children and Food 107

6. On the Trail 108
    Loving the Backcountry to Death 110
    "Leave No Trace" Guidelines .111
    Walking Lightly 113
    Navigating 115
    Weather 126

River Crossings 127
Venturing Off-Trail 132
Loading Your Pack for Various Terrain 136
Traveling at Night 137
Going Solo 137
Older People and Children 140
Sharing the Trail 141

7. Making Camp 144
Selecting a Site 145
Roughing It Comfortably 148
Low-Impact Camping 152
Campfires 155
When Nature Calls 158
Sharing the Backcountry 160

8. Bloodsuckers, Slithering Things, and Opportunistic Carnivores 162
Ethics of Human-Animal Encounters 164
Avoiding Animal Problems 165
Insects 173
Nasty Flora 174
Other "Opportunistic Carnivores" 175
Resources 175

9. Leadership and Decision-Making . .176
Think Things Through .178
Anticipate and Head Off Problems 180
Know When to Take Charge 182
Maintain a Positive Attitude 185

10. Wilderness First Aid 186
You Can't Dial 911 187
How Much Should You Know? 189

Reacting to an Emergency 190
Patient Assessment 191
SOAP Note 195
Backcountry Ailments: Avoidance, Symptoms
    and Treatment 196
Long-term Patient Care 210
Women's Issues 210
The First-Aid Kit 211
Resources and Training 212

11. Winter in the Backcountry 213
Staying Warm and Dry 215
Environmental Hazards 219

12. Outdoor Adventure
Photography 224
Cameras, Lenses, Film 225
Taking Photos 227

About the Author 232
About the Appalachian Mountain Club 233
Index 235

INTRODUCTION

IT'S BEEN SAID with regard to being safe in the outdoors that good judgment comes from experience, and experience comes from bad judgment. My first eager forays into the mountains were made with pitiful clothing, crappy gear, and a body of knowledge about the backcountry that could fit on an index card. The combination produced innumerable moments of misery but many more wonderful times that have kept me going back for more.

There's a comic irony in the fact that one can become expert at something by spending enough time making mistakes, but it's true of most human pursuits, from careers to growing up. Fortunately, we are just smart enough that not all learning has to come from personal error—we can actually glean knowledge from the experience of others. Most of us begin learning about the outdoors through a combination of personal experience and the tutelage of others; that's good, but it's also a random and scattered way of acquiring skills. Frankly, I wish I'd had the foresight to pick up a book like this way back when; it might have saved me a lot of unnecessary discomfort and risk.

I decided some years ago to make my living in the outdoors—essentially to remove the barrier separating work from play. I get to spend many days every year in the backcountry, play with new gear, and constantly explore new places. And through making an infinitude of mistakes large and small, I've formed my own ideas about how to maximize my enjoyment and safety while minimizing my discomfort, risk, and impact on the land—which is really what traveling in the backcountry is all about.

But just as importantly, I wanted to write this book to remind people that this is supposed to be fun. Somewhere along the line, the fun part seems to have gotten lost in the fog of marketing and rained on by the self-righteousness of some outdoorspeople who are severe about their outdoor activities and seem contemptuous of anyone who doesn't share their attitude.

Of course, preparedness and knowledge go hand in hand with safety and enjoyment. But most of us don't have to be outfitted for Everest. Our decisions will be largely between degrees of comfort and challenge, not life and death. Lacking in some knowledge of wilderness esoterica is not a mortal sin. We all learn from mistakes, and are usually able to laugh about them later. As long as you're thinking about safety and acting conservatively, you're likely to make good decisions even in situations where past experience may not inform you.

Respect and awe are more appropriate responses to raw nature than paralyzing fear. This book's goal is to provide a solid backcountry foundation, a springboard to launch yourself in any direction you choose—and to provide you with some entertaining reading along the way.

Have fun out there.

ACKNOWLEDGMENTS

FIRST, I want to thank AMC Books Editor Mark Russell for not telling me to get a real job when I approached him about writing this book. My appreciation goes out also to Jessica Church, marketing and publicity manager at AMC Books, and her predecessor, Ola Frank, as well as to the many others at the Appalachian Mountain Club with whom I've worked and whom I've come to know and admire.

I owe a special thanks to several people who volunteered to read parts of this book and offer their knowledgeable suggestions. They include my wife, Dr. Penny Beach; my good friends Kathleen Adams, Jerry Hapgood, David Ports, Keith Ratner, and Lance Riek; the AMC's backcountry campsites and shelters field supervisor Kevin "Hawk" Metheny; Alex Kosseff, who coordinates leadership training and trip policies with the AMC's volunteer trip leaders; and AMC leaders Andy Cohen, Joe Kuzneski, Pete Mason, and Kathryn Yousif. Buck Tilton, director of the Wilderness Medicine Institute in Pitkin, Colorado, offered valued advice on wilderness medicine and other topics. I also received technical information from the experts at SOLO, Cascade Designs, Columbia Sportswear, Eastern Mountain Sports, Ex Officio, Leave No Trace Inc., W. L. Gore & Associates, L. L. Bean, Nikwax, the North Face, Peak Exposure, Recovery Engineering, Suunto USA, and Wild Things.

Personally, my gratitude goes out to my favorite backcountry travel partner, Penny; to my parents; and to all the family and friends who have shared with me many enjoyable trips into wild places all over this continent. I look forward to many more good times with all of you.

chapter
one
TRIP PLANNING

YOSEMITE'S CELEBRATED WILDS *seemed to call to us as we walked out of the valley ranger station with our backcountry permit. They beckoned with promises of a grandeur so unrestrained that we scarcely noticed that our loaded packs were nearly fat enough to cast a shadow across the face of Half Dome, or how their bulging heft knocked scowling tourists rudely about when we clambered onto a bus bound for the trailhead. As we started panting and sweating up the John Muir Trail, the wilderness seemed to whisper our names on the wind.*

And in the tradition of young, novice backpackers, we answered the call with overzealous ignorance.

Looking at a map of Yosemite now, I'm stupefied that we believed we could walk our intended route in the five days we planned to be in the backcountry. We'd already scaled back the distance once during pre-trip talks over the phone, but it wasn't enough: On the trail, hard reality would demand that we moderate our distance goals a couple more times. Apparently, all those squiggles on the map where the trail compressed itself like an accordion had left little impression on us. The contour intervals leaping upward through numbers like 7,000, 8,000, and 9,000 feet seemed unimposing from our kitchen tables. We either neglected to look into, or simply ignored, how hot the midsummer days get—even in the Yosemite high country—and didn't consider that we might wilt in that heat beneath packs that resembled family-size refrigerators.

Ignorance, we would learn, does not always beget bliss.

Our first night out, we were awakened around midnight by the unmistakable sound of a large animal clawing up a tree—and the sound came from the direction of our hanging food. Quaking in our underwear in the cold blackness, banging cook pots, we managed to chase off the black bear and rescue most of our food, but the specter of him coming back for more kept us up all night. On the trail the next day, the lack of sleep, the heat, our unwieldy loads, and a long uphill slog all conspired to slowly crush our spirits.

Ascending an endless series of switchbacks, we began to embrace that blindly obdurate conviction—known to many backcountry travelers—that the top must be around the next bend, that the campsite we sought had to be within a half-mile at most. It was in this condition of extreme emotional fragility that we met two backpackers coming down the trail.

Dispensing quickly with the usual pleasantries, we moved on to the question preoccupying our thoughts: How far to the next camping area? Unfortunately, the man who responded failed to perceive just how much we had invested in his answer being what we needed to hear.

"Oh, a couple miles or less," he told us.

My friend Gary—his grasp of social decorum badly slipping away under the strain of a total physical exhaustion which had rendered him, as he would admit later, "mentally broken"— responded to this good Samaritan's show of helpfulness by spitting out a four-letter epithet rarely heard in such a tranquil setting. Right up there among the nastiest of nasty words, quite possibly the mother of all profanity, it is normally reserved for only the most antagonistic exchanges. This offensive verb is commonly followed by the third-person pronoun, which was exactly how Gary completed his thought, leaving this stranger with no doubt that he was the object of the sentiment.

Understandably, Gary's outburst left the man visibly shaken. His eyes widened with what looked to me like the sincere fear that he'd happened upon an escapee from a hospital for the criminally insane. In the awkward silence that ensued, I seized the opportunity to avert any escalation of the misunderstanding, thanking the man and ushering Gary onward.

To this day, Gary doesn't recall saying what he did, although our other friend on the trip, Mike, remembers Gary's two-word conversation killer as well as I do. So, if the man whom Gary insulted that day on the John Muir Trail is reading this, please understand that my friend really is a peace-loving person who was, simply, mentally broken.

I've deliberately related a tale from that trip's hardest day. All in all, we had a wonderful time, enjoyed some stunning backcountry, and look back on the experience fondly. But with a little better preparation—not overpacking, choosing our route better, finding a campsite where we could better protect our food from bears—we easily could have reduced the level of physical suffering we endured, and maybe avoided an embarrassing outburst of misguided invective.

We all accept some measure of pain on any backcountry journey as part of the bargain; if not for that, everyone would be out there, right? But that measure of pain can affect the quality of a backcountry trip as much as the views, and you can manipulate it dramatically through the decisions you make before taking step one on the trail. With experience, you'll develop a refined sense of the sort of trip you enjoy best—and traveling self-supported in the backcountry can vary tremendously from relatively easy trips to physically demanding outings. Better to dictate your place along that easy-to-difficult continuum than let your lack of preparedness dictate it for you. What I hope to accomplish in this chapter is to get you thinking about ways to do just that, and ultimately make the trip safer and more enjoyable for you.

Choosing a Route

In Maine's 100-Mile Wilderness, the stretch of the Appalachian Trail that crosses no paved or public roads for more than 99 miles, I bumped into a backpacker who offered an honest, blunt response to my innocent query, "How ya doin'?" He wasn't very pleased, it seemed, with this mostly wooded stretch of the AT. Too many trees, he griped. I laughed and said, "Yeah, Maine's got a lot of trees." What I thought was, "Duh. Appalachian Trail? Maine? You didn't expect trees?"

The first step in choosing a route has to be big picture, broad perspective. You may be told or have read good things about a certain trail or mountain range, but deciding to go there based purely on a recommendation, without knowing what to expect, may be setting yourself up for disappointment—or difficulty. Think about the quality of trip you want, and get enough information about your destination to form a clear mental picture of what awaits you there. Are you looking for forest lakes or alpine meadows? Do you prefer a remote wilderness experience with few other people, or a great view

Plan a route that takes advantage of scenic views along the way. (The Mist Trail, Yosemite National Park.)

reached with little effort that may draw hordes? Would the presence of large carnivores like bears prompt you to consider an alternative destination? (See more on critters below.) These are just a few of the questions to consider as you begin to narrow your choices.

Many of us get through that first phase quickly: we know where we want to go and need to focus the planning. Start with a guidebook and a good map. Other possible resources may include Web sites, outdoors magazines, literature from the management agency (national park or forest, state park, etc.), friends, members of an outdoors club, employees in the local outdoor-gear store, and rangers who know the area. How many resources I tap depends on my familiarity with the area and with the terrain and climate. But regardless whether I'm heading into the Maine mountains or the Rockies, the Southwest or Sierra, I'll get as many maps as necessary, consult at least one guidebook, and scan the management agency's Web site if there is one.

Gather as much detail as you can about the several factors that will affect any backcountry trip's level of difficulty and potential for unforeseen complications: trail mileage, terrain, climate, the maximum altitude you will reach, the amount of elevation gained and lost along your route, the availability of campsites and water sources, and animals. I'll get into greater detail on all of these below.

Get and use the relevant **guidebooks and maps**; good ones will provide most of the info you need on the factors listed above. New computer software packages allow you to map out your route on your home computer. But bear in mind that, while some maps and books are quite accurate on distances or the precise location of trails, others can be way off—or two sources may offer conflicting information. See what year the book was published—it's printed on one of the first pages, indicated by a copyright symbol. If the book is old, some of its information may be dated; some trails may have been relocated or closed since it came out. Some U.S. Geological Survey (USGS) topographic quad maps are decades old and inaccurate on the location of trails, or do not show all the trails in a region.

The condition of trails varies greatly, too; some are easy to follow, others rough, not well maintained or not obvious. Not all trail systems are as well signed as those under the AMC's aegis. Even in the relatively well managed public lands of the Northeast, I've hiked or skied trails I thought led to a certain place, only to discover the

tips on choosing a map and guidebook

❖ Ask a knowledgeable source (management agency, local gear store, club, etc.) to point you to a good guidebook and map.

❖ Flip through two or three different guides to the same area, comparing their formats and the accessibility and completeness of their information. Check a book's detail: its driving directions to trailheads and trail descriptions, and whether those descriptions show that the author has an intimate knowledge of the place, or may not necessarily have hiked the trails you're planning to hike. See whether the trails are described in the direction you plan to travel. Guidebooks are written in different formats; choosing one is a matter of personal preference.

❖ A good map for traveling in the backcountry is in a scale of between 1:24,000 (like standard USGS 7.5-minute topographic quad maps) and roughly 1:95,000 (like the AMC's White Mountains maps). The larger-scale maps—which, in the range described here, would be those with a 1:24,000 scale—provide greater detail than smaller-scale maps but also cover less area. (See more on maps and navigating in chapter 6.)

❖ Look for a map that shows topographic contours—the lines that connect land points at the same elevation—in intervals of anywhere from 20 to 100 feet. The larger contour intervals are adequate for backpacking on trails, while the smaller intervals provide the detail needed for off-trail travel.

error later and have to double back—adding unanticipated miles to my day. Pushing your limits in an unfamiliar place invites exhaustion, which can lead to bigger problems. And it's generally not very much fun.

The importance of **planning your distance** requires little explanation. But anyone whose hiking experience is limited to a certain region often finds trails in a different region easier or more difficult. If you know someone who's hiked in your destination and you know what that person considers "hard" and "easy," that's possibly the best source of trail data. Determine how far to hike each day based on finding answers to the factors listed above and detailed below, and on your group's experience and fitness level. Paying attention to how fast you hike—how many miles you cover per hour—in a variety of situations will help you plan trip mileage too. Fit hikers may average 2 mph on a moderately difficult trail, but that rate will be affected by many factors, beginning with differences in individual ability.

As much as anything, **terrain**—that is, the ground you walk on—will affect how quickly you tire out and how far you can walk. A fit hiker who can move along at 2 mph might see his pace cut in half over exposed or rugged ground. Anyone who's hiked the King Ravine, Huntington Ravine, or Madison Gulf Trail in New Hampshire's Presidential Range understands how steep slabs or large, loose talus slow you down. By contrast, the same hiker might make the steady climb of about 2,000 feet over two miles or more on the John Muir Trail from Yosemite Valley to Nevada Falls in an hour—the trail, originally built for horses, is a well-graded, easy path up gentle switchbacks.

In planning the distance you'll walk, ask these questions: Does the trail cross talus, exposed slabs, boggy tundra, or extensive muddy areas? Does it cross rivers or creeks that may be dangerous or impassable in certain seasons? Similarly, is the trail or are waterways affected by high and low tides? Are there spots, such as in some Southwest canyons, where short cliffs or boulder jams necessitate special equipment like a rope and the expertise to use it? Are there no maintained trails at all?

Know the climate where you're headed before leaving home, so you can pick the best time of year to go and know what to bring along. Are there rainy and dry seasons? How late into summer does snow linger at higher elevations? How much snowpack remains from the most recent winter and spring? Is there a thunderstorm season that increases the threat of lightning at high elevations, or flash floods inside a canyon? What are the average high and low daily temperatures in each month? What's the average monthly precipitation, and does it fall as rain or snow? I know a certain writer (all too well) who's packed snowballs in New Hampshire's Presidential Range in early September, and clung helplessly to high cliffs in Colorado's Flatirons and Wyoming's Tetons during frightful electrical storms. He says it's no fun getting caught in bad weather.

High altitude is not an issue in the East, but throughout the West it becomes a major consideration in trip planning. You don't have to be attempting a 14,000-foot summit in Colorado or the Sierra to feel the effects of altitude either—many popular trails reach heights that can take the wind out of your sails. Backpack the popular four-day loop through the Maroon Bells–Snowmass Wilderness on Colorado's western slope and you'll climb over four passes, each surpassing 12,000 feet. Well-traveled hiking trails lead to 12,000-foot summits along the Continental Divide in Rocky Mountain National Park. The John Muir Trail in Kings Canyon National Park traverses long stretches of mountain terrain between 10,000 and 12,000 feet. Trails through the Grand Tetons routinely exceed 9,000 feet, and you'll reach similar heights on numerous "smaller" peaks in the Pacific Northwest's Cascade Range and trails in the mountains of Montana and Idaho.

I'll save a discussion of the symptoms and ailments associated with altitude for chapter 10. But in planning a multiday trip in high country, you have to anticipate the effects of altitude on the physical performance of everyone in the group. It varies between individuals, but many will experience some difficulty breathing, and consequently adopt a slower walking pace, beginning as low as 7,000 to 8,000 feet. Obviously, the higher you get, the more pronounced the effect. Between 8,000 feet and 10,000 feet, most people will slow down significantly if they are not acclimatized. Many people coming from sea level will become ill above 10,000 feet if they don't acclimatize. While fit hikers have no greater physiological ability to combat altitude illness than less well fit hikers, hiking at altitude is more exhausting than at sea level, and your fitness level may affect your stamina up high.

It's best to take a day or more to acclimatize by slowly walking up to higher altitudes. But most Americans live at or near sea level and have limited time for their trips into the mountains. Given that, adhere to this golden rule for treks into high backcountry: Expect high altitude to slow your party down, and plan ahead your options for changing your route or retreating if someone becomes ill. If possible, plan your route, or your climbs, so that the highest altitudes you will encounter are toward the end of the trip.

As any hiker knows well, altitude's double whammy is that you don't have to go very high for it to hurt. As much as terrain and high altitude will affect your hiking time, so will **elevation gain and loss**, and that rings just as true in the East as the West. In fact, many people who've logged their share of miles on the right and left sides of the country will maintain that the Northeast's trails are harder, mile for mile, than many western trails. The East's tallest peaks rise abruptly out of low valleys, and their trails often take direct lines upward rather than the more gentle switchbacks prevalent in the West. It's not uncommon for 5,000-foot summits in the Northeast to entail more than 4,000 feet of climbing, while some of Colorado's 14,000-footers involve only a 3,000-foot ascent from the trailhead.

The old East vs. West debate notwithstanding, you might roughly expect every 2,000 feet of elevation gain to add an hour of hiking time at a 2 mph pace—on a good footpath. That can vary greatly depending on influences like actual altitude, terrain, your fitness level, and the weight of your pack. And going down may be no faster. On steeper terrain, you may find that a more accurate way of estimating your ascent time is by getting to know how much elevation you typically can gain per hour, and placing less import on distance (a standard tactic among mountaineers).

Experience is the best teacher when it comes to anticipating your own speed and stamina when confronting significant elevation gain and loss, so attempt harder trips in incremental steps rather than great leaps.

The most critical consideration in mapping out a route through the backcountry is the availability of **campsites and water sources**. In some places, water and campsites will be abundant; in others they will be very limited and will dictate how far you travel every day. Most water sources fluctuate with the seasons; some dry up completely at certain times of year. Wherever water is scarce, contact a source with direct knowledge of its availability, usually the management agency. In certain national parks and public lands, backpackers are required to camp in designated backcountry sites and to reserve a permit for them in advance; their availability may also affect your itinerary, so plan ahead, particularly when heading for a popular destination.

The discussion of campsites is probably the best place to mention **critters**. Predators that consider us lower on the food chain—grizzlies, mountain lions—still retain footholds in the West. Rattlers and other snakes are fairly widespread around the country. Public lands sometimes have recommendations or rules unique to their own situation regarding wildlife. If there is a management agency, find out what precautions it recommends to avoid unfortunate encounters with the residents whose home you're visiting.

Where human presence is heavy, problems with animals like bears going for human food tend to be the most pronounced. Smaller animals, from raccoons to mice to desert kangaroo rats, also can be quite persistent in pursuing your grub, not to mention unattended clothing and gear. Our sloppy practices at campsites are often to blame, and only we can solve the problem by practicing better

Always consult a map when planning your trip. Take note of features like river crossings, exposed ridges, escape routes, and potential campsites.

campsite habits. And while your mind may be preoccupied with bears, at certain times of year in certain places your body will be busier with insects. Find out what biting insects reside in your backcountry destination, and what time of year they are most numerous. (See chapter 8 for more on hiking and camping amid wildlife.)

Turn to chapter 6 for more-detailed advice on traveling the trail, from weather and river crossings to navigating your way; and to chapter 7 for more on selecting a campsite.

Long-distance hiking, or setting out for weeks or months continuously on the Appalachian Trail, Pacific Crest Trail, or the like, raises the task of pre-trip planning to another level, and this book isn't intended as a guide to such a trip (although I do offer a few more thoughts about planning food consumption for a long-trail hike in chapter 5). Many of the same logistical issues come into play as on a two-day or five-day backpacking trip, though. Certainly maps, guidebooks, and land or trail managers are a good place to start planning. Among the major differences between a weekend or week-long trip and a long trail are that, on the latter, you should give greater consideration to your physical condition, gear, traveling as lightly as possible, and at what points along the route you can resupply with food, stove fuel, and other necessities.

One final word on trip planning: **roads.** They aren't much of an issue in the Northeast, where most roads to trailheads are open year-round, and even gravel forest roads are usually passable to autos. In some parts of the Northeast, however, privately owned logging roads that allow access to trailheads become impassable during winter and spring mud season, and there may be a toll for driving the road. Gates are closed and locked across some public roads year-round or seasonally, and a few major roads are not maintained in winter. Check with the management agency or state police.

In the West, where freak snowstorms occasionally close interstate highways, getting to the trailhead can be the most harrowing leg of your adventure. On a late-April trip to Utah's canyonlands, for instance, we flew into Las Vegas a day after a storm had temporarily closed Route 14 through Utah's Cedar Breaks, a road we planned to drive. You can encounter the same thing on innumerable roads throughout the West well into summer.

Some trailheads lie at the end of long gravel roads that are only accessible by high-clearance, four-wheel-drive vehicles. The condition of those roads can vary greatly between seasons. (My wife and I once drove my aged, creaking Geo Prizm up an increasingly rough and steep gravel road in western Colorado until it literally could go no farther, then parked it, put on our packs, and walked the last quarter-mile to the trailhead.) Roads described as accessible for cars are not always—we were glad we had a four-wheel-drive truck on the rough, sometimes sandy, sometimes steep forty miles of gravel road we drove to the Upper Muley Twist Canyon trailhead in Utah's Capitol Reef National Park.

Predominantly clay desert roads may morph to a dangerously slick gumbo after a downpour, making them unsafe even for a four-wheel-drive truck, although chains might provide the needed traction. And private-vehicle access has been restricted on some paved roads, like the Maroon Creek Road to the popular Maroon Bells trailhead near Aspen, Colorado. Consult the management agency for current road-access information. Consider leaving extra water, food, and stove fuel in your vehicle, in case you find yourself stranded at the end of a backcountry trip because the road has become impassable.

Avoiding the Masses

The more I travel through backcountry, the more I crave a real sense of remoteness and solitude—and the more elusive those qualities seem to become. If solitude is your goal, the obvious formula is that the crowds grow thinner as the trail grows steeper and rougher, and the farther you walk from the nearest road, the fewer people you will see. But there are other tactics for achieving solitude in our nation's increasingly popular mountains, forests, and canyons.

First of all, close proximity to population centers always spells crowding, as anyone knows who's paid a summer visit to Maine's Acadia National Park or Great Smoky Mountains National Park in Tennessee and North Carolina. Look for destinations away from major cities. And avoid the marquee destinations. They comprise quite a long list, from 14,000-foot summits, or "14ers," in Colorado, to 4,000-footers in the Northeast, and any place which, by dint of its renown for scenic splendor or its national-park status, attracts backcountry enthusiasts like grizzlies to a salmon run.

In July and August, for example, you'll have company on the Teton Crest Trail in the Grand Tetons, in Glacier National Park's Many Glacier area, on many stretches of the Appalachian Trail or

Pacific Crest Trail, hiking to the Cirque of the Towers in the Wind River Range, and on any trail within a day's walk of Yosemite Valley, among many other popular backcountry areas. The masses gravitate to these places, leaving opportunities for quietude in mountains that are just shy of the magical elevation numbers—be it 4,000 or 14,000 feet—and in the relatively anonymous national forests, preserves, monuments, and other public lands that suffer no shortage of natural beauty.

Find these obscure gems by consulting any of the trip-planning sources mentioned above. Contact the National Park Service, U.S. Forest Service, or Bureau of Land Management (see Resources list at the end of this chapter) and request information about their properties, especially their lesser-known units. Stop in at any of their regional offices, load up on free literature, and talk to the staff.

Even in the best-known national parks, you can lose the crowds by knowing where to look and what questions to ask. Park rangers often direct the bulk of hiker traffic onto the best-maintained and best-marked trails, both to keep novice hikers from getting lost and to concentrate use on a few trails that are designed to handle large numbers of people. If you ask only for "a nice hike," that may be where they send you. To avoid those crowds, find out which are the most heavily used trails, and avoid them. When a ranger understands that you're a seasoned backcountry traveler who prefers solitude, he or she will often direct you to the loneliest trails.

In our most-popular backcountry areas, you can also enjoy moments or long stretches of solitude by hitting the trail when most people don't—early morning or late in the day, midweek, or off-season. Instead of taking your vacation in August, try late September in the Rockies, mid-October in New Hampshire's White Mountains, or winter in the desert Southwest. One friend advises people to hike in the rain to avoid crowds—"It's a whole new world out there," he claims. (See chapter 11 for advice on winter backcountry travel.)

Play by the Rules

It was the first trip to the Grand Tetons for three friends and me, and we were on the fourth day of a five-day loop around the heart of the range. Before noon, we reached the area for which we had a permit to camp that night (poor pre-trip planning, perhaps?). It seemed too early to stop for the day; we wanted to push over the next pass and shorten our walk out the next day. Well, we figured, we had yet to see a backcountry ranger in four days, so why not?

Sure enough, shortly after we pitched our tents illegally in another backcountry camping area a few hours later, a ranger hiked up, offered a friendly greeting, and asked to see our permit. We sheepishly acknowledged our deliberate violation, feeling like jerks as she explained the need to control the numbers of people in the backcountry, both to protect the land and to provide an optimal experience for backcountry travelers. I haven't repeated the mistake since.

Many of us who love spending time in the backcountry are guilty of having violated some rule established by a management agency. Perhaps the offense seemed innocent enough at the time. But the more time we spend exploring wild places, the more we develop an appreciation for the necessity of managing them well to ensure they remain wild. There are a whole lot of us out there these days, and we're capable of an awful lot of damage arising from nothing more malicious than ignorance and negligence.

I've yet to encounter a place where the regulations imposed too great an inconvenience to follow, or where information about regulations was not readily available. The management agency usually provides any information you request. If you have concerns about particular issues, like disposal of human waste, ask (see more on low–impact hiking and camping in chapters 6 and 7). Many managed areas have regulations regarding where and how to camp, fires, dogs, and other issues related to your impact on the land, some of which are specific to the place. New Hampshire's White Mountain National Forest, for example, prohibits camping in alpine zones (except on a two-foot snow base) or near trails. In the popular Enchantment Basin of Washington's Alpine Lakes Wilderness, backpackers are asked to urinate in the pit toilets, or dig a hole in sand and bury their urine afterward, rather than peeing on vegetation, because the resident herd of mountain goats has become habituated to consuming human urine.

In national parks, you have to obtain a permit to spend one or more nights in the backcountry, and most parks restrict the number of permits issued daily. If you want to backpack in the Grand Canyon, for instance, you'll have to reserve a permit four months in advance. Many public lands, including the Grand Canyon, also impose recreational fees on backcountry users, including backpackers, climbers, and river runners.

Heavy demand creates stiff competition for permits in public lands other than national parks too. Parks and forests that restrict the numbers of visitors to prevent overuse—such as Maine's Baxter State Park and Washington's Alpine Lakes Wilderness—see people snapping up available permits for summer and fall weekends months in advance. Federal Wilderness areas, found in all categories of federal land, impose the most stringent restrictions.

Learn the rules wherever you intend to play, and follow them. Be aware of any restrictions on group size—some places limit the number to ten (see more on this in the Sharing the Trail section of chapter 6 and the Sharing the Backcountry section of chapter 7). Respect the rights of private landowners whose land you may be crossing—their generous permission to traverse their land can be revoked if people abuse the privilege. See the Resources listing at the end of this chapter for where to turn for information on federal lands.

Getting in Shape

Whenever I'm asked the question, "How fit do I have to be to go backpacking?" I answer, "Well, how much do you want to enjoy it?" Simply put, the better your physical condition, the less likely you'll find yourself hurting on a trip. Then again, you don't have to undertake an Olympian training regimen to head into the backcountry for a few days.

If you maintain a regular exercise program, getting in three or four cardiovascular workouts a week of at least thirty minutes each—that is, intense workouts that elevate your heart rate to around 80 percent of its maximum rate for your age—and preferably at least one workout (or hike) that's at least twice as long as your daily workouts, you're probably going to be fine on any backcountry trip short of moderate difficulty. If you've fallen out of shape, ease yourself into a regular exercise routine well before your trip. Do what you enjoy and is convenient, whether it's running, cycling, fitness walking, exercise machines—anything that provides an aerobic and muscular workout. If you're in your midthirties or older and have not exercised in some time, you should get advice from your doctor before starting a program.

Don't ignore the importance of stretching. Along with staying well hydrated, stretching while on the trail is the best way to avoid muscle and joint injuries, as well as the soreness and stiffness that can follow a hard day. This book isn't a forum for detailed instruction on stretching routines—you can get information on that at a local gym or in any number of books on exercise. Basically, you want to find stretching exercises that loosen up your major muscles, especially your calves, quads, hamstrings, buttocks, back, shoulders, and neck. Doing regular abdominal exercises like crunches will help guard the lower back against injury, provided you do them correctly. Ten or twenty minutes of easy stretching at the start and end of a day of hiking will greatly reduce your aches and chances of injury.

The best way to train for hiking with a heavy pack, of course, is to hike with a heavy pack. Hit the trails on the weekends leading up to your trip. Get your body into condition for lugging around the extra weight imposed by a pack—abruptly boosting your body weight by 25 percent or more has a very noticeable effect on your back, shoulders, feet, knees, and leg muscles. Begin with a light or moderate weight, depending on your physical condition, and increase the weight gradually on each hike.

If you'll be heading to high altitude, try to get in some hikes at higher altitudes in the two or three weeks leading up to your trip to start acclimating your body to the thinner air—the more hiking and the higher the altitude, the better, but don't overdo it. (See more in chapter 10 on acclimating to altitude.) If you live in flatlands where training at altitude or even on a big hill isn't possible, wear a pack while working out on a Stairmaster or hiking up and down stairs, or simulate hiking in a pool as a form of resistance training.

Make an honest assessment of your own and your companions' physical abilities and limits and plan your itinerary accordingly. Don't attempt a long, arduous route if everyone in the party is not ready for it. Those trails will still be there for a future trip when you are ready for them.

Finally, think about the mental and emotional limits of everyone in the group. Experienced backcountry travelers sometimes forget that a relative novice—even someone very fit and active in outdoor sports—may be intimidated by the exposure of a high ridge with long, steep drops off either side, or just by the notion of being days from the nearest road, or of camping in bear country. Making that person an integral part of the planning process, so that he understands what he's getting into beforehand, can often head off such issues and make him more comfortable with the plans or a sudden need to change plans. Similarly, someone pushed beyond his physical limits can come crashing down emotionally, suddenly overwhelmed by the exhaustion-enhanced fear that he's in over his head. Don't push a group member too far—it's not fun for anyone on the trip.

At the same time, maintaining a positive attitude in the backcountry keeps small problems from seeming big, and makes the trip more enjoyable for everyone. Things go wrong: weather turns lousy, gear breaks, you get blisters or bitten by bugs, or you just become plain tired and sore. The backcountry offers rewards we can't find in civilization, but we're sacrificing some comforts. Head out there knowing that there's no reason to attempt anything you consider unsafe or beyond your ability, but also feeling that you might be willing to try something you've never tried before.

A few years ago, my mom and I went to Yosemite Valley together. She was fifty-eight at the time. Previously, she had only day-hiked in New England, but in Yosemite we did an overnight backpacking trip and hiked to the top of Half Dome. Neither of us will ever forget the long time we sat at the base of the steel cables that lead hundreds of feet up a steep and exposed granite slab to Half Dome's summit, while Mom wrestled with the decision on whether she was up for it. I had no doubt she could handle the physical challenge; she had to make the mental leap herself. Well, she did, and she loved it. She was willing to push the limits of her comfort zone, to try something she had never before thought herself capable of doing, and that helped make it a special trip for both of us.

Keep Your Gear Organized and Make Sure It Works

So, you haven't taken your gear out in months—are you really willing to head out again without checking it out first? Leather boots may need waterproofing, a tent may need seam-sealing, a stove may need cleaning and maintenance—failing to examine your gear before a trip is a recipe for frustration or disaster. Don't wait until the day you depart. Take time to organize all your stuff in advance to see whether you need to get batteries or a bulb, replace something, fix something else. See chapter 2 for details on gear care.

Always check the condition of your gear before you pack it for the final time.

I like to store my gear together, well organized, so that I can put my hands on any particular item immediately and literally have my pack loaded and ready to go in little more than an hour. I also keep a checklist that I'll consult before a trip to make sure I'm not leaving behind anything I need, and some backpacking food, extra stove fuel and batteries, and other supplies in the house. Equally important is keeping everything organized within your pack so that you can find it once on the trail. (See chapter 6 for advice on loading a pack.)

It's a bit anal-retentive, I know, and certainly not absolutely necessary. But I find that the ability to prepare quickly for a trip helps me get out more often. It eliminates the excuse, "I'd love to get out this weekend, but I don't know where half my stuff is and don't have time to find it."

Need This, Don't Need That

I have a good friend—let's call him Lance—who takes the light-is-right ethic of backcountry travel very seriously. Lance once gently lectured me for having too bulky and heavy a toothbrush holder. Nothing enters Lance's pack without first being weighed and severely scrutinized for its necessity and multiple functionality.

My friend Lance represents one polar extreme in this discussion.

I have also walked trails with backpackers who seemed never to have made the intellectual connection between the objects they stuff into their pack and the weight they bear on their back. I have seen friends produce more toiletries and food from a single backpack than small convenience stores keep in stock. For a five-day trip along the Appalachian Trail in Maine, a friend—let's call him Topher—brought along a block of cheese the size of my head. As we cooked our final dinner, he pulled a can of beans from his pack and exclaimed, "Wow. I forgot I had this."

These people represent the other pole in this discussion.

Once you get past the essentials, deciding what to bring or not bring on any trip comes down to a trade-off between the benefit provided by something and the weight it adds to your burden. You may laugh at Lance's extremism—I certainly do at every opportunity—but his basic premise is correct: ounces count.

A widely accepted guideline for determining a good backpack weight is that it not exceed one-quarter to one-third of your body weight. But we all have different tolerances for what we're willing to carry—one-third of their body weight is a hurtful load for many people, while technical climbers might cart half their weight because of the additional gear they need. And even lightweight items occupy valuable space. Don't carry unnecessary clothing (see more on this in chapter 3). On my first trips, I packed a T-shirt for each day. Not anymore. A couple of years ago, on a 17-day trek around Nepal's

Annapurna Range, I wore the same synthetic T-shirt for 15 days. (One garment on which I will not skimp, though, is socks; see why in the section on blisters in chapter 10.)

Take a hard look at everything before it goes into your pack. Does it serve multiple purposes—such as an emergency space blanket doubling as a tent ground cloth—or is it something whose single purpose isn't likely to be needed? Is there something else you're already taking that's smaller and lighter and could replace it? Do you, for instance, need two mugs, or could one person or both people eat from the cooking pot? If you want to bring along something to read, will it be a magazine, a small paperback, or an unabridged hardcover edition of *Les Miserables*?

Trim weight anywhere possible. Unless you're skiing across Antarctica, there's really no need for that family-size tube of toothpaste. Leave the economy-size bottle of contact lens solution at home and just take what you need in a small plastic bottle. Remember that the comfort some items provide in camp can be more than negated by the discomfort of lugging those things around on your back. If there's something you routinely carry into the backcountry but never use—and it's not a safety item, like a first-aid kit—maybe you don't need it.

Your decisions may justifiably change from trip to trip, depending on the sort of trip you want, the season, and the destination. (I'll talk more specifically about basic mountaineering in chapter 6, and about winter in chapter 11.) One weekend, I may carry the extra weight of a backcountry oven because I'm excited about eating some tasty meals; next trip, I might leave it at home because I'm carrying climbing gear or food for several days, or simply want go as light as possible. A simple repair kit for certain gear, or a second light source, may be important for a week-long trip but not so critical for an overnight hike. When traveling in a group, coordinate who's carrying items you can share, like stoves, a first-aid kit, or toothpaste, to avoid unnecessary redundancy. If you're bigger and/or stronger than your companion, offer to take the lion's share of the load; it might make the trip more pleasant for both of you.

If you're hitting the trail for several days, weeks, or months, going as light as possible becomes critically important. Get the lightest and most compact tent and sleeping bag you can afford. Many Appalachian Trail thru-hikers carry a pack that weighs thirty-five pounds or less, but they can often get away with bringing no tent because of the availability of shelters along that trail, and potential resupply points are more frequent. Conversely, Pacific Crest Trail trekkers don't have the convenience of a network of shelters or frequently spaced towns for buying food.

No matter what kind of trip you're planning, be critical about what you bring—nothing in your pack should take you by surprise, least of all canned foods. But if there's some luxury item you really want to bring along, well geez, bring it. Remember, this is supposed to be fun.

Traveling with Your Gear

My good friend Rod was once detained in an airport for having a backpacking stove in his luggage. It was a liquid-fuel model—i.e., it burns white gas, like the widely available Coleman brand—and it was empty of fuel. The person at the check-in counter told Rod that the stove smelled of fuel and insisted he "clean it with soap." Well, to make a sad story short, after several trips to the bathroom to bathe his stove, and several olfactory inspections by the airline counter person, Rod's stove never worked again.

I first discovered the airline prohibition against stove cartridge fuels in luggage while checking in for a flight out of the tiny airport in Chico, California, at the conclusion of a bike tour. I dug through my panniers to find my stove, an old-fashioned Camping Gaz model which couldn't be detached from its cartridge without leaking its butane-propane fuel. You might imagine the reaction of other people in that terminal when a strong-smelling, pressurized gas started hissing loudly from a cartridge in the hands of a strong-smelling, dirty, and unshaven young man traveling alone.

In Boston's Logan International Airport, I once attracted an audience of carry-on-baggage inspectors when I tried—the foolishness of it struck me only afterward—to board a jet with a mountaineering ax attached to the outside of my climbing pack. One astonished inspector-supervisor kept shaking his head and repeating to me, in understandable disbelief that I had not perceived this on my own beforehand, "That's a weapon!"

Flying with your gear is generally not a problem, but there are a few things to be aware of—beyond resisting any temptation to carry on any tool that might be mistaken for a weapon (pack it in your checked bags). Any fuel stored under pressure, such as stove cartridge fuels, are banned for obvious reasons. Cartridge fuels are widely available throughout the United States and Canada and many foreign countries, so plan on buying them after arriving at your destination. Similarly, no airline will let you board a jet with a liquid fuel like white gas in a stove or fuel bottle, for equally good reason. Purchase the fuel after landing. (See chapter 2 for more about stoves and fuels.)

If you're checking a backpack, the counter employee may ask whether it contains a camp stove, and the airline may have a rule prohibiting camp stoves from checked luggage. If it's a cartridge stove, which generally will not carry an odor of fuel, you could try showing it to the counter person, and perhaps you'll be allowed to pack it in your luggage. A white-gas stove, or fuel bottle, however, can carry an odor long after being emptied of fuel, and it may be difficult to persuade an airline employee to let you take it on the plane. My own experience has been that, if an airline has a policy on camp stoves, enforcement of it depends more on the person you deal with than the relative danger of the stove. But to avoid a hassle, ask the airline before arriving at the airport. An alternative to flying with your stove, though inconvenient, is to ground-ship it ahead of you. Most post offices will hold mail addressed General Delivery, with your name on it, for a week or two.

In the many times I've flown with gear, I've never had anything damaged, but take simple precautions. Pack clothing around hard and breakable objects within your pack or bag. You will be asked to secure all loose pack straps to prevent them from snagging on conveyor belts. Pull all straps snug and tuck them in somewhere. If a sleeping pad or anything else is attached to the outside of your pack, make sure it's secure, and turn an inflatable pad so that the valve is against the pack rather than sticking out from it, to protect the valve. You can buy a stuff sack for most inflatable pads to guard against punctures. Lastly, buckle the hip belt backwards around your pack and pull it tight, so no part of it sticks out. Airlines typically will not cover any damage to a backpack checked as luggage, and will ask you to sign a waiver acknowledging that fact. If you're really worried about it, look into one-time flight insurance, or buy a tough nylon duffel large enough to fit your loaded pack. The airline may also have a large plastic bag you can use as a pack duffel.

With skis, definitely get a bag to protect them. Most airlines allow you to check skis as luggage and will cover any in-transit damage to them. A bicycle has to be partly disassembled (saddle, handlebars, pedals, cranks, wheels) and packed in a bike box. While skis often count as one item of luggage, most airlines impose an unreasonably high extra charge for checking a bicycle. Ask your airline well before your departure about their policy; it's usually much cheaper to ground-ship the bike before your trip.

The only thing I worry about is my camera gear and film. I'll keep them in my carry-on bag. X-ray machines in many industrialized nations are film-safe, but it's probably wise to inquire first. And X-ray machines are not film-safe in much of the nonindustrialized world. Politely request that your carry-on be hand-inspected rather than putting your film through an ancient X-ray machine. I encountered no resistance to that request in the airport in Kathmandu, Nepal, for example, but I'll always seek advice on dealing with that issue before I travel to any unfamiliar foreign country—moving against the tide can get you into trouble in certain places.

What if Something Goes Wrong?

Hopefully, much of the discussion above led you to the conclusion that you cannot be too well prepared for a trip into the backcountry. Later chapters will address how to avoid accidents and how to deal with specific incidents.

But as you're mapping out your backcountry trip, think about what options you would have in the event of an emergency. Look at how far you'll be from help—e.g., a road, ranger station, or town—at various points along your route, and consider how long it would take to get help. Note "escape routes": trails, river and creek drainages, forest and logging roads, and any other avenues for fleeing to safer ground or to a public road in the event of bad weather, illness, or accident.

How you analyze all this information, and how it affects your trip planning, will logically be influenced by the composition of your group—whether there's a child, a relatively slower adult, or someone with a specific medical condition, for instance. Having at least examined these options before the trip will help effect a more rapid escape or rescue if one becomes necessary while you're out there.

Be Flexible

Don't be excessively goal oriented. Begin the trip with the notion that things may not go as planned. Keep an open mind about changing the itinerary as the situation dictates; this is especially important in winter, in any climate where weather can change abruptly, at high altitude, or when you're unsure of your companions' abilities.

Whenever I've set out to climb a peak in winter, I've gone thinking that chances are good I won't make the summit. When you're focused narrowly on a goal, you're easily blinded to the unanticipated barriers to reaching that goal which can arise, and your mind is slower to accept the idea that maybe it's time to turn around, to change your plans. While backcountry accidents are generally attributed to a concrete event or series of events, you can often trace them back to the victims' failure to take steps to avoid the accident when they had the opportunity. (See chapter 9 for more on decision-making and leadership.)

Finally, before heading out, let at least one responsible person know your route and when you expect to return. If you need help,

Be flexible. Something as simple as a blistered ankle can change your plans drastically. Remember, your goals are safety, responsibility, and fun.

that person can make a difference of hours or days in how quickly it arrives. For the same reason, register your trip with land managers or at a trailhead hiking register whenever possible.

Resources

The Washington, D.C., main offices of federal land-management agencies listed below can provided general information about their public lands and contacts to specific parks and areas. Usually, the best source for specific information about the park is its own backcountry office or ranger headquarters; get that phone number and mailing address from area directory information or the agency's headquarters. The Web sites are also quite useful.

- The Bureau of Land Management (BLM), within the U.S. Department of the Interior, manages 264 million acres of land—about one-eighth of the land in the United States—mostly in the western United States, including Alaska. Its Web site provides links to specific BLM lands. Bureau of Land Management, Office of Public Affairs, 1849 C Street, Room 406-LS, Washington, DC 20240; 202-452-5125, fax 202-452-5124, www.blm.gov.

- The National Park Service (NPS) manages more than 80 million acres of national-park land. Its Web site provides links to individual parks and is an excellent trip-planning tool. National Park Service, 1849 C Street NW, Washington, DC 20240; 202-208-6843, www.nps.gov.

- The U.S. Forest Service manages 191 million acres of national-forest land across the country. Its Web site provides links to individual national forests and recreation information. U.S. Forest Service, 201 14th Street SW, Washington, DC 20250; 202-205-1706, www.fs.fed.us.

One very useful Web site is www.recreation.gov, which provides links to information for recreational uses of federal lands under the Army Corps of Engineers, the Bureau of Land Management, the Bureau of Reclamation, the Fish and Wildlife Service, the Forest Service, and the National Park Service.

Other Web sites providing interesting information for backcountry travelers include:

- www.gorp.com, which provides numerous links to recreational opportunities and other information of interest to outdoorspersons.

- www.lnt.org is the home page of the organization Leave No Trace, where you can find its guidelines for low-impact backcountry travel for backpackers, climbers, river runners, and other users.

- www.gearfinder.com is an excellent way to begin shopping for an item of gear. The site allows you to select specific criteria in ten gear categories, then shows you what's available on the market. It also provides a listing of manufacturers.

- www.thebackpacker.com provides an almost infinite number of links to information for backpackers, from articles to gear to destinations.

- www.bpbasecamp.com, *Backpacker* magazine's base camp, has lots of info relevant to backpackers and backcountry travelers.

- www.lexicomm.com/views/index.html provides updates on trail and ice- and rock–climbing conditions; pictures; trip reports; and the latest weather reports from the Northeast, Northwest, and northern and southern Rockies.

- http://parkscanada.pch.gc.ca/parks/main_e.htm, and www.canadianrockies.net are two sites with information on Canada's parks and the Canadian Rockies.

- www.orca.org, is the home page for the Outdoor Recreation Coalition of America, the trade group for the human-powered outdoor-recreation industry, and a source for a variety of information about gear, government issues, and other things.

- http://weather.noaa.gov/weather/ is the National Weather Service Internet Weather Source, where you can find information on the current conditions, forecasts, and climates for sites across the country.

- And, of course, there's the AMC's home page, www.outdoors.org.

chapter
two

GEAR

OUR OUTDOOR GEAR *has a funny way of forging a sentimental bond with us, especially the first pieces of gear we own. Maybe it's because we associate them with our first outdoor experiences, which always command an exalted place in memory. Sometimes our attachment to gear has little to do with how well it performs.*

My first tent was a flimsy nylon dome I considered a steal at, if I remember right, $79. A crime it was, though I was confused for the longest time as to who was the victim. Nonetheless, I coaxed several enchanting years of mediocre performance out of that tent. In its twilight summer, as my wife (who was then my girlfriend) and I traveled the Mountain States backpacking and climbing, I dubbed that tent the "Wind Sock" for its ability to make the least detectable breath of air sound like a cyclone. The tent all but disintegrated during a week-long stay in a national forest campground in Colorado's Front Range—the zippers breaking one after another, the rainfly leaking like mesh, the elastic cords connecting the fly to the tent so stretched out that the fly flapped about like a poncho in a tornado.

I think that tent may still lie beneath an entombing layer of dust in my brother's house. Unable to chuck it into the trash—as would have been appropriate—I clung to the stubbornly optimistic notion that the Wind Sock still possessed some intrinsic value. I actually gave it to my brother's kids. My niece Brittany, five years old at the time, immediately rubbed through my superficial sheen of sentimentality when she sized up the tent in two words: "It's dirty."

My first hiking boots were a canvas pair that set me back about 45 sawbucks. Though woefully inadequate for anything more than hiking with a light pack on dry trails, I wore them backpacking, in mud and in snow—although not in severe cold. I even wore them for three magical days in Alaska's Denali National Park, during which my feet remained perpetually cold and wet and I began to wish I knew how to recognize the symptoms of trench foot. I think I squeezed about five years out of those boots, using them until they had worn so badly I could practically clip my toenails without taking the boots off.

You've no doubt detected a consistent theme to these anecdotes: My first gear purchases were what I could afford at a time when I didn't know better anyway. They served the purpose of letting me get out into the woods and mountains. I own better stuff today not because I couldn't get outside without expensive stuff, but because I'm more discriminating about how gear performs, and I can afford gear that enhances my comfort—whether that comfort is measured in the weight of the gear, how well it fits me, or in the trouble I avoid because my gear performs its desired function.

Go out shopping for outdoor gear today, and the choices are dizzying. There's a lot of stuff on the market; in a nutshell, some of it's junk, most of it's pretty good, some of it's excellent. Avoid the junk if you want to use it more than three times, but think hard about how you plan to use something before shelling out the bucks for high-end gear. Those items are worth their price to someone; it may or may not be you.

As with most things, there is a correlation between quality and price when it comes to gear. For most of us, price matters. But while fiscal reality may dictate what you can spend, don't base your choices primarily on price. Instead, choose gear that's designed for the demands you will place on it—that's the best way to assure that your new gear doesn't fail you in your time of need, and may also protect you from spending more for features you don't need. If what you think you need is beyond your budget, either wait until you can afford more or see a better deal, find the best affordable alternative, or mold your activities to fit the gear you can afford. I'll get into specifics about different items of gear below.

My early gear provides evidence aplenty that you don't need expensive stuff to get out into the backcountry—provided your activity doesn't require high-end gear for safety, and backpacking generally doesn't. But if you're bothering to read this book, you're probably fairly serious about outdoor recreation and already may have come to a conclusion on your own that I reached some time ago: The more you travel into the backcountry, the more importance you will place in gear that's lightweight and *comfortable and performs well. You usually pay more for these qualities, but it's money well spent.*

Finally, don't spend more time shopping for gear than using it. Educating yourself can only help the decision-making process, and this chapter will help you sort through the morass of information. But don't let it intimidate or consume you, and don't be sold on the notion that you can't wander into the mountains without all the latest gadgets. Heading into the backcountry is supposed to be, first and foremost, fun.

Packs

On a backpacking trip in Colorado's Weminuche Wilderness, I passed a woman who appeared to be in her seventies, not five feet tall, and was hiking alone with all her stuff in a frameless rucksack which hung awkwardly from her hunched back. She strode past me without a pause, but another backpacker I encountered minutes later said of her, "She's famous around these parts." Pondering the discomfort of all that weight resting on her shoulders, my first thought was, "Wow, she's tougher than I'll ever be." My second thought was, "She's tougher than I ever want to be."

You may be tough enough to handle it, but today there's no reason to wear an uncomfortable pack. Pack design has evolved into one of the most competitive arenas within the outdoors industry, with dozens of manufacturers producing packs of all sizes for all purposes. That's good for you and me. Virtually every year, pack makers are introducing innovations that improve comfort by providing a more individualized fit and better load control.

If you go for a high-end backpack, you should be able to find something custom-fit to your torso, and the retailer should be able to swap out parts like hip belts and shoulder straps to achieve an ideal fit. Packs priced in the midrange are generally adjustable to a broad array of torso sizes and shapes, and have a plethora of straps to fine-tune the fit and how you bear the load. The cheapest packs will compromise fit, comfort, and features, feeling a bit boxy and not having all the extra bells and whistles available on better packs. If you're looking for a bargain, you should nonetheless search for the best fit you can find, and look for solid construction: durable pack cloth, seams that aren't going to rip open on your second trip, decent padding in the hip belt and shoulder straps.

tips on buying gear

❖ Shop around; compare products. Look for sales and discounted or second items rather than buying on impulse or last-minute. Buy at out-of-season close-out sales.

❖ Don't settle for something that doesn't fit well, unless it's the best you can afford and you're willing to sacrifice some comfort and performance. Manufacturers today are designing gear for people of all shapes and sizes—men, women, and children. If you're willing to spend extra, you should get a perfect fit.

❖ Don't go on a spending binge, buying everything you think you need based on limited experience with gear. Accumulating gear over time, as your outdoor skills mature, will give you a finer sense of the kind of gear you want.

❖ Read gear reviews in outdoors magazines that are devoted to your activity.

❖ Ask your friends for recommendations, or to borrow a piece of gear before buying.

❖ Check out what other people you meet in the backcountry are using.

❖ Buy from someone who knows the product and seems more interested in selling you what you need than selling you what costs the most.

❖ Take any major purchase for a test drive before laying down your plastic: Fill up the packs with real weight, put on the boots, and walk around the store for an hour or two. Set up the tents or stoves yourself in the store. Look into renting the tent, snowshoes, sleeping bag or whatever for a weekend trip first.

Packs range in size from hip packs with just a few hundred cubic inches of capacity, which hold no more than a water bottle or a thin jacket, to expedition backpacks with more than 6,000 cubic inches of capacity. Those numbers measure a pack's interior space without extending its sleeve, or collar (if the pack has one), although a measure of the extended capacity is often also provided. The industry lacks a standard for measuring capacity, so regard the numbers as approximate when comparing packs from different makers.

Get a pack with a capacity ideal for the kind of trips you take. Having too small a pack results in you lashing things to the outside of it or having to choose which critical items to leave at home. But having too large a pack can result in either taking more stuff than you really need— thus lugging a bear around on your back—or toting a pack that's underfilled, and some packs don't carry well when underfilled because contents shift around.

Unfortunately, it's just about impossible to find one pack ideal for all the uses most outdoorspeople demand of their packs. A good two-pack combination is a backpack between 4,500 and 6,000 cubic inches and a streamlined pack of 2,000 to 3,000 cubic inches for climbing, skiing, or day trips when you need extra gear and clothing.

Backpack frames fall into two categories: internal and external. Internal frames were introduced two decades after the external ones and immediately rendered the latter obsolete in the eyes of most backpackers. Internal frames hug the torso better and carry the load lower and closer to the back than an external frame, making them more stable on steep trails and for scrambling, climbing, backcountry skiing—any activity where maximum freedom of movement is important.

External frames probably suffer lax sales in part because the design looks ancient—we tend to associate them with old photos of sideburned hippies hiking in worn jeans—and because you don't see external-frame packs featured in cool ads. But they have certain advantages over internals. They are cooler because air circulates between the frame and your back—especially appealing to big men who tend to perspire heavily. They have a higher center of gravity, thus transferring more weight to the hips and allowing you to walk more upright. They often have many pockets that make organizing your stuff easier. And they cost much less than internal-frame packs.

A second fundamental difference is in how packs are loaded. **Panel-loading packs** have long, vertically oriented side zippers which provide ready access to pack contents. **Top-loading packs** are easier to load and overstuff, but offer more-limited access. Some top-loaders have side zippers to combine the attributes of both designs. Choosing between styles comes down to personal preference and how you like to load your pack. I've used many packs of both types and prefer top-loaders because they generally have at least a few points of access (various pockets, the top opening, and a zipper on the sleeping-bag compartment) where I can keep things like snack food, a jacket, and first-aid kit. And I find that once you've opened a panel-loader's side zipper once or twice while on the trail, the contents shift around, sometimes affecting how the pack carries, and it becomes difficult to stuff things back into the pack.

The bones of backpacks are lightweight aluminum frames (in externals) or stays (in internals). The skin is durable nylon, reinforced in places of high abuse, such as the bottom and lid. Designers put a great deal of thought into **pack suspension systems**—the hip belt, shoulder harness, and connected parts which determine how the load rides on your back. Hip belt foam comes in two types: dual-density, in which two layers of foam of varying density conform to your hips, while compromising some stiffness; and compression-molded, which provides the stiffness desirable for supporting the pack's weight but may be uncomfortable if the hip belt's shape doesn't fit yours. Most important, suspension systems come in different sizes and often can be adjusted, or parts like the hip belt swapped out for another size, to fit your contours.

Try on as many packs as necessary to find a good fit. When properly fitted, the suspension system should focus about two-thirds of the pack's weight on your hips. If your shoulders or neck grow uncomfortably stiff from hiking with the pack on, and it's not grossly heavy (its weight is within one-quarter to one-third of your body weight), the pack is either not the right size or not fitted properly.

To **properly fit a backpack,** measure your torso. While you stand at attention, have someone extend a soft tape measure from your seventh vertebra (the prominent bone at the base of your neck) along your spine to the top of your hipbones, which you can find by placing your hands on your hips and drawing a line between your thumb tips. Use that measure to determine what size pack you wear, bearing in mind that manufacturers do not all size their packs the same. Women can find packs designed for their shorter torsos and wider hips.

pack size by category

- Less than 2,000 cubic inches: Small, so-called day packs and hip packs for nontechnical day-hiking. Few features, no frame, a thin belt, possibly a chest strap. Fancier hip packs have stabilizer straps to pull the weight closer to your hips, but overloading them can be uncomfortable on the lower back.

- 2,000 to 3,500 cubic inches: Typically streamlined packs for gear-intensive day trips like rock climbing, backcountry skiing, and mountaineering, or for trip leaders or anyone who carries extra gear for safety in the mountains. Often have thin foam back pads. Hip belts range from thin to wide, and straps draw the load close to your back, but in general the suspension system is minimalist, to keep the pack's weight and bulk down.

- 3,500 to 4,500 cubic inches: Backpacks large enough for three-season weekend trips. They vary greatly in price, features, and fit. Packs at the lower end of this size range are really big enough only for someone who travels very lightly or whose partner carries more than half the gear. If your gear is bulky, or you go places that demand plenty of warm clothing, get a pack closer to 4,500 cubic inches for weekend trips.

- 4,500 to 6,000 cubic inches: Backpacks large enough for trips of a week or more, or for winter trips. Many recreational backpackers buy a pack with a capacity of around 5,000 cubic inches, which expands to near 6,000 cubic inches with the pack collar extended, allowing them to do weekend as well as longer trips, or long trails where resupply points may be several days apart. These packs also vary greatly in features and fit.

- More than 6,000 cubic inches: Backpacks generally used only for long expeditions into areas where one is days from the nearest source of food and fuel supplies.

Most modern packs can be fine-tuned for fit once you've selected the right size. You should have to do this only once, and it will enhance your comfort tremendously. Load the pack first; an empty pack naturally rides differently. Put the pack on so that it rides atop your hips, rather than slipping down over them. The hip belt should fit your waist with ample leeway to tighten or loosen it. With all the straps pulled snug, the shoulder straps should wrap cleanly around your shoulders, without gaps or bunching, and extend about a hand's width beneath your armpits. They should fit so that you have leeway to tighten or loosen the straps while wearing the pack. The load-lifter straps attach to the pack behind your ears, and should be angled at about 45∞ to your shoulders. The chest strap, which usually can be slid up or down, should sit about three inches below your collarbone.

To adjust fit for torso length, most packs have some kind of shoulder yoke above or behind the back padding which allows you to slide the shoulder harness up or down. You may have to put on and remove the pack a few times to get it right. Some hip belts can be adjusted, but you may have to ask whether the retailer can change the hip belt to one that fits you better.

Pack features is an area where designers try to set their models apart. Packs vary tremendously from very Spartan models to those replete with bells and whistles. Features are the little things that make a pack more functional, but they also increase its weight and the blow to your wallet. Ideally, you want a pack with features desirable for your activity without features you don't need.

Here are some extras to seek or avoid, depending on your own needs: ready access to your water, whether in the form of mesh side pockets or "hydration systems," internal bladders with external sipping hoses (see chapter 4 for more on methods of carrying water); a top pocket that detaches for use as a day pack; a divider between the main compartment and sleeping bag compartment to prevent contents from falling down when you pull out the bag; a shoulder yoke for fine-tuning the pack's fit to your torso; load-lifter straps above the shoulder straps for shifting the load from shoulders to hips, and stabilizer straps from the hip belt to the side of the pack to pull the load in closer to your hips (see more below on loading and adjusting a pack); horizontal compression straps around the pack body for pulling the load closer to your back and preventing the shifting of contents; a shovel pocket for a shovel or other gear you want handy; daisy chains for lashing gear to the pack; external pockets in the right places for your purposes (for instance, water–bottle pockets on the sides of a pack aren't very useful to someone planning to carry skis on it); ice–ax loops; and the flexibility of swapping out hip belts and shoulder harnesses to custom-fit the pack.

How well you **load and organize a pack** will determine whether you fumble around in it looking for a jacket as the rain drums on your back, and whether, over the miles and mountains, that pack rides comfortably or feels like a body bag. This is a bit anal-retentive, I know, but I have a system for loading my back-pack—a designated place for just about everything, with slight variations depending on the type of trip. I always know where to find anything, which has proven useful on the countless occasions that a sudden storm has materialized, or my headlamp batteries expired, or I reached a mountain pass and felt a pressing need for a hat and gloves, or I stopped for sunblock or bug dope or blisters. Having a system also actually expedites the task of loading the pack: I can practically do it blindfolded now, without thought.

The general guideline for backpacking on trails is to place light and bulky items at the bottom of the pack, and the heavy and compact items up high and close to your shoulders. Women, whose legs are long relative to their torso, may prefer centering the weight slightly lower. (See chapter 6 for more on how to load a pack in various terrain.) I always place my sleeping bag at the bottom of my pack, rather than lashing it to the outside, where it's exposed to weather and sharp things that want to puncture it. My bag is compact, so I can squeeze a few other light items in that bottom compartment of my pack. I'll keep things I may need to get at while on the trail, like wind pants or a first-aid kit, right inside the compartment zipper.

Just above the sleeping bag goes the clothing I won't likely need before we camp, with bottom layers like socks and long underwear always packed in zip-lock plastic bags—the so–called "freezer" kind that are more durable, and which I can reuse many times rather than throw out after each trip. Nearer to my shoulders go heavier items like the water filter, stove and fuel, cook kit, and food stuff sack, arranged so that I can quickly get the things I might want while on the trail—the food and filter. Also near the top of the pack goes whatever jacket I think I may want, depending on how the skies look on a given day. Small items like snacks, hat, ear band, gloves, sunglasses, map, film, and headlamp generally fit into my pack's lid pocket or an exterior pocket.

Backcountry travel means carrying everything you need in a pack—choose one that rides comfortably. (Bigelow Mountain, ME)

On a weekend trip, when I can fit my tent and sleeping pad inside my pack, I'll stand the tent, in its stuff sack, so that it sits right against my spine and place my rolled-up pad, which is relatively light, to one side of the tent. I'll counterbalance the relatively light weight of the pad with clothing on the other side of the tent. The tent poles usually get tucked into compression straps on the outside of the pack.

If I can fit only one of the two inside the pack, the tent gets preference and the pad goes on the outside. An inflatable pad, which I want to protect against sharp branches and rocks, I tuck inside compression straps on one side of the pack, so that the pad is aligned vertically behind one arm, where it's relatively safe while I'm hiking a trail or when I set the pack on the ground. You can get a protective nylon stuff sack for an inflatable mattress pretty cheaply too. A foam pad I may strap horizontally across the outside of the sleeping-bag compartment, where it helps the pack stand up on the ground.

When the tent does not fit inside, I usually tuck it beneath or lash it atop the pack's lid. If your pack's that full, it's also probably pretty heavy, so be careful not to load the weight up too high, making it top-heavy and unwieldy in steep, rugged terrain.

Lining your tent and sleeping-bag stuff sacks with a plastic trash bag helps keep them dry in a drenching rain. If they are both inside your pack and you have a waterproof pack cover, that may not be necessary. If you live in a wet environment, like the Northeast or Northwest, you might want to line the inside of your backpack with a large plastic garbage bag as added insurance against leakage.

Once the pack is loaded, cinch all compression straps down snugly to prevent any shifting of the contents, which can send you reeling while scrambling up or down a steep trail.

Before donning your pack, loosen all the load-lifter, shoulder, and stabilizer straps that connect the suspension system to the pack body. Put the pack on, buckling the belt and chest strap. With the hip belt resting atop your hipbones, not sliding down over them, pull the belt comfortably snug. Then tighten the stabilizer straps, which are the straps connecting the hip belt to the pack, beginning with the lower strap if there's more than one. Next, tighten the load-lifter straps, which are above your shoulders and adjust how closely the pack rests against your shoulders. Then tighten the shoulder straps and chest strap as desired. Ideally you feel most of the pack's weight resting comfortably on your hips, the pack does not shift around while you're hiking, and the shoulder straps do not interfere with circulation to your arms, making your fingers numb or swell.

Pack covers are light and thin nylon shells with a waterproof coating that fit over a backpack to keep out precipitation. Because no backpack is absolutely waterproof, I always carry a pack cover. They generally run from $15 to $30, and you can get a good, functional cover at the lower end of that range. Look for taped seams so you don't have to seal them yourself, and a size large enough for and designed for your pack. Internal-frame packs require a more trim profile than external, but any cover with a draw cord in a continuous sleeve that cinches with a cord lock should let the cover fit snugly over your pack without restricting your access to hip belt or stabilizer straps. Some covers come with a stuff sack.

Backpack care is basically a nonissue: If you buy a cheap pack and load it up, it may fall apart at critical stress points, and you will learn a valuable lesson about cheap gear. A good pack, though, should withstand anything you put it through, and if it doesn't, send it back to the manufacturer. Any respectable pack maker should be willing to repair or replace the pack for no more cost to you than the shipping.

Boots

I've already talked about my first pair of lightweight day-hiking boots. It was no mystery that my feet ached and were often wet when I wore those boots backpacking, and it wasn't the fault of the boot manufacturer; those boots weren't built for what I put them through. Today the choices in outdoor footwear continually expand—which can make the process of buying boots seem more complex, but actually translates to greater assurance that you can find boots suited to your needs and that truly fit your feet. Gone are the days of settling for a mediocre fit, or women having to wear boots designed for a man's feet.

The most important trait of any boot is fit. Sizes vary slightly between manufacturers, as does the "last" around which boots are constructed, meaning your foot may swim in one size nine, and feel like it's wrapped in a comfy sock in another maker's size nine. See more below on how to fit boots.

The traditional all-leather waffle-stomper is the classic backpacking boot, and is still great for providing support while you're carrying a big load and for keeping your feet warm and dry. But it's overkill for any other use, and certainly much less friendly to the earth than more-lightweight boots—its weight, stiffness, and deeply lugged sole tear up ground more than a lighter boot. Before shopping for boots, decide which of the categories of footwear listed below best meets your needs.

Some boots on the market will overlap categories, and your own experience, demands, and hiking style will determine what you use. As a general rule, go for the lightest boots that serve your purposes—they will be more comfortable out of the box, cause less erosion on the trail, and probably set you back less than a beefier boot.

Finding one pair of boots to cover a range of hiking and backpacking demands is difficult but not impossible. Consider the categories described below, pick the two you want to wed, and look for boots that meet as closely as possible both sets of criteria. For instance, if you want boots for day hikes and three-season backpacking trips of five days or less, look at light backpacking boots with a waterproof-breathable liner. A leather backpacking boot will be too heavy and

Few other pieces of hiking gear take more abuse than your boots. Find a durable pair that won't cause blisters.

cumbersome for day hikes, while a light backpacking boot offers decent protection and support for carrying a big pack (although you have to be more careful where you step, to avoid a twisted ankle).

On the other hand, if you want boots that can be used for backpacking and three-season mountaineering, there are full-shank, all-leather backpacking boots which, while not designed for use with crampons and lacking a lip at the heel and toe, are stiff enough to accept some crampons—provided you're not doing anything that creates greater stress on the crampon than hiking up low-angle snow or ice, and that the crampon has a secure, adjustable strap and preferably a bale that can be secured over the toe.

boot categories

- Sneakers or almost any versatile athletic shoes with a decent sole are fine for day-hiking with a light pack. The boot industry's trend toward more-lightweight models serves as a reminder that those things you run or work out in make an adequate first pair of trail shoes. But they provide limited support for the arches and ankles and little protection against a rugged trail, and won't keep your feet dry. Frequent trail use will wear out sneakers quickly. The more you hike, the more you will want appropriate boots.

- Approach shoes are the sneakerlike models used for hiking and scrambling when traction takes priority over support and protectiveness, especially by climbers approaching the base of cliffs. They are usually low cut and lace up snugly, have breathable fabric uppers and soft soles of sticky rubber, and are not waterproof. They are certainly adequate for hiking with a light pack, but their sticky-rubber soles wear out more quickly than soles of day-hiking boots.

- Day-hiking boots put a bit more protection between your foot and the hard ground and often provide more support than approach shoes, yet are still lightweight, low to midcut, and usually not waterproof. They are not as durable, or nearly as expensive, as backpacking boots. They are best for day hikes of any length with a light pack.

- Light backpacking boots are mid- to high cut, for greater ankle support with significant weight on your back, have a fairly stiff midsole (sometimes with a half-shank) for support and protection, and may have a waterproof-breathable liner. Still, they rarely require any breaking in and have fabric uppers that make them cooler than all-leather boots. They are ideal for weekend backpacking trips, and, depending on how much weight you're carrying and how careful a hiker you are, they can be used for longer trips. But they will wear out sooner than leather boots, especially if you frequently carry a heavy pack.

- Backpacking boots have thicker, deeply lugged soles of hard rubber, a high cut, and a stiffer midsole to provide more support and protection for your foot than a light backpacking boot. Leather uppers provide additional support and protection, repel water, and make the boot warmer. Frequently, they have a waterproof-breathable liner. They typically require breaking in, cost more, and are best for backpacking with a heavy pack.

- Mountaineering boots are high cut and made of leather, plastic, or a combination of the two. A full shank and thick hard-rubber outsole make them stiff and difficult to hike in for long distances (see the chapter 6 section on hiking in varied terrain for advice on lacing mountaineering boots for hiking a trail). They are waterproof, and some have a removable, insulated booty for warmth in extreme cold. With their stiffness and a pronounced lip on the toe and heel, these boots are designed for wearing with crampons. For steep, technical terrain and ice climbing in deep cold, get plastic boots, but for general, three-season mountaineering where you expect to do a lot of hiking, get leather.

- I will use the term "winter boots" for that growing category of footwear designed for nontechnical activities like snowshoeing. They are high cut, heavy, bulky, waterproof, sometimes breathable, and warm, typically made of rubber or a combination of rubber, leather, suede, and synthetic insulation. Many have a removable insulated booty. They are far less expensive than mountaineering boots, but most will not accept a crampon.

As with other gear, you can educate yourself to the fine technical details of boot construction before choosing the right shells for your feet, or you can ignore this fundamental stuff and skip ahead to the most important element of buying boots: getting the right fit (below). Herewith, for the devoted gear geek, a tutorial on the basics:

Hiking–shoe uppers show increasingly varied appearances, yet are still essentially variations on leather, suede, and lightweight fabric or mesh. Full-leather uppers, found on backpacking and mountaineering boots, offer the most support and protection to your feet and ankles. If you regularly treat the leather with any of the weatherproofing treatments on the market to prevent it from drying out, it will shed water and keep your feet dry splashing through streams and down muddy trails—especially if the upper is seamless, meaning it has few places for water to leak in. Suede's waterproofness and durability is a grade below leather's, and any boots with multiple seams and/or uppers made of fabric or mesh panels will not keep out water. Fabric also wears out much faster than leather. Fabric/mesh, however, is the lightest and most breathable (read: coolest) type of upper, making it preferable for lightweight day-hiking and approach shoes.

Many backpacking boots and some light backpacking boots now come with a **waterproof-breathable liner** to ensure waterproofness, which some argue is redundant and adds unnecessary expense to all-leather boots. But it is a popular feature, and a liner will ensure that the boot remains waterproof even immersed in water—provided, of course, the water does not wash over the boot top. Despite the breathability, a liner inevitably makes a boot warmer, which may be desirable on cold days and uncomfortable on hot days. Whether you prefer having such a liner will depend on the type of hiking you do, the typical trail conditions and weather, and how easily your feet sweat or get cold. Different types of waterproof-breathable materials differ in how warm and breathable they are, and they change too frequently to comment on here, so shop around. Another feature of boots is a synthetic liner that wicks perspiration away from the foot and sock.

Outsoles vary from deeply lugged rubber that prevents slips on mud, snow, dirt, and gravel—typical of backpacking boots—to the smoother, softer, often stickier rubber more suited to traction on smoother surfaces like granite and slick rock. You'll find the sticky rubber on lightweight day-hiking and approach shoes. Advances in the way outsoles and midsoles are attached to the uppers have made boots lighter and easier to resole. Resoling is a good option for holding on to leather boots that have become like a protective second skin on your feet over the years, but it is rarely worth the cost with light hiking shoes which wear out more quickly and are less expensive to replace.

Midsoles are basically comprised of either expanded vinyl acetate (EVA), which is used in running shoes for its cushioning ability but has a short life span; or polyurethane (PU), which is stiffer and more durable. The other key element of a midsole is the shank, present in boots designed for backpacking and mountaineering. Traditionally made of steel but now increasingly made of nylon, the shank may run the length of the boot or only to roughly the ball of your foot. The shank provides support and protection against sharp objects and makes a boot stiffer and heavier. The **insole** is a stiff piece of fiberboard (in cheaper shoes), molded nylon, PU, or polypropylene above the midsole which offers a little more protection for your foot and improved torsional, or side-to-side, rigidity. When a boot is board-lasted, it means an insole layer has been added.

How to fit boots. Start by trying on the boots with the socks you intend to hike in. (See more about socks in chapter 3.) Even the first time in new boots, you should feel little movement around the heel and ankle. Too much rubbing will create blisters.

Look for a good fit in the length and width of the boot (women's feet are typically much more narrow than men's, which is why they need boots built around a women's last). In lightweight day-hiking boots and approach shoes, like sneakers, the toe box will fit snugly; in heavier boots, the toe box is bigger to prevent your toes from getting jammed while walking downhill under a big pack. If you hike in mountainous, steep terrain, you may prefer a boot with a large toe box even for day hiking, to prevent jammed toes. For similar reasons, trail-running shoes should have an ample toe box.

Lightweight backpacking boots, and anything lighter, should fit correctly out of the box. The stiffer the boot, the more time it will require breaking in to flex with and fit your foot. Don't break in a pair of stiff leather boots on a week-long backpacking trek. Remember that any boot's fit will loosen up over time, so don't buy a pair so big you have to pull the laces as tight as you can to fit well. Sometimes trying a different boot insert can make the critical difference in fit and comfort; some inserts greatly reduce the abuse your sole suffers on the trail, particularly under the weight of a pack.

Boot care. Leather boots should be treated with any of the several waterproofing products available, to keep the leather from drying out and help it repel water. Treat your boots at least at the beginning and end of each hiking season, or as often as you feel necessary if you backpack frequently; you can't really overdo leather treatment. Never leave a leather product close to a heat source like a fire or radiator; it will dry out the leather and may irreparably damage the boot and shorten its life. Lightweight fabric boots require little maintenance, but cleaning off excessive dirt or mud and drying them out thoroughly will prolong their life.

Use an antibacterial foot or shoe spray in boots after wearing them. Anytime you go backpacking for a weekend or longer, or get rained on, or even just sweat a lot in a pair of boots on a day hike, moisture remains inside the boot after you take them off. Stuff balled up newspaper into the boots for a few hours to absorb that moisture and prevent the buildup of mildew that causes odor and the premature degradation of boots. If possible, remove the insert and let it dry thoroughly. If you have a waterproof-breathable liner like Gore-tex, it's a good idea to swish a little clean water around periodically inside the boot to clean the liner; then let the boot dry out in a warm, dry place.

Tents

My first nights in a tent were with the Boy Scouts. I was in junior high school, and we slept under prehistoric army pup tents, those floorless, canvas **A**-frames supported by two wooden poles at either end and stakes along each side. They weighed nearly as much as I did at that age, and rolled up not-so-conveniently to the size of an Oriental rug.

Besides allowing our active imaginations to court a notion of ourselves as rugged wilderness explorers, the coolest thing about those tents was that you could reach out under the side flap of your tent and pull up the stakes of your neighbors' tent while they slept through a rainstorm—precipitating great hilarity when your neighbors began shouting and cursing about getting soaked. The worst thing about those tents was their susceptibility to the same prank by your neighbors after you fell asleep.

Although my days of army pup tents are far behind, even modern tents have not spared me from my share of wet nights or waking up to find my pad and bag in a puddle. But those minor disasters could be traced to poor tent maintenance, poor campsite selection, or just miserably torrential rain that even a good tent could not repel. They may be imperfect, but today's tents are remarkably resistant to the harshest weather. They also come in myriad designs, sizes, and prices. Choosing the right one for your needs is simplified tremendously by a fundamental knowledge of how tents differ.

The box below describes three categories of tents designed for backcountry use. Within each category are other options and characteristics to consider, described on page 47.

The first decision you'll make is on the **tent size.** Tent capacity is measured in two ways: the number of people it will fit and the square footage of its floor space. The first number is an approximate measure; the second provides a finer comparison. Most three-season backpackers will go for a two-man tent, but even within that broad category interior space can vary by several square feet. If you like keeping stuff inside your tent, look for a roomy model (i.e., at least thirty-eight to forty square feet of floor space), and make sure you set it up and crawl inside before buying. If you're a winter camper or have other reasons for keeping lots of gear in your shelter, you may prefer a three-man tent even for two people. The trade-offs for more space, of course, are that the tent is heavier and usually more costly.

Most tents designed for backcountry use, except some of the lightest models, are **free-standing**, meaning their poles will support the tent without it being staked out—provided the weather remains calm and dry. In practice, even free-standing tents function better when staked out, which prevents the walls from sagging, lets the zippers slide more easily, and reduces the risk of your shelter getting blown away. (While staying at the Gros Ventre campground on the edge of Grand Tetons National Park once, we were approached by people in the adjoining site who asked whether we'd seen anyone make off with their tent while they were out. We shook our heads, contemplating the disturbing thought that someone would actually dismantle and steal a tent at a campsite—until I noticed a brightly colored spot a few hundred yards away across the grasslands.) For all but the weight-conscious who aren't concerned about weather or having a tent that's more difficult to erect, free-standing is the way to go.

Two **basic tent designs** are most practical for backcountry travel: the inverted bowl shape known as the dome, and the modified **A**-frame, in which poles are looped over the tent to keep its walls from

types of backcountry tents

- Three-season tents are designed for the conditions most recreational backpackers encounter: late spring to midautumn in the middle latitudes; temperatures ranging from hot to below freezing; and rain, light snow, and fairly strong winds. This is the broadest category of backcountry tents, with great diversity and variation between models in sturdiness, ventilation, and warmth, as well as in the other characteristics described below. In general, they consist of a breathable tent with a zippered door and often a zippered window, and they are supported by poles and stakes, over which is attached a waterproof rainfly.

- So-called convertible tents are three-season tents that can be modified to make them warmer and sturdier for use in strong wind and winter temperatures. This is typically accomplished via solid nylon panels which zip in over mesh walls, and adding another pole for support. They're great for people who occasionally encounter harsh cold and whose summer and fall outings are in mountains like the Rockies or those in northern New England, where even August nights can be chilly. Their drawbacks are increased weight and price, that they can be too warm on balmy evenings, and they collect condensation more easily below freezing than a true winter tent.

- Four-season, or expedition, tents are built to contain heat while ventilating well and to stand up to powerful winds and heavy snow. These highly specialized tents have a lower profile and more poles than three-season tents and are considerably more expensive. Their weights vary. Some sport a single-wall design that forgoes the traditional rainfly for a tent canopy made of a waterproof-breathable fabric, making them very lightweight but quite expensive, and they tend to trap more condensation inside than traditional double-walled tents (that is, tents with a rainfly). Expense aside, they're not a good choice for three-season backpackers because the interior is more cramped and too warm. But if your primary activities include mountaineering or serious winter travel, look at these tents.

sagging like the old **A**-frame pup tents of my Scouting days. A dome has extra space for stashing gear but tends to be bulkier and heavier. The modified **A**-frame is often more streamlined and lighter at the expense of space, although some models are certainly spacious. Well-built tents in either style will be equally tough against the elements.

With modified **A**-frame tents, **tent entry** takes one of two forms: from the side or from one or both ends. Side-entry tents provide easy access to any corner of the tent, and a big doorway for coming and going, but someone is always crawling over someone else. Tents entered from one end are a little more cramped to get in and out of, but you're not as likely to wake up your partner when nature beckons in the middle of the night. It's a matter of personal preference, although many side-entry tents feature ample mesh in those big doors, making them better suited to warm weather. Some high-end tents, in both the dome and the modified **A**-frame designs, have two doors, a very nice feature—especially when there are also vestibules at either end—but one that adds weight and significant expense.

The number of **poles** is the biggest factor determining a tent's weight and sturdiness. Ultralight one- or two-person tents, which are fine for warm weather backpacking or bicycle touring, may have just two poles and may not be free-standing. Three-season tents have two to four poles, and convertible three-season tents add an extra pole. Most winter and mountaineering tents sport at least four poles. Look for poles that are shock-corded, meaning they come in detachable sections held together by a single elastic cord running through them, and made of aluminum or carbon-fiber, the latter being more expensive but having a good strength-to-weight ratio. Fiberglass poles are heavy, prone to shattering, and an indication of a cheaply made tent.

Ventilation and warmth are opposing objectives in tent design, so give appropriate weight to which is more important to you. Obviously, the more mesh in the walls, the cooler the tent; but how well a tent ventilates or contains heat is also affected by how low to the ground the rainfly reaches; whether or not there's a vestibule (which inhibits ventilation); and the size, number, and position of windows and doors. Getting a tent that is warm may seem like the safe decision, but if your backcountry trips are in warm places, you may be uncomfortably hot without lots of mesh on the walls. Also, condensation builds up inside a tent that does not adequately ventilate, a problem occurring more often on nights below freezing (see more in chapter 7 on dealing with condensation). Tents that allow you to adjust the rainfly coverage and area of open mesh panels are good at preventing condensation in varied temperatures, and of course, you pay extra for that versatility.

Unless you always backpack in warm weather and never see rain, you'll benefit from having a **vestibule**, an extension of the rainfly beyond the door that acts something like a mudroom in a house. The vestibule on many three-season and convertible tents is supported by stakes; some high-end tents have a vestibule supported by poles, or even vestibules and doors at either end. A good vestibule provides enough space—several square feet—to store wet boots and other gear or to cook when the weather makes "eating out" an unsavory option. Just make sure you know your stove well, and that it won't flare up and set your shelter ablaze. And make sure the vestibule and door are secure, so that they do not blow into your stove and catch fire.

Check out a tent's **ease of setup** in the store before buying. Ideally, you can set up a tent alone within minutes. Manufacturers have various ways of connecting poles and rainfly to tent, and personal preference will determine your favorite system. Once you've narrowed your choices according to the above criteria, set up a few tents. Remember that a tent with more points of attachment between its parts will take longer to erect, but also will prove sturdier in a gale.

A tent's color may not seem all that important—especially if you're like me, and mix and match technical clothing in the most unfashionable combinations imaginable. But bear in mind that a dark tent will absorb much more heat than a light one, which may or may not be desirable, depending on where you typically camp. Also, the color of the rainfly will affect how dark or bright it is inside the tent during the day. And a brightly colored tent can be more intrusive on the backcountry experience of others.

The **profile of a tent** is something to be aware of but probably won't be a primary factor in your decision. Mountaineers camping on wind-beaten ledges need a tent with low-angle walls and a low peak, and for that they tolerate cramped quarters and less headroom. Tents designed for three-season backcountry use have somewhat more upright walls and better headroom. There is variation in the profile and vertical space in three-season tents, though, and long-torso campers should make sure they're comfortable inside a tent before buying.

A tent is a significant gear investment and probably something you'll have for years. Be picky about it, right down to the small

Pick a tent that keeps you warm, dry, and offers enough elbow room for you and your tentmates.

details—understanding that these things can cost extra. For example, some **nice features** I've seen in tents I've reviewed for outdoors magazines included plastic windows in the tent and rainfly to let me look at the stars at night; plastic clips that make setting up the tent quick and easy; mesh pockets in various sizes on the walls for storing items like a book, hat, and headlamp; loops in the tent canopy for hanging things to dry; and the ability to roll up the foot of the tent like a pant cuff, and roll back the vestibule for improved ventilation on steamy nights. Manufacturers are constantly introducing unique features. See which you like best.

See chapter 7 for pointers on setting up a tent and choosing a site in the backcountry.

Tent care is important only if you don't have a few hundred bucks to throw away every two or three years on a new tent. You don't? OK, for starters, do not store the tent and rainfly in their stuff sack at home; doing so stamps creases into the fabric which will inevitably mark the first places that leaks appear. As with a sleeping bag, store the tent in a big cotton sack or anything that breathes, so that no moisture is trapped inside (plastic trash bags are a no-no). Many tents come with such sacks, but a big old pillowcase will do.

For similar reasons, always stuff your tent rather than rolling it up, whether in its stuff sack while on the trail, or at home in that cotton sack. Rolling a tent the same way all the time creates creases. After a trip, even a dry one, set up your tent indoors to dry it thoroughly. Storing it damp promotes the growth of mildew, which breaks down a tent's waterproof coating. Keep it in a cool, dry place, out of direct sunlight and away from heat sources.

Ultraviolet rays from the sun cause any synthetic fabric, including tent nylon, to fade, lose strength, and ultimately disintegrate; the higher the elevation, the more intense and destructive the UV rays. Whenever possible, camp in a shaded place, set up your tent late in the day, and take it down early. Using the rainfly protects the tent, and a rainfly is cheaper to replace than the tent. Using a ground cloth protects the tent floor and prolongs the tent's life, because otherwise the floor is often the first part of a tent damaged. Make sure your ground cloth does not protrude out from under your tent, or it will catch and pool water.

Don't snap shock-corded poles together. Connect them gently, and always dismantle them starting from the pole's center, to reduce stress on the cords during storage and help them last longer. Keep zippers clean and avoid using a lubricant on them, because dirt will stick to it. Also, do not yank on zippers; it can stress seams and cause tears. If a zipper isn't sliding smoothly, it may be because the tent is sagging slightly; holding the fabric while manipulating the zipper will get it to slide. Zippers eventually break; send the tent to an authorized repair shop or the manufacturer to have the zipper replaced, or look into whether a zipper repair kit is available for that model. Dirt can be washed off tent fabric with a little nondetergent soap (no dishwashing liquid or spot remover) and water and a clean cloth; don't stick a tent in the washing machine or dryer.

Tents that are not factory seam-sealed should be seam-sealed at home before your first trip, and any tent will need periodic—maybe once a year—seam-sealing to prevent leaks. Make sure the tent is dry first, then seal only the seams on the rainfly and tent floor, not the more-lightweight fabric of the tent canopy. Apply the seam sealer on the side of the fabric that does not have the waterproof coating, which is easy to identify because the coated side is shiny, and water will bead up and run off it. There are several products on the market. I like those that come in a liquid form with an applicator—it makes the task much cleaner and faster, although you may have to apply a second coat. Follow instructions that come with the tent and the seam sealer, and let it dry for twenty-four hours.

Sleeping Bags

On a three-day backpacking trip one recent Thanksgiving in Utah's Capitol Reef National Park, my friend Bill developed his own definition of the temperature ratings given to sleeping bags. On nights that dipped just below freezing, Bill wore a hat and long underwear and closed up his 32° bag so that no part of him was visible as he slept— and still could not get warm enough for a restful sleep. The bag's rating, Bill concluded, "means you'll survive at 32°."

Having a bag that doesn't quite keep you warm is no fun, but having a bag that's too warm is rarely any better. I once brought a 30° winter bag on a late-March backcountry skiing weekend in the Gulf of Slides on New Hampshire's notoriously frostbitten Mount Washington. As it turned out, the weather was freakishly warm, with nighttime temps in the twenties—roughly 50° higher than conditions for which my bag was intended. When I zipped it closed, I perspired feverishly. Leaving it open, I shivered. Laying it over me like a blanket didn't work because the ground beneath my sleeping pad was still frozen and I could feel its frigid breath. I got very little sleep that night.

Your sleeping bag is one of those critical gear items that can make the difference between comfort and misery in the backcountry. It can also save your life. Like packs, bags should fit you well, are designed for different uses, and come in two basic types.

Synthetic-fill bags are stuffed with one of several kinds of synthetic insulating material. Compared with similarly rated down bags, synthetic bags are much less expensive, dry out more quickly, and are easier to clean, but they are also heavier and bulkier and do not last as long. Their primary advantage over down is that synthetic fills retain much of their ability to trap heat when wet—meaning that, while you won't be dreaming of tropical beaches lying in that soggy bag, your chances of surviving the night are much better than in wet down. Among the most commonly used synthetic fills are Hollofil and Quallofil, longtime occupants of low-end bags because they are inexpensive, but the bulkiest and heaviest of fills; Polarguard, of which the 3D version is the most lightweight and compressible, though still not as good as down; and Primaloft, Lite Loft, and Micro-loft, which compress fairly well and insulate when wet but tend to lose loft at a younger age than down.

Down-fill bags are more pricey and all but worthless when wet, but they are much lighter and compress more compactly than synthetic bags. I'd pit any high-quality down bag against any synthetic bag of comparable rating in a contest of warmth anytime. They also last longer if given the proper care. Down "fill" is a numbered measure of how many cubic inches of space an ounce of a particular type of down can fill: an ounce of 550-fill down will puff up to occupy 550 cubic inches of space. Manufacturers keep getting more fill capacity out of down, so that bags are now pushing 750 and 775 fill. The higher the fill rating, the higher the cost, but you're also getting a warmer, higher-quality bag which will probably last longer.

My first bag was a synthetic three-season—what I could afford at the time—and I got lots of use out of it. But once I purchased my first down bag, my old synthetic one was relegated to indoor bedding for friends crashing on my floor. If you're a polar explorer or big-wall climber and concerned about the bag getting really wet or holding moisture for long periods of time, go synthetic. If you're on a budget or expect to use the bag only two or three times a year, you'll probably be satisfied with synthetic. But if you spend at least a few weekends and one or two longer vacations a year sleeping in a tent that generally keeps you dry, and want a bag that's toasty, light, and compact and will probably last several years or more, think about investing in down. (See more in chapter 7 about keeping your bag dry in the backcountry.)

While sleeping bags come in different shapes, so-called **mummy bags,** which taper from the opening to the foot and can be closed up around your head for maximum heat retention, are the only type to consider taking into the backcountry. Features to look for include a draft tube along the zipper which keeps out unwanted cold air and keeps the zipper's cold metal from brushing against you; a snap, hook-and-loop tab like Velcro, or another type of closure at the top of the zipper to prevent it from unzipping when you toss and turn at night; a taffeta inner lining, which is comfortable, lightweight, and wicks moisture away from your body; an insulated draft collar; and the ability to adjust the snugness of the hood and draft collar independently through draw cords. Some bags come with fleece-lined stuff sacks for use as a pillow. You can purchase compression sacks to squeeze your bag into as compact a package as possible. A bag's features will vary depending on price and temperature rating.

A **bag's shell** ideally breathes very well (because your body releases quite a bit of moisture at night, which would otherwise reduce the loft of the bag's insulation); fights off water, wind, and UV rays; and boasts of light weight and great durability. The shell materials used in today's bags all have their strengths and weaknesses—and none is truly waterproof, or else it wouldn't breathe adequately. To summarize them briefly: DryLoft is very breathable and wards off condensation or frost; is warm and windproof and the most expensive material. Microfiber is very lightweight, but not as water-resistant or windproof as DryLoft. Ripstop nylon is highly resistant to tearing but sacrifices some breathability. Polyester taffeta offers good resistance to moisture and UV rays and is soft. Nylon taffeta is also soft, but not as durable as others.

A **bivy bag** offers the option of traveling without a tent. It is an uninsulated shell, made of a waterproof-breathable fabric, that fits over a sleeping bag. Options include mosquito netting and a hoop for lifting the fabric off your face. A bivy bag is good, but in a downpour it will not keep you as dry as a tent.

The outdoor gear industry has yet to establish a standard measure, so bag temperature ratings remain arbitrary—each manufacturer rates its own bags (read: not all 20° bags are made equal). Use the rating as a base point from which to begin narrowing your choices. A bag is usually comfortable in temperatures from around its rating to about 20° above its rating, depending on your metabolism. How warm a bag you need depends on how "hot" or "cold" you sleep. Do you complain about your bedroom being cold on cool fall nights, or do you like to throw open a window? When other people are wearing a sweater, are you in nothing but a T-shirt, or bundled up in thick fleece, a hat, and gloves?

My wife and I have two down sleeping bags, both rated at 15°. One has 700 fill, the other 550 fill. The 700-fill bag is, without question, warmer, and she uses it whenever we're out together. Still, I may sleep with the less-warm bag partly unzipped, while she mummics deep inside the warmer bag. We have to look no further than basic physics to explain why. She's tall and lean; I'm short and—as one friend has described me—"dense."

sleeping bag categories

- Summer bags, rated 30° and higher, provide the minimal insulation you need on summer nights when temps are 40° or higher. They're great for that purpose, but as my friend Bill will attest, they feel like thin sheets when the mercury dips below freezing. (I have an old three-season down bag that's lost so much loft over the years it functions now as a summer bag—giving new life to an old sleeping bag.)

- Three-season bags, rated roughly 10° to 25° and the most common bags among backcountry travelers, are useful in conditions most recreational outdoorspeople routinely encounter—e.g., summer to autumn in the Rockies, New England, and most other lower 48 mountain ranges. There's a big difference between the warmth of a bag rated at 10° and one rated at 25°, so think hard about how warm a bag you want before buying (see below).

- Winter bags are those rated approximately 5° and lower and are absolutely necessary for backcountry trips in the coldest season, when the air around you and the ground below conspire to turn you blue. Again, there's a huge difference between a 0° bag and a -30° bag; know what you need. These are the bulkiest, heaviest, most expensive bags on the market. Shop around, because many stores will have a limited stock. Many retailers rent winter bags, which is a more economical way to use them if you go winter camping only once or twice a year.

Women tend to "sleep colder" than men because women, on average, have less body mass relative to their surface area; thus they lose heat more quickly. The same law of physics applies to men who are long and lean too—they often get cold more easily. While many men will be comfortable with a three-season bag rated between 15° and 25° on nights below freezing, many women may prefer one rated somewhere between 0° and 15°—about 20° colder than the chilliest temps they anticipate encountering. Some manufacturers are now marketing "women's" bags, which have a little extra insulation and are shaped more to a woman's contours—shorter, wider in the hips, and narrower in the shoulders.

Getting the right fit. There's a reason bags come in different lengths and differ slightly in their widths at the shoulders, hips, and feet. A bag keeps you warm by trapping the heat released by your body in the tiny air pockets between its insulating fibers. That's why a bag's "loft," or the ability of its insulation to puff up thickly when you lay the bag out, relates directly to its warmth, especially in down bags. Try on a bag in the store before buying it; see that it feels comfortable in the shoulders, hips, and feet, allowing you adequate movement without being too capacious, because the more air around you inside the bag that your body has to heat up, the more energy your body expends staying warm, and the colder you feel. Besides finding comfortable widths, make sure the bag's length is appropriate for your length. Many bag models come in at least two sizes: standard for people of average height and shorter, and long for taller folks.

Liners that can be stuffed or zipped into your bag, and overbags that your bag slips into if your mummy's fit is too snug to accommodate a liner, **improve a bag's rating** by up to 20° at less expense than purchasing another bag. So does wearing extra clothing to bed. (See more tricks for keeping warm at night in chapter 7.)

Proper sleeping-bag care will extend its life and help it keep you warm. The most important thing to do is not store it in its stuff sack at home; keeping it so tightly compressed for long periods of time will crush its insulation fibers, ruining its loft. Instead, drape it over a clothes hanger in a closet, or better yet keep it in a bulky cotton sack with a drawstring (never in plastic or anything that doesn't breathe). After each trip, even if the bag did not get noticeably wet or damp, open it up and spread it out inside your home to dry it out thoroughly before putting it away. In the backcountry, avoid dragging it through dirt and avoid contact with objects that could tear its shell.

Keeping warm with a sleeping bag and inflatable mattress in the Pemigewasset Wilderness, White Mountain National Forest, NH.

On a trip of more than a couple of days, it's wise to lay the bag out in the sun each morning for long enough to dry it out—especially a down bag. Wearing a layer of clothing while sleeping helps protect the bag from the perspiration that's dried on your body and can contribute to the growth of mildew. Occasional laundering of the bag is recommended if it's gotten smelly or dirty, but laundering also can reduce the bag's loft, especially with down bags, and quicken wear in places like seams.

Sleeping Pads

My nephew Stephen was probably four years old the first time he camped with me—in his backyard. At first he seemed to be enjoying the not-so-remote-wilderness experience. But as the evening wore on, he grew increasingly disgruntled over two issues, which eventually drove him indoors. "There's no TV," he bemoaned, "and there's bumps." The TV situation I had not the means or inclination to change. But next time I'll make sure Steve has a good sleeping pad.

The sleeping-pad industry has seen increased competition and dramatic innovations in recent years, mostly with self-inflating mattresses. The choices today give new meaning to the phrase "roughing it," and prices remain reasonable for good, basic pads. Selecting the right one entails choosing between two types and deciding whether light weight or comfort is more important to you. Both types come in different lengths to accommodate taller and shorter people and offer another way of shaving a few ounces.

Closed-cell foam pads are lightweight and do not absorb water because the foam bubbles are closed and airtight—distinguishing them from the even cheaper open-cell foam pads, which soak up water like a sponge and really aren't worth the small saving compared to the cost of closed-cell foam. They provide a Spartan comfort which doesn't compare with that of an inflatable pad. But they are very lightweight—basic, full-length pads are less than a pound and three-quarter-length pads may be a half-pound or less—virtually indestructible, and insulate well against a cold ground. You can lay a foam pad out on the bare ground of a campsite to sit or lie on and not worry about puncturing it on a sharp rock.

Self-inflating mattresses are the waterbeds of the backcountry. While two or three times the price and weight of foam pads, they have become the bed of choice for the majority of backcountry travelers, based on my own unscientific survey. Personally, I'll gladly tote around an extra pound for the added comfort at night. Twist open a valve, and the mattress inflates in minutes, though you usually have to give it a few breaths to firm it up. They come in different thicknesses, the thicker generally being heavier and more comfy, although I've tried thinner, lightweight inflatable pads that were pretty comfortable. Look for a nonslip surface on the mattress to keep your bag from sliding off it, or the mattress from sliding if your tent's on a slope. Some inflatable pads have features like a built-in pillow, ergonomic padding, and independent air chambers that allow you to customize your bed.

Self-inflating mattresses will spring a leak when you least want them to—as my wife discovered one frigid, wind-blasted night at 9,500 feet on Washington's Mount Baker—and a flat inflatable pad offers virtually no padding or insulation against the cold, hard ground. Many models come with repair kits, and you can purchase them separately; get one and carry it. The glue in many repair kits will dry up after the tube is opened, so check it before a trip. Tiny pinholes often can be repaired without a patch by smearing a little glue into the hole and letting it dry. A stuff sack protects the pad while in transit, and a chair kit—besides elevating your campsite quality of life by degrees—often will have a tough nylon bottom that's virtually puncture-proof.

Sleeping–pad care is pretty simple. With closed-cell foam, you don't have to do anything more than store it dry to prevent mildew buildup. A self-inflating mattress should be stored unrolled—because long-term compression eventually will kill its self-inflating capability—and with the valve open so that mildew-causing moisture is not trapped inside. In camp, avoid sharp objects and heat sources. Carry an inflatable mattress vertically along one side of a backpack, tucked under compression straps (see Packs section above on how to load a backpack).

Stoves and Cookware

A number of years ago, I set off to bicycle across the country with the misguided notion that I could cook all my meals, for three months, over a campfire. That fantasy dissolved in the ashes of a couple of very unsuccessful dinners. So somewhere along California's coastal highway, I stopped at the first gear store I came upon and laid out my plastic for a butane stove that set me back around $29. Long since rendered obsolete by modern descendants, it consisted of a tiny burner that screwed into a butane fuel canister, and it served me well for some years—although the contents of my backpack would sometimes reek of leaked butane.

I brought that stove on my first winter camping trip, in New Hampshire's White Mountains, and learned the hard way that butane does not vaporize in temperatures below freezing. Fortunately, my friends had white-gas stoves that fired up even after a night that dropped to about -20°—which illustrates an important point. A stove is one of those critical pieces of gear, like a sleeping bag or tent, that can make the difference between a comfortable and safe trip, and one that's miserable and potentially dangerous.

In January of 1996, two winter campers discovered this truism in New Hampshire's White Mountains. After they were unable to light their stove to prepare a hot meal and melt snow for water, one of them became severely dehydrated and hypothermic during the night, shivering violently. They made it out safely the next day, but a working stove probably would have prevented a situation that could have degenerated into tragedy.

In recent years, I've used just about every backpacking stove on the market while testing and writing about them for an outdoors magazine (an assignment which has, well, "fueled" some exciting moments—like nearly setting a shelter ablaze when a lit stove leaked white gas, instigating a frenzied scramble to hurl sleeping bags and other gear out of the path of a spreading, flaming puddle. I finally lifted the fuel bottle and carried a swinging, still-burning stove at arm's length out of the shelter, as drops of flaming white gas dripped onto the floor). The industry has seen tremendous leaps in stove technology. While all models have their strengths and weaknesses, as a whole, backpacking stoves are more reliable and versatile than ever before. Technological advances happen too quickly to review specific models here, but a basic knowledge of the two types of stove will help you pick one that best serves your needs.

Butane, or canister, stoves burn a butane-propane blend in a pressurized cartridge. Operation is beautifully simple: just twist the burner head or a fuel-line valve onto a fuel canister, open a valve, and put a match to the burner. These stoves are lightweight, compact, and may last your lifetime without needing maintenance. They are capable of delicate flame control, making them great for simmering. Contemporary models can be detached from their fuel cartridge before it's empty, then reattached later, making them easier to stow in a pack. Fairly recent innovations include push-button lighters, which eliminate the need for matches, and a collapsible two-burner butane stove that weighs just twenty-five ounces and has separate burner controls.

With some models, flame output tapers off considerably, and eventually dies out, in temperatures below freezing, although newer stoves have remedied that problem with a higher propane-to-butane fuel mix. Some of those new models also generate a flame nearly as strong as that of the best white-gas stoves, but the big rub against butane flames remains that they do not hold up well in wind.

The smallest and most basic butane stoves are inexpensive, but they can be tippy because the burner sits atop the fuel canister (bigger, wider canisters make a better base). Even among these smallest butane stoves there are differences in the width of the burner; the wider burners, naturally, will be more stable and cook more evenly under a big pot, but these little stoves generally aren't suited for cooking for more than two people. More-expensive butane stoves stand on legs and attach to a cartridge via a fuel line, making them more stable.

Whether you choose a butane stove over a white-gas model should be dictated by the kind of trips you take—they are ideal for fair-weather outings and campsites protected from wind, so don't overlook these stoves. I often take only a butane stove into the backcountry because they're so lightweight and simple to use.

A lightweight cooking stove makes hot, tasty meals with a minimum of effort.

White-gas, or liquid-fuel stoves are heavier, more complicated, and more expensive than cartridge stoves and they also require periodic maintenance. But they still rule in the heat-output department, even in strong winds and deep cold—although some stoves handle the frost and wind better than others. Using them involves a few steps: attaching and pressurizing a fuel bottle with a pump; and priming, or pre-lighting, the burner with a little gas. Some models have a tendency to flare up until you learn the stove's idiosyncrasies, which can be dangerous if you're cooking in a vestibule (see advice below on avoiding flare-ups). They typically have a low profile and stand on collapsible legs, making them sturdy under a heavy pot. Their other advantage is that, while they need periodic cleaning, some can be cleaned in the field—delaying but not canceling dinner. A few models have self-cleaning needles that clear the jet, which needs frequent reaming to prevent clogging.

White-gas stoves traditionally were characterized by high-output flames that could not be adjusted for simmering. You had to use a heat-deflecting plate over the burner, or underpressurize the fuel bottle, to reduce their BTUs. But some contemporary models boast flame control that nearly competes with butane stoves. They all burn white gas, such as the familiar Coleman brand, which burns cleanly and doesn't clog the works as quickly as other liquid fuels. Multifuel stoves also will burn kerosene, diesel, auto gas, and other fuels, making them useful in countries where white gas is not available—for the most part, anyplace outside the United States and Canada. If I anticipate encountering freezing temperatures and/or wind, I want a white-gas stove in my pack.

Advances in this field also brought us the first stove that runs on both butane-propane cartridges and several kinds of liquid fuel, including white gas.

You can pretty much ignore information like burn time and boiling time used to promote many stoves. The numbers are provided by the manufacturers, and are derived under ideal conditions. In case you're curious, though, **burn time** is how long it takes to expend a full liter bottle or a cartridge of fuel at high power; **boiling time** is how fast a stove will bring a liter of water to a boil in windless, warm air at sea level. Your own cooking habits and menu, and conditions like ambient temperature and wind, will determine how long your stove takes to boil water or how long it runs on a full bottle or cartridge.

On extended backcountry sojourns, when **conserving fuel** is an issue, bring foods that require only minimal cooking time or to which you merely have to add boiling water. And as experienced long-distance hikers know, you can shortcut the cooking time for some packaged foods that come with instructions to cook the meal over low heat for several minutes. Instead, long-distance hikers will throw the dried meal into boiling water, cover the pot, bring the water back to a boil, then turn off the stove rather than turning it down to simmer. Leaving the lid on the pot will trap sufficient heat to cook the meal; keep the lid on for a little longer than the prescribed simmering time. Experiment to find out which packaged foods are best suited to this method.

stove care

Butane canister stoves

- Keep the stove clean of food, dirt, mud, or dust.

- Avoid damaging the valve that connects the fuel cartridge or fuel line to the burner.

- Some fuel cartridges are designed to lie on their side while in use; others stand upright. Make sure you know which kind you have. With either kind, avoid jostling or tipping over the cartridge while the stove is lit; that may cause a flare-up.

- With a cartridge fuel that does not perform well in freezing temperatures, when condensation droplets appear on the canister and the flame weakens, warm the canister with gloved hands, or stand it in a pot in an inch or so of cool (never hot) water. Or keep a second canister in a warm place, like a jacket pocket or a sleeping bag. If the canister in use gets cold, turn off the stove, swap canisters, then relight the stove.

White-gas stoves

❖ Carry a maintenance kit (available for most models).

❖ Whenever possible, burn white gas, which is cleaner than kerosene and other liquid fuels. If stored for months, white gas will break down and not burn well, and may have to be replaced. Clean the fuel bottle by rinsing with fresh fuel.

❖ In stoves that don't have a self-cleaning jet, use a wire to poke the jet regularly and clean out carbon residue. With some stoves, you will have to unscrew and remove the jet, soak it in white gas, and wipe it clean.

❖ A poor flame may be the result of a clogged fuel line. If possible, disassemble and clean it with a rag dipped in white gas. Use that rag and white gas to wipe any black carbon residue from the burner; otherwise it may wind up clogging the jet.

❖ The pump failing to pressurize the fuel bottle, or leaking fuel, may mean that its rubber O-ring is dry. Lube it with maintenance-kit oil or saliva; it that fails, replace the O-ring.

❖ Before storing a stove for an extended period, clean it and lube the O-ring. Before any trip, make sure the stove works.

❖ Flare-ups result from overpriming. Prime just enough so that fuel squirts from the jet for about three seconds. Turn the stove off and light that fuel, then wait until the fuel nearly burns away and the yellow flame is barely lapping above the burner before slowly turning up the gas. You can also let the flame burn out completely, then open the valve slightly and hold a match to the burner to light it; but don't open the valve too much or release the gas for more than a few seconds before lighting it, especially inside a tent vestibule, or you may get a brief flash.

Backcountry cookware has come a long way since the first lightweight stainless steel pots were introduced. Today, nonstick surfaces are the rage, making campsite cleanup not such a bad job anymore. They may not last forever like stainless steel, but I swear by 'em. Some manufacturers are marketing titanium cook pots, but they're pricey and usually come in smaller sizes than more-affordable cook kits—no doubt to keep the price down. Frankly, you have to be awfully concerned about weight to make them worth the expense.

Shop around, because cook kits come in a great variety of combinations of pot sizes. Don't carry more than you need, but having too small a set means someone waits for dinner. I personally prefer a set big enough to cook for two or three people, with two pots and a frying pan that efficiently doubles as a pot lid. I take only the smaller or larger pot when I don't need both. With utensils, get something lightweight like Lexan or titanium. If you want to get exotic with meals, go for a backcountry oven, which fits over just about any stove but works best with stoves that simmer well (if your stove doesn't simmer well, get a heat–deflecting plate).

Other Essential and "Luxury" Gear

Beyond the primary gear explained in detail above, of course, there are numerous smaller items that might be divided into two categories: essential gear and "luxury" gear. In these lists, I am deliberately omitting clothing (chapter 3), water (chapter 4), food (chapter 5), and first-aid kits (chapter 10), to cover them in later chapters.

Below are items essential to any backcountry trip of at least one night:

Compass

Whistle

Map and guidebook

Permit where needed

Water bottles

Waterproof/windproof matches and/or working butane lighters

Lip balm and sunblock

Sunglasses

Cap with visor, to keep the sun off your head

Flashlight, headlamp, and/or candle lantern, and spare batteries

Swiss army knife or multitool

Bug repellent

50 feet of 3mm nylon cord (for bear-bagging and other uses)

Food stuff sack, especially for hanging food

Space blanket for emergencies

Toilet paper, trowel

A basic repair kit for gear

Enjoying some "luxury gear"—a Thermarest lounger—in the Yosemite backcountry.

Below are optional items which can help make a trip more enjoyable:

Camera and film (see chapter 12 for more on outdoor photography)

Notebook, pens, reading material, playing cards

One or two trekking poles to reduce the strain on knees

Pack towel

Extra footwear such as sandals or old sneakers

Toiletries

Earplugs (for sleeping with loud companions)

Low gaiters to keep sand, stones, or rain out of your boots

Duct tape for minor repairs

In winter, or for mountaineering in any season, minimum additional gear needs, depending on the type of trip, may include an ice ax, crampons, helmet, goggles, gaiters, skis or snowshoes, ski poles, wands, technical boots (plastic mountaineering, backcountry skiing, or insulated double boots), a backcountry shovel, avalanche transceiver, and a stove base. More important is the knowledge of how to use this gear and survive in a winter or high-angle mountain environment. While chapter 6 covers some mountaineering fundamentals and chapter 11 offers more on winter in the backcountry, this book is no substitute for real training and experience in both disciplines.

chapter
three

CLOTHING

IT WAS JANUARY, *time for the "cabin weekend," as we called it. The annual gathering of several of my high school buddies had begun just a few years earlier and would survive ten years or so, through a time in our lives when these occasional, men-only getaways were cherished and foolishness was revered as great sport.*

Actually a three-bedroom cottage at a Boy Scout summer camp, the cabin had a wood stove but no insulation. The stove had an annoying habit of belching smoke into the cabin, forcing us to throw open windows until the bitter cold became less tolerable than the dissipating smoke—though the open windows had the added benefit of masking the odor of untold numbers of mice who'd made the ultimate sacrifice in the cabin walls. As you might imagine, we spent these weekends cycling through drastic temperature swings inside the cabin—and learning about layering clothing before we'd ever heard the term.

The cabin sat in the shadow of New Hampshire's Mount Monadnock, a bald-topped, 3,000-foot peak which has somehow acquired over the years the unverifiable but enduring legend as the world's second-most climbed mountain—out-tramped only by Japan's Fuji, which apparently is so well traveled that even unverifiable legends risk credibility problems by challenging its claim to number one. And while our cabin weekend had little to do with wholesome outdoor pursuits, from the very first it pivoted around an ascent of Monadnock.

To a man, we were poorly equipped for hiking even a little mountain in winter. Jeans, cotton long underwear, flannel shirts, ski gloves, lined windbreakers, wool sweaters and hats, and leather work boots comprised our wardrobe of technical clothing. But that particular January, I did some research and shopping, and showed up prepared—or so I thought.

As we readied for the climb on Saturday morning, I marched out into the dim haze of our smoky living room to show off my newly acquired first layer to my climbing partners: midweight polypropylene long underwear and turtleneck, and thick socks of a wool-polypro blend. The lads responded with a mix of approving nods, disinterested shrugs, and one or two gastrointestinal declarations.

I ducked back into a bedroom and emerged moments later clad in my outer layers: a neon-bright nylon winter jacket that wouldn't breathe any better than those mice in the walls, and a pair of heavy—really, really heavy—wool pants I'd purchased for around twenty bucks at an army-navy surplus store. This time eyes widened, and I grinned the grin of someone who figured he had just serviced an entire people with the noble gift of enlightenment.

The day was a bluebird for January—not a wispy thread of a cloud to be seen, a thermonuclear sun, and temperatures comfortably in the twenties. Dressed as I was, I probably began sweating on the drive to the trailhead. But I recall vividly that runnels of perspiration began streaming off my head before we'd been hiking for fifteen minutes. Inside of thirty minutes, the fabric against my skin felt like a wetsuit. Taxed far beyond its wicking capabilities, my polypro was floating.

As we trudged up the steepest stretch of trail, an oily sheen covered every square inch of my body as thickly as anything I'd ever experienced in the hottest, hardest physical workouts of my life—even though I'd deliberately slowed to a crawl, falling to the rear of the group. I think the sweat had begun to pool in my boots, and I could imagine its level rising until it spilled over the boot tops. I removed the jacket, but taking off those wool pants would have left me hiking in long underwear so wet that later, at the cabin, I would wring the sweat out of them. The greater risk of removing the pants, of course, was the ridicule of my friends after I'd tried so hard to portray myself as the superior mountain man.

So I hiked, sweating an ocean of water, a mountain of salt, all the way to the summit—where, in my wetsuit, I was probably colder than anyone else and possibly five pounds lighter than I had been at the trailhead.

I still own those wool pants, and they're great for sitting around the campsite in winter or crawling into a damp, wet cave on a cold day. But I learned that day on Monadnock that layering clothing serves the end not only of keeping warm, but also of not overheating.

Dress for Success

Decisions about backcountry clothing basically come down to a few questions: how far you're going and for how long, the likely temperature range and potential for the weather worsening while you're out, and how quickly you can escape the backcountry. The answers to those questions, of course, still leave you to make a subjective judgment based on your own experience and objectives.

A cotton T-shirt and shorts may be fine for hiking on a warm day, when you know you can get back to your car quickly or there's little risk of cold wind or precipitation. But the variables change with increasing commitment of time, distance, altitude, and remoteness; look at all of those factors as lengthening your lifeline to civilization. Plenty of serious backcountry accidents—broken limbs, even fatalities—have their origin in the victims simply not having adequate clothing for bad weather. The resulting hypothermia, or the victims' panicked rush to get back to safety because they knew they had inadequate clothing, precipitated their accident.

Other considerations affect clothing choices. Weather patterns in different geographic regions present their own concerns (see more on that in Regional Climate and Clothing at the end of this chapter). Spring and fall present greater temperature fluctuation and shorter days than summer (see chapter 11 for advice on traveling in winter). Your activity will certainly affect how quickly you can escape foul weather.

At some of Colorado's highest mountain passes, above 12,000 feet, backpackers laden with clothing, gear, and food for several days in the backcountry can bump into hard-core trail runners in nothing but shorts and a mesh tank top, with perhaps a light jacket and water bottle in a small hip pack. Yet both the runners and the backpackers are properly outfitted for their objective. On the other hand, some places are difficult to escape from expeditiously: a perch several hundred feet up a cliff will suddenly seem an unfortunate choice of locale when a thunderhead rolls in and your only escape option entails the time-consuming task of setting up multiple rappels to the ground.

We all have different metabolisms and react to heat, cold, and wind differently. Experience in various temperatures, weather, and seasons is the best way to learn what kind of clothing you'll need for any type of trip, whether for an hour or two or several days. But weather exhibits an annoying trait of unpredictability. The only way to assure comfort, particularly on all-day or multiday outings, is to have clothing with enough layering versatility to keep you warm and dry through whatever you encounter.

Layering

This word is recited like a mantra among backcountry travelers of all stripes today, but there seems to remain nonetheless an incomplete understanding of the concept. The goal of an efficient layering system is to keep you comfortable through the hottest and driest, as well as the coldest and wettest, conditions you may encounter, while being as lightweight and compact as possible. How close you come to that ideal is partly a product of your budget and experience and the natural limitations of any fabric, but also of knowing the climate and environment where you're heading (see chapter 1 on trip planning).

I'll talk about specific fabrics and garments later in this chapter. On a more fundamental level, think of layering as a method of balancing your clothing with existing weather conditions (ambient temperature and the presence of wind or precipitation) and your level of physical exertion.

The **first layer** should help keep you either cool or warm, depending on the weather. On a hot day, if that layer against your skin retains moisture, it will have a desirable cooling effect by accelerating the rate at which heat escapes your body—one reason you're actually cooler when wearing a wet shirt than wearing no shirt at all. (The other reason is that the sun can make you hotter when you're shirtless by evaporating moisture from your skin and, if you're not wearing sunblock, by burning the skin.) The lower the air temperature or the stronger the wind, though, the more important it becomes to counter that cooling process by wearing a first layer made of a synthetic fabric that wicks moisture away from your skin. That's true of both your torso and your legs, and whether you're wearing one or more layers.

Socks are the exception to what I've said above about using a damp first layer to cool the skin on a hot day. That's because you wear boots over socks and, in all but the coldest conditions, feet perspire. If you're reading this book, you probably don't wear cotton socks while hiking, knowing well enough that they retain sweat,

Use a layering system like this to stay warm and dry when you hike. (Seven Devils, ID)

bunch up, and facilitate the formation of blisters—not to mention how uncomfortable they are in boots.

Socks are among the most important articles of clothing you will bring into the backcountry because they protect your feet, and without your feet you're not going anywhere. On most trips of two to five days, I like to have a clean pair of socks for each day. (See more in chapter 10 about prevention of blisters and foot care.) Comfort is a big issue too: If your hands feel cold, you might stuff them into your pockets and not think much about it; but if your feet feel cold, your whole body feels cold. Hot, sweaty feet can similarly darken your mood. The right socks make a difference.

Trail socks have become highly specialized in recent years, with models designed for specific uses from trail running to expeditions. They are often a blend of wool, a synthetic fabric like polyester, spandex for elasticity, and some type of wicking fabric. Socks may be extra thick for cushioning and durability in high-impact areas like the toes, heels, and balls of the feet, and have greater elasticity in places that do a lot of stretching and contracting, like above the ankle and in the arch.

A thin liner sock helps prevent blisters and keeps your feet drier and more comfortable by wicking moisture off the skin; wear a liner beneath a warmer sock, especially if you're carrying significant weight or hiking for a full day or longer. I often get a couple of days' use out of a pair of liners. "Outer socks"—for want of a better term—come in a variety of thicknesses. A midweight sock is good for most three-season hiking; a heavier sock is needed for cold hikes or sitting around the campsite at night. Wear the right socks to prevent your feet sweating too much or becoming cold. (See chapter 11 for advice on using vapor-barrier liners in socks in extreme cold.)

Middle layers provide insulation and are the most versatile garments you can buy, functioning either as a middle layer or an outer layer, depending on weather. Look for wool or a synthetic like fleece because it is warm even when wet, dries quickly, and breathes well. Fleece is manufactured in different thicknesses, or weights, each of which retains body heat to varying degrees. The outdoor enthusiast who hikes, backpacks, climbs, skis in the backcountry, and/or snowshoes—in other words, pursues activities with widely ranging levels of physical exertion in widely ranging temperatures and other weather conditions—will get tremendous mileage out of a middle-layer combo of one lightweight fleece vest or jacket and one heavier fleece jacket.

Fleece jackets with a windproof layer sewn into them are popular, though that wind-breaking ability comes at the expense of some breathability. For that reason, the windproof fabric may be sewn only into the front of the garment, which is good for nordic skiers and mountain-bikers, who typically get more wind in their faces, or for someone whose back is protected from wind by a large pack. But a fleece jacket with a windproof layer will not be as warm as a jacket truly designed as a wind shell worn over a fleece layer; anytime you add a garment, you gain insulation by adding a layer of trapped air that will be warmed by body heat. Just as a sleeping bag keeps you warm because your body is actually warming the air trapped in pockets within the bag's insulation, slightly baggy middle layers will be warmer than tightly fitting garments.

Outer layers are those garments designed to protect you from the elements: wind, rain, snow, sleet, etc. I will cover them in the Technical Outerwear section below.

No one can tell you what combination of layers to wear for any given weather situation; only you know whether you're warm or cold, and you get better at predicting and making those decisions with experience. But adjust layers whenever necessary for fluctuations in precipitation, wind, temperature, and your level of exertion (whether, for instance, you're walking uphill or downhill). Dress as lightly as you can to prevent overheating, bearing in mind that once you begin walking you will warm up quickly. In steady or heavy precipitation, most people prefer to wear a waterproof-breathable shell, even if it's too warm to wear anything else but a first layer underneath it.

Recognize conditions that can cause hypothermia (defined in chapter 10), like wind or getting wet. Change into dry clothing or put on middle and/or outer layers to guard against the slow cooling that can sneak up on you.

Synthetics and Wool versus Cotton

This debate is an old one, and most of us have heard cotton disparaged a bit melodramatically as the "death fabric." Cotton has its merits, however; namely that it's comfortable and inexpensive—and, as we all know, a cotton T-shirt and shorts are fine while hiking in warm weather. But we also know that cotton has its limitations in the backcountry—in cold temperatures, wind, or precipitation, dry

Cotton is a poor choice of clothing for winter travel. (Mt. Monadnock, NH)

cotton offers little protection, and wet cotton will accelerate the loss of heat from your body.

Unlike cotton, the synthetics keep getting better. T-shirts, jerseys, shirts, pants, shorts, and long underwear made from various incarnations of nylon and wicking fabrics are comfortable and durable, breathe well, dry quickly, and hold their shape—even after days in the backcountry. Cotton, on the other hand, gets smelly and dirty easily and stretches out once wet. Because synthetics hold up better, you remain more comfortable and need to carry less clothing.

On a seventeen-day trek around Nepal's Annapurna Range a few years ago, I wore the same wicking T-shirt for fifteen days (and I maintain it didn't start to grow ripe until around day thirteen, although my wife insists it became offensive a few days earlier). On short backpacking trips, I'll hike every day in the same synthetic T-shirt or jersey, then put it on between dry layers while hanging around the campsite at night to let my body heat dry it thoroughly for the next day's hiking (see more in chapter 7 on staying warm and dry around the campsite).

Synthetic pants and shirts come in different fabrics. In general, the softer fabrics are a bit less durable, though certainly tough enough for most trail hiking. Look for desirable features, like a front zipper in a jersey for ventilating, or pockets on pants that are accessible while you're wearing a pack. Any first-layer garment like pants or a jersey should fit well and not restrict mobility at all.

Technical Outerwear

Probably more than any other garment, technical outerwear—parkas, jackets, anoraks, and pants—have changed the nature of backcountry travel and outdoor recreation. They have improved safety by keeping participants warmer and drier, and opened up the backcountry to greater numbers of people by enhancing their comfort—and perhaps their perception of the inherent safety and comfort. Looking for a measure of the impact of technological advances in outdoor clothing? Consider this: Gore-tex and Polartec are household words even among people who have never set foot on a trail.

The choices in technical outerwear today are numbing, and change every year. These garments are also among the most expensive items most outdoor recreationists purchase. Getting a good buy begins, as it does with most gear, with determining your needs, then finding the garment that best suits them.

Outerwear basically falls into three categories.

Waterproof means just that and nothing more. These garments will repel a drumming rain and are windproof, inexpensive, lightweight, and usually compact. Their inability to breathe, however, means all the heat and moisture you produce at almost any level of activity remains trapped inside, and you will sweat prodigiously—except perhaps while walking in the cold—which at the least is uncomfortable and at worst can increase the risk of hypothermia and injury. These garments are too hot to wear for most three-season hiking or backpacking, and are absolutely inadequate for activities like mountaineering or anything similarly extreme. But if you're on a tight budget, a simple, cheap jacket may be the rain shell to go with until you can afford better. (See Buying Outdoor Clothing below.)

Waterproof-breathable fabrics like the ubiquitous Gore-tex are designed to allow the tiny molecules of water vapor rising from your pores to escape through the garment, while keeping the larger molecules of rain and other precipitation out. These windproof shells come in the form of a laminated membrane, like Gore-tex, or a waterproof-breathable chemical coating. Two-layer laminate construction means the outer layer is bonded to the laminate, plus there's a free-hanging layer inside that wicks moisture to the outside. In three-layer laminate construction, the shell, laminate layer, and wicking layer are all bonded together, making for a somewhat lighter but stiffer garment than a two-layer. Gore-tex came first, but other companies are producing fabrics that are waterproof and breathable and less expensive.

Waterproof-breathable garments are usually treated with a durable water-repellent finish (DWR), which is what causes water to bead up and run off it like rain off a newly waxed car. This finish will eventually wear off, leaving the fabric less waterproof (see Care of Technical Clothing below).

Waterproof-breathable garments are the best for extended backcountry travel, such as a multiday backpacking trip, in any place that presents the possibility of foul weather, and they are virtually indispensable for the sort of extreme conditions faced by mountaineers, ice climbers, backcountry skiers, and their ilk. How well they breathe and stave off the elements depends on the effectiveness of their waterproof-breathable fabric and how well the garment is constructed, including whether its seams are sealed. Price offers a pretty good measure of performance in this respect, although price is also affected by the features built into a jacket or pants (see below). In other words, some models will lose a fight against wind-driven rain before others.

Technical outerwear like this Wild Things Anorak allows you to stay dry and cool with an array of zippers, linings, and other features.

Being waterproof does compromise a garment's breathability: Gore-tex and its competitors are too heavy and do not breathe well enough for a highly aerobic activity like mountain-biking; they can even be too steamy for backpacking in a warm rain. These fabrics are also relatively bulky compared to the other two categories described here, and bulk increases proportionately with additional features.

How much should you spend? It really does depend on how much jacket you need. You're not likely to be disappointed with a high-end mountain parka, but you might wisely ask yourself whether you really need it. The most expensive and feature laden of these parkas and jackets are designed for extreme activities like mountaineering. Less-expensive waterproof-breathable rain jackets often function well for three-season backpackers. Conversely, getting a jacket or pants that offer minimal protection in extreme conditions, if that's what you expect to encounter, is a formula for disappointment. I offer more thoughts on this in the section below on buying outdoor clothing.

Water-resistant/breathable jackets were developed in response to the plaint that waterproof-breathables are too hot and do not breathe well enough for highly aerobic activities like mountain-biking or trail running. These lighter and trimmer jackets are not intended to shield you from the wet stuff, but to breathe extremely well while beating back a little wind or mist. Basically, they provide the minimum protection from the elements that you need while working out for an hour or two. This jacket should fit into a small hip pack or stuff into one of the jacket's own pockets and clip to your belt. While they're great for that kind of backcountry activity, they are not designed for extended backcountry travel—more than a day—or extreme cold, wind, or precipitation. The one environment that might present an exception to that rule is the desert, assuming you're traveling in a season of warm temperatures and expect little or no precipitation.

Fit should not be compromised when you're spending this kind of money, right? Shop around for a good fit. Make sure the sleeves and hood move with you—that the jacket doesn't ride up when you lift your arms, and your face isn't half lost in the hood when you turn your head to one side. Waterproof and waterproof-breathable jackets should be long coverage down to midthigh and spacious enough to fit two or three layers underneath. Water-resistant and breathable jackets are waist-length and close-fitting, not something you would likely wear with more than one or two thin, tight-fitting layers beneath.

Parka, jacket, or anorak? While parkas are often designed for more-severe cold and wind and heavy precipitation in any form, and include plenty of extra features, and jackets are more typically designed primarily for rain and warmer conditions, the terms are used interchangeably. An anorak is a pullover with a zipper that goes midway down the chest. But these terms are not very helpful in distinguishing between different shells; more important are the fabric, fit, and features. Remember also that shells are just that, and while they can be warm while you're moving, they offer little insulation, and you may need middle layers at times of inactivity.

The extra **features on a jacket** are often what ultimately sway your decision on what to buy—and, of course, features jack up the price, so look for the combination you want. For starters, I would not buy a waterproof-breathable jacket, parka, or anorak that lacked pit zips, the zippers that run from around the elbow to the ribs under each arm. No matter how breathable the jacket, without pit zips to open up when you're working hard—like hiking uphill with a pack on—no jacket will ventilate well enough to keep you comfortable.

The better jackets have storm flaps over the pit zippers to keep water out when they're closed, and stay open via hook-and-loop tabs like Velcro when you want the zips open. Waterproof zippers forgo storm flaps over the pit zips for a waterproof coating on the zipper itself, translating to a bit less bulk in the sleeves, but in a driving rain, my experience has been that a waterproof zipper will leak before a storm flap.

A two-way front zipper allows you to ventilate from the neck or waist; the front zipper should have storm flaps, preferably ones that secure with hook-and-loop tabs. Cuffs are generally either elasticized or adjustable with hook-and-loop tabs; you don't want a cuff that doesn't snug tightly around your wrist. Pockets should be easily accessible with a pack on. Many jackets have a hem draw cord, and nicer ones have a draw cord at the waist too.

Hoods that roll up and secure on the collar with a hook-and-loop tab are easier to manipulate, and usually more comfortable when rolled up, than hoods that zip into the collar. Think about whether you prefer a stiff bill on a hood for keeping rain out of your face (important to folk who wear glasses) or one that's lighter and less bulky while sacrificing stiffness. Either way, the hood should extend out past your nose, and have a draw cord to cinch it tight around your face and another (usually in the back) for adjusting the hood's depth. Mountaineers and climbers should make sure the hood is spacious enough to fit over a helmet.

Pants come in many forms for three-season backcountry travel. Rain pants that are strictly waterproof but do not breathe are simply too steamy for virtually any backcountry travel. Waterproof-breathable rain pants are very useful in places where rain is almost constant and steady—like the Hoh River Valley rain forest in Olympic National Park—though they may leak in a wind-driven downpour and are not really necessary for weekend or vacation trips in most North American mountain ranges in summer and early fall.

Nylon wind pants, while they do not breathe, are relatively inexpensive and a good shell for pulling over shorts or long underwear when you reach a wind-blasted alpine ridge or summit. They are not waterproof, but they will shed some water and help retain body heat when wet if you have to wear them in the rain. Lightweight pants made from a breathable synthetic are comfortable for three-season backpacking and provide more protection than shorts against cooler temps, wind, and UV rays.

Features to look for in pants include ankle zippers that come up high enough to pull the pants on and off over boots, and pockets accessible while wearing a pack. Some pants have at least one or two pockets secured with either hook-and-loop tabs or a zipper so you don't lose anything. Bear in mind that the roomier and bulkier the pockets, the warmer the pants can feel. Lightweight synthetic pants with zip-off legs are a nice feature on hot days, though some people find the midthigh zippers too bulky.

Buying Outdoor Clothing

They're not giving away modern outdoor clothing—the stuff's expensive. The flip side is: much of it's worth the price. While I've logged my time in the backcountry in decidedly low tech garb, I wouldn't trade the technical duds I have today for those old rags. The new stuff is simply much more comfortable, durable, lightweight, compact, and for many reasons safer.

Still, most of us look at the price first when deciding what to buy. Many of the tips on buying gear that I offered in chapter 2 (see box page 30) apply to outdoor clothing too. But there are other things to consider if you're on a budget.

Prioritize your clothing wish list. The waterproof-breathable mountain parka is a prudent investment if you're a climber or backcountry skier, or a backpacker who frequently encounters extended periods of foul weather. But some three-season backpackers on a budget would more wisely invest the considerable cash outlay required for such a parka into more-versatile middle and bottom layers and a cheap, nonbreathable but waterproof rain jacket.

If you're a backpacker who does not often have to deal with foul weather—because you avoid the backcountry when the forecast looks iffy, or simply because you live in a dry region—that expensive parka will spend a lot of time in your pack. Sure, you usually can't hike in a cheap rain jacket because it doesn't breathe. But it will perform the basic function of protecting you from rain and wind around a campsite or on a summit. Finally, if you're hiking in the rain and it's too warm for the cheap rain jacket, good insulating middle layers will at least keep you warm even when wet. Not to mention that you'll get far more use out of them.

Also, in virtually every clothing category there are the high-end, expensive garments, and there are more "competitively priced" garments. With the high-end stuff, you usually get superior materials, workmanship, durability, comfort, and features. But manufacturers compete for budget buyers by striving for the perfect marriage of frugality and function in the less-expensive garments. Don't assume the cheapest item on the rack is junk (there may be reasons to ignore it, but price is not one). I still own and wear some garments I bought at incredible bargains years ago. But be careful, because some of that cheap stuff isn't worth even its low price. Stick with familiar and reliable brands.

Care of Technical Clothing

Stretching the life of technical clothing begins with trying to keep the material free of dirt, which can take the durable, water-resistant finish off waterproof-breathable garments and ultimately accelerate the deterioration of any fabric. You get dirty outdoors, but don't hurry the demise of your expensive clothing by throwing it in the dirt. Some synthetics, like polypropylene and other wicking fabrics used in underwear, are damaged by dryer heat, so hang them to dry indoors (UV rays from the sun also break down synthetics).

A common misconception about waterproof-breathable jackets is that machine washing damages them. Actually, they should be washed whenever they become dirty, because keeping them clean maintains their effectiveness. All of these garments are treated with a durable water-resistant finish, or DWR, which is what causes the shell to shed water. The DWR can be "masked," making it appear to have worn off, by dirt, campfire smoke, even oils from your skin, and sometimes washing and drying alone will restore it. Check the manufacturer's recommendations on washing; some will advise using a nondetergent soap like Nikwax Tech Wash; others say a small amount of powder laundry detergent is fine. Usually the heat of a normal dryer cycle helps to reactivate the DWR. Some garments, however, should be dried on low heat.

Eventually, the DWR will wear off and even a wash-and-dry cycle will not prevent the jacket from "wetting out," or appearing to soak up water while not breathing properly, which makes you feel clammy and cold. It's time to reapply a DWR. There are different products for this, and they are applied in different ways. Again, see whether the manufacturer recommends a particular DWR-restoring product for its garments. Among the waterproofing agents available are Nikwax TX Direct, which is applied in a wash cycle. Other agents, like Gore's Revivex, are sprayed onto the garment after it's been washed and before the dryer cycle.

If the garment's layers are delaminating, no treatment will revive it. Similarly, if seams are coming apart, it's often a good sign the garment's life has run out. You can try to retape the seams, or, if you think the jacket has some mileage left in it, try sending it to a vendor recommended by the manufacturer for repair.

Nylon wind pants last a long time and are pretty tough, but they will eventually wear out in high-use areas like the seat or knees. Small tears from a sharp branch or crampon point can often be patched, and cheap patch kits are widely available, as is duct tape.

Finally, most manufacturers of outdoor duds market them as durable, and will repair or replace anything that fails or breaks, within reason. Contact the manufacturer's customer service department directly. You should be able to get a toll-free number from a local outdoor-gear shop, or from magazine ads.

Clothing Ethics

Ever since modern technical clothing began replacing the wool generation, and designers of the new stuff saw bright colors as an effective sales tool, some folks have begun raising questions about how conspicuous these clothes make us. Given that we wear them in places where most of us prefer an inconspicuous human presence, the ethical question seems a legitimate one. But I don't expect manufacturers to stop producing brightly colored jackets—or, for that matter, brightly colored tents—or consumers to suddenly eschew flash for a style Chairman Mao might have endorsed.

You will make your own ethical choices in that regard, but consider a couple of other points. Bright colors certainly make you easier to spot than earth tones in the event someone comes looking for you, especially if they're looking from a helicopter or from a distance. For certain activities—mountaineering and backcountry skiing, among others—this becomes important. Dark-colored garments blend more readily into a backdrop of rock or trees, yet make you visible on snow. When I put on a fleece jacket, it's to satisfy a desire to feel warmer; if the sun's shining, dark colors achieve that more effectively than bright colors.

The ethic of not making your presence conspicuous in the backcountry is a good one, and it can be accomplished through practices beyond the choice of color in your clothing, like not making excessive noise or camping in view of others. (See more on ethics in chapters 6 and 7.)

Deciding on Your Wardrobe

So, you're packing for a trip and facing that ominous decision: What clothes do I take? You know yourself better than anyone else does; you know whether you get cold easily, or prefer backpacking in a jersey even on cool, blustery days. As a general rule, if you're not sure how many layers to bring, err on the side of having too much rather than too little. As someone who has sat around a campsite feeling uncomfortably chilly in every stitch of clothing I brought, I've learned that it's better to carry a little extra than to wish you had more, especially in spring and fall.

Another guideline I like to follow is that any garment that cannot be worn in more than one situation or combination is too inflexible and not a good choice for the backcountry—with the possible exceptions of a big down parka and thick fleece pants for sitting around a campsite when you expect evening temperatures well below freezing. In other words, the vest I wear while descending to a campsite in late afternoon will become one of my insulating middle layers that evening. If you're hanging out at the campsite wearing all the layers that fit together, including your shell jacket and pants, yet there's still extra clothing in your pack—other than socks or maybe one more jersey—then ask yourself whether some of those articles are superfluous.

Regional Climate and Clothing

Clothing choices depend on climate and your season of travel, and the research you do before your trip (see chapter 1) will aid in deciding on your backcountry wardrobe. But below is some general advice for three-season travel in various regions of North America.

No matter where you go, always carry a hat. Actually, I mean two hats—a baseball cap or wide-brimmed hat to ward off sun or rain, and a good warm wool or fleece hat. A warm hat may be the single most important clothing item you carry. No other garment helps retain as much body heat for the weight and volume of actual fabric. Always carry one.

On any peaks where you can encounter strong, cold winds and precipitation in any form year-round—including the Appalachians (especially the Northeast mountains), the Rockies, and the Cascades, a wind shell jacket and pants are required gear. Wind protection is also critical in low-altitude places exposed to strong winds, like the shores of big lakes in the upper Midwest, or prairie parks like South Dakota's Badlands National Park. In rainy climates, you'll want the jacket and perhaps the pants to be waterproof and breathable.

Warm, insulating middle layers are indispensable anywhere, whether in the mountains or the desert, which can cool off dramatically at night—especially at higher elevations. At a minimum, bring one thick fleece jacket or wool sweater, preferably something that ventilates with a front zipper. A lighter middle layer, like a fleece

Dress according to the climate. In the desert, a cotton shirt and convertible pants make for cool hiking.

Clothing 85

vest, comes in handy when you're working hard in cool air or as another warm layer when sitting around the campsite at night.

The layer against your skin should be synthetic whenever the air is cool enough that staying dry is important. That generally includes anyplace at high altitude or any exposed summit or mountain ridge. You can, however, get away with wearing a cotton T-shirt and shorts on warm and humid days, but you may want to change from that wet T-shirt into a dry synthetic shirt once you reach high ground exposed to wind.

In regions where precipitation is scant and too much exposure to the sun becomes a primary concern, such as California's Sierra, the Rockies during spells of clear weather, the desert Southwest, or anyplace at high altitude, you need to use clothing to protect yourself from sunburn or heat exhaustion (see chapter 10). Use long sleeves, pants, and a wide-brimmed hat or baseball cap to keep the sun off your head and skin. Lighter colors are cooler. Synthetics are far cooler and more comfortable than cotton.

Pants and long sleeves may also be necessary to guard against biting insects or ticks (see chapter 8) during spring and summer in regions like the Appalachians and the Pacific Northwest, and against thorny plants, snakes, or scorpions in the desert Southwest. Thick socks help too. If ticks are a serious concern, tuck your pant legs into your socks.

Waterproof boots are indispensable anywhere precipitation is possible, including virtually any North American mountain range, or where you may encounter a lot of water or mud along the trail. (See more in chapter 2.)

Other clothing accessories to consider include low or high gaiters, great for keeping your boots free of snow, mud, and small stones; dark sunglasses, absolutely necessary to protect your eyes; a bandanna or some other sweatband for hot days; and mesh head netting in places with a lot of mosquitoes.

chapter four

WATER

WHERE THE FOOTPATH turned abruptly away from the stream it had been following and started climbing uphill, the four of us dropped our packs. We knew from the map that this was the last water source we'd see for at least thirty hours. Backpacking along a high ridge in New York's Adirondacks would reward us with a gorgeous sunrise and sunset and long views of an endless forest painted in some of the most brilliant fall colors I have ever seen. But the price was having to lug all the water we'd need for a day and a half.

So we broke out every bottle and water container we had—and I pulled the short straw. It seemed I was the only one to have brought along a collapsible two-gallon water bag. In the silence that followed this revelation, I quickly ascertained which of us would play the role of yak humping two gallons of water up the mountain.

On a hike up any of the Northeast's steep, high peaks, this task would be only slightly more enviable than receiving notice that you're the subject of a special prosecutor's investigation. But we were following so-called herd paths, the narrow, unmaintained trails tramped into the Adirondack backcountry by peak-baggers. Although the path had been easy enough to hike through the lower-elevation deciduous forest, in the dense conifer jungle above us, walking would be something of a cross between bushwhacking and running the gantlet between two rows of military-academy cadets armed with sharpened pencils.

Straightening up beneath my top-heavy pack, feeling myself sway drunkenly as its liquid load swished side to side, I resolved to bear my cross without complaint. At that moment, on my first trip to the Adirondacks, I had only a vague idea how ugly things were about to get.

Adirondack herd paths are a lot like deadbeat dads—just when you need them, they disappear. At the foot of an old landslide scar several hundred feet high, quite steep and wet, our path evaporated. We started up the slab, weaving from one island of dry rock to the next while edging across the slick, wet patches only when necessary. Near the top of the old slide, where the rock grew so steep we had visions of slipping and cartwheeling hundreds of feet back down it, the spruce jungle alongside the slab suddenly appeared more alluring than it ever would have under any other circumstances. We dove into it.

Ridiculously hunched over beneath the pack, I pushed and pulled through a tangle of branches so thick that two hands weren't enough to part them. Each step up was a knee-to-the-chest clamber and lunge through stubby branches that lashed at my arms, legs, and clothes and snagged my pack. My heart thumped against my ribs as if trying to break out so it could just leap to its death off the mountain and end its agony. Perspiration stung my eyes, it dripped off my elbows when I lifted my arms, it practically sprayed from my pores like water from a sprinkler. My T-shirt could not have been more wet if I'd thrown it into a pond.

By the time we reached the top of the ridge and found a distinct herd path, I felt like I could have guzzled the entire two gallons on my back at once.

How Much to Drink and When

We can go days without food, but without water our bodies shut down. Anyone who's gone even a half-day without something to drink knows the terrible discomfort of real dehydration, how it weakens you physically and focuses all of your mental energy on one objective: finding water.

The average person needs about two liters of water per day—when not exercising. Physical exertion increases your body's fluid needs by a factor of two or more, and that demand is made even greater by hot temperatures and deep cold, very high or very low humidity, sustained exposure to the sun, and a high level of exertion. Big people need more water than smaller people. The fact that you're not perspiring very much does not mean you need less water. The best indicators of sufficient hydration are the need to urinate frequently and that the urine is clear. Remember the battle cry of the well-hydrated backcountry traveler: "clear and copious."

Keeping hydrated maintains appropriate pressure in your cells so they can metabolize the nutrients that maintain your energy level. It allows your kidneys to function the way they should. Dehydration is often the first stage in a process that can degenerate into hypothermia, physical weakness, frostbite, impaired judgment, injury, hypovolemic shock—a host of bad scenarios easily avoided simply by drinking enough fluids. (See chapter 10 for more on wilderness medicine and prevention techniques.)

Dehydration occurs commonly in the backcountry. More people become dehydrated than ever realize it, especially on hot days, but their level of dehydration usually does not become severe enough to be a problem. The indications of dehydration are there, though: reduced urine output and a dark yellow color to the urine, not to mention a raging thirst.

The fact is, it's difficult to stay hydrated while exerting yourself outdoors, because your body is constantly losing water through your perspiration, breath, and urine, yet the body can absorb water only at a certain rate, which varies from 1 liter to 1.5 liters per hour. Guzzling a liter all at once will only result in you peeing out much of that fluid a little while later. If your mouth feels dry, you're already dehydrated and have not been consuming enough fluids for some time.

To stay hydrated, you have to drink water frequently. That's going to happen only if you keep water within easy reach (see the section below on water bottles and hydration systems). When I'm working hard enough to perspire heavily in the outdoors, I'll pay attention to my watch and gulp several mouthfuls from my bottle every fifteen minutes. In a hot and dry environment where water sources are limited, such as the desert or a high ridge in the Rockies, it becomes particularly important to sip water frequently rather than guzzling less frequently—make sure every drop is put to good use rather than just being peed out.

Keep extra water in your vehicle at the trailhead for when you get back. Another thing I do is steadily sip a liter or more of water while driving to the start of a trip. Two or three hours on the road without a drink, and you're on your way to dehydration that will quickly worsen as you hit the trail, especially going uphill. Ditto when you wake up in the backcountry: Your body has dehydrated overnight, and you need about a liter to hydrate before hitting the

Staying hydrated is one of your primary concerns on the trail. (Glacier Peak Wilderness, WA)

trail again. Dehydration is also encouraged by drinking a diuretic—anything that causes you to urinate—like coffee or caffeinated tea.

The various electrolyte-replacement drinks available today are especially helpful when you're sweating a lot, or moving for several hours a day. Many powdered soft-drink mixes provide a similar benefit.

How Much Water to Carry

The day had been a long one—backpacking along the ridge of Little Bigelow Mountain, then the steep, rocky climb of more than 2,000 vertical feet to Avery Peak, one of the two summits of Maine's majestic Bigelow Mountain. The views of mountains to every horizon and the blue expanse of Flagstaff Lake far below made the effort worthwhile. But we were ready to call it a day.

At the Avery tent site, in the saddle between the two summits of Bigelow Mountain, Mike and I dropped our packs, took long drinks from our nearly empty bottles, then walked down a path toward the only local water source, a spring. There we found a few ounces of water in a stone basin, and the spring all but dried up on that September weekend. Darkness loomed less than two hours off, and we had no choice but to continue three hard miles farther, over another summit, to the next camping area to spend the night. We did not walk those miles at a spirited pace.

Failing to have enough water with you is potentially one of the worst mistakes you can make in the backcountry. The other side of that coin, though, is that carrying more water than necessary places undue strain on your energy reserves—and makes you sweat more. Water is weight—about two pounds, two ounces per liter, to be precise. Where you have to carry lots of water, it will be the single heaviest item in your pack. The trick is to have enough water without lugging around more than you need.

During pre-trip planning (see chapter 1), find out about the availability of water and the location of water sources before heading out. If there's a question about water availability, play it safe and carry enough to cover yourself. Day-hikers often carry two liters per person because their packs are relatively light anyway, and having the water saves them the inconvenience of having to purify water during the day. When traveling in the backcountry for more than a day, though, you have to identify the existing water sources beforehand.

In some mountain ranges—the Cascades, the Appalachians, and the Rockies, among others—creeks and streams are abundant and usually carry a strong flow through the drier months of summer and fall. If it's clear you'll come across a reliable water source every two or three hours and you're hiking mostly in the shade or in moderate temperatures, you probably need to carry only one full liter, and simply refill it frequently (I often still carry a second water bottle, even if empty, in case I need it). Check beforehand with a management agency or another good source about the reliability of streams and creeks.

Where water sources are less frequent—say, you'll encounter them only once or twice during the day—carry at least two full liters. High temperatures or constant exposure to the sun may mean you'll need three or four liters; this is the case on many backcountry trips in the desert Southwest.

Water 91

In many places, streams and creeks are seasonal and dry up. Your route may take you through high country with few water sources or, as in parts of the desert, no water sources. (Often the lack of water is the single greatest limitation on how far you can travel in the desert backcountry—you can carry only so much water.) You may decide to camp someplace with a great view but no water, including no snow to melt. In those cases, you're lugging water. At the last certain source, "water up"—that is, drink plenty to hydrate yourself—and fill all the water containers you have. A collapsible water sack that holds at least two gallons becomes a necessity. Plan on each person needing at least a gallon of water per day, five to six liters per day in the desert, including cooking meals. And make sure you know where you'll next find a reliable water source.

Treat It Right

I've met plenty of backpackers who insist they don't worry about drinking directly from streams. I've done it myself out of desperation, but only a few times, and I've been lucky enough never to contract problems because of it. I've also heard from many people who have had a bout with the intestinal turmoil caused by a few invisible little swimmers, and to a person they've sworn never to drink untreated water again.

A little awareness of your surroundings probably will tell you all you need to know about how safe the water is. Are you in a narrow canyon bottom where it's impossible to walk 50 feet from the creek running through it, never mind 200 or 300 feet? A mountain cirque or canyon, like Garnet Canyon in the Tetons, where dozens of climbers and backpackers are concentrated around one water source every weekend? A shallow watering hole in the desert, or the Alaskan tundra, surrounded by the tracks of several kinds of animals? A meadow in the Rockies dotted with cow pies? A New England stream within shouting distance of a campsite overrun by thirty people?

You don't need a Ph.D. in biology to figure out what's getting into that water. The reality is there are few places, if any, in the American wilderness where you don't have to worry about fecal contamination of water. Chemicals, agricultural and mining runoff, viruses—all add another dimension to the concerns. Our waters are

View wilderness water sources with suspicion: filter, purify, or otherwise treat your drinking water.

no longer as pristine as they were in the days of Lewis and Clark, or even when the Appalachian Trail thru-hikers of the '60s and '70s were routinely dipping their Sierra cups into brooks and drinking from them.

Consider any water source in the backcountry unsafe unless treated—and even then, be discriminating. If there's any possibility of people being upstream from you, treat the water. If that creek looks or smells funny, find another one. If the waters have traveled many miles to reach the point where you stand, odds are good they're tainted by agricultural, industrial, or mining runoff, and you don't want that water even if it's boiled or purified.

There are three **proven methods for treating water:**

Boiling kill protozoans like public enemies number one and two, *Giardia lamblia* and cryptosporidium, as well as bacteria and viruses. Boiling is the most effective and sensible method for purifying cooking water, because you generally have to boil the water for whatever you're cooking anyway. There's no need to filter water you plan to cook with—it just puts undo mileage on your filter and is unnecessarily redundant. Conversely, boiling water for drinking—except for a hot drink like tea—consumes fuel and leaves you with drinking water that's hot or warm. Use iodine or a filter to purify drinking water.

There's no consensus on how long water has to boil to make it safe. Some say that reaching a boiling temperature is sufficient, others insist you have to maintain a rolling boil for at least a few minutes. I generally boil water for about a minute, and my health record after innumerable pots remains free of illness. While the boiling temperature of water drops as altitude increases, you can't go high enough on this planet to drop water's boiling temperature so much that it fails to purify water.

Treating water with **iodine**, which comes in tablet, liquid, or crystal form, kills *Giardia*, bacteria, and viruses but does not kill cryptosporidium, which appears to be spreading through the waters of North America. Iodine is lightweight and inexpensive, but some people don't like the taste it leaves in water (personally, it doesn't bother me).

Follow the directions for iodine use. While one tablet is usually sufficient for one liter, if the water is very cold, use two tablets. Leave the cap screwed loosely on the water bottle while the tablet dissolves, then shake the bottle so that the treated water swishes through the bottle cap and screw threads before tightening the cap. Wait ten minutes before drinking the water. Wait thirty minutes after dissolving the tablets before adding something to improve the taste, like a powdered drink mix. Iodine tablets are also sold with a neutralizer that's usually added at least twenty minutes after the iodine has dissolved.

Filtering or purifying is the third method for treating water, and popular because it's easy, effective, and leaves no bad taste. Anytime your only water sources are standing water that's murky, shallow, or silted—common in the desert Southwest and any rivers that originate in glaciers—filters are the way to go. Filters and purifiers are more expensive than treating with iodine or boiling, though, and add a bit of weight to a pack, and filtering water is more time consuming than treating with iodine.

The terms "water filter" and "water purifier" are often used interchangeably, but they are different products. A filter, or microfilter, removes things from water by physically straining them out. A filter's effectiveness depends on the size of its pores, and here you face a Catch-22: The smaller the pore size, the safer the filter, but the easier it clogs. A filter rated to 1 micron or smaller will remove *Giardia lamblia* and cryptosporidium, but only a filter rated 0.2 microns or better will remove bacteria. The minimum protection you want is one that removes bacteria. Filters are generally considered adequate protection when you're at high altitude or near the source of the water you're using.

Viruses are tiny enough to slip through any filter. Viruses carry diseases like hepatitis and are a bigger concern in developing countries, although some experts maintain they are a growing problem in North America. While inoculation is the best protection against viruses, some people will want to spend a little more money for a water purifier that eliminates viruses.

A purifier is essentially an enhanced filter that adds an iodine element to kill viruses and a carbon element to remove the iodine taste. The carbon also reduces organic chemical contaminants like pesticides, herbicides, and chlorine, as well as heavy metals such as those found in the runoff from strip mines. To call a product a water purifier in the United States it must have EPA approval, acquired through passing a battery of tests to remove all microorganisms from water, including viruses. Purifiers are a little more expensive than filters, but they are increasingly popular.

The most visible performance differences between filters and purifiers is how quickly they pump water and how long they last before clogging. The best ones spit out well over a liter per minute—which makes a big difference when two or three people are each pumping two or three bottles a day—and will regurgitate at least 100 to 150 gallons before you need to change a filter element. A backcountry filter should weigh a pound or less. Features like an easy-to-grip pump handle, a long intake hose, a bottle adapter for the output hose so it stays in the mouth of your bottle, and a floater to keep the intake from dragging on the creek bottom all make the task easier.

Filters, including those in purifiers, eventually clog, which becomes evident because the pump sticks and water squirts out hoses. Do not force a pump that's sticking. Some filters can be cleaned by scrubbing or regularly backwashing; check the instructions. Many can be disinfected after each trip by adding a capful of bleach to a gallon of tap water and pumping the water through the filter. Using a pre-filter greatly extends the life of your filter.

Sediment is the nemesis of filters, clogging many of them long before their time. Just three days of pumping water from glacially silted rivers in Alaska killed a filter of mine. Try to remove sediment from water before pumping it through a filter, either by filling a cook pot with the water and letting the sediment settle first, or putting a bandanna or some other thin cloth over the pre-filter; a paper coffee filter held in place with a rubber band works well. Face the intake downstream rather than upstream in a river that's carrying lots of sediment. Make sure the intake isn't dragging on the creek or pond bottom.

Water Bottles or Hydration Systems?

How you carry and consume water isn't as important as having it handy so that you consume enough of it. But water bottles and hydration systems each have advantages and disadvantages.

Water bottles are easier to use around a campsite. Many have measurement markings on them that are useful when cooking. They are a bit less cumbersome than hydration bladders when filtering water or treating it with iodine. There are collapsible "bottles" available that mimic one advantage of bladders in that the space they occupy diminishes as you empty them. (If I'm carrying two or three bottles, one of them is usually a collapsible bottle.) And the caps on wide-mouthed bottles are not likely to freeze shut in the cold. If your pack does not have water bottle pockets that you can reach while wearing the pack, though, you have to get a separate accessory for that. Holsters are available that clip onto a shoulder strap or hip belt and hold a half-liter bottle, which is less obtrusive than a full liter bottle.

Hydration systems typically employ a bladder stored inside a pack with a hose that extends over one shoulder. Their great advantage is the constant availability of water—the hose is positioned near your mouth, allowing you to grab frequent sips. They also shift the weight of your water from your hips—where water bottles are often carried in pockets—to your shoulders and upper back, where, ideally, most of a pack's weight is placed. But you can't conveniently drink out of a hydration system around a campsite, when you're no longer wearing your pack, and its hose will clog with ice when the mercury drops below freezing. Hydration systems are definitely advantageous for strenuous outings of a day or less, like a mountain-bike ride.

Children and Water

Children dehydrate faster than adults and don't acclimatize to heat as quickly. A child can lose a great deal of fluid in just an hour of activity in heat. Go easy for the first few days of a trip in heat to which the child isn't yet accustomed; he will slowly adjust. Fluids help a child or adult combat the effects of exposure to sun and heat, including sunburn.

Kids may need reminders about drinking enough water along the trail. (Mt. Cardigan, NH)

While it's important that children consume plenty of fluids, they don't feel thirst as readily as adults, and it can be difficult to get them to drink. Establish before the trip that their participation in it depends on them following some basic rules, among which is drinking when you ask them to do so. Drink frequently—a good idea for adults too—and watch how much they drink. Use a powdered drink mix, diluted somewhat, if they object to plain water.

Watch for a dark yellow color to their urine, which is a sign of dehydration. Symptoms of more advanced dehydration include a headache, unusual fatigue, loss of appetite, nausea, and other complaints that are similar to a flu. Serious dehydration in a child is indicated by restlessness and unusual loss of interest in what's going on around them.

chapter five

FOOD

I THINK THE FIRST INKLING *that our plans might not materialize quite as we had laid them out hit us a few hundred feet up the cliff. As a cold wind blew in powerful gusts, we inched up the face of Pingora Peak in Wyoming's Wind River Range more slowly than we had anticipated. It was our first time rock-climbing the route, so we had to figure out which of its myriad granite corners and cracks to follow upward. For that matter, just finding our way through a zigzagging maze of grassy ledges to the base of the cliff had consumed a precious chunk of the morning.*

On one narrow ledge, Penny and I examined our situation and agreed there was not a high likelihood that we would finish the climb, get down off the mountain, hike a couple miles back to our campsite, load everything into our packs, then hump about nine miles back to our car and drive forty-five miles of gravel road to the nearest town in time for dinner—the itinerary we'd mapped out the night before. In fact, we shrewdly realized, we wouldn't even be hiking out to the car until the next morning.

This normally would not have bothered us. But one salient fact cast a dark cloud over the prospect of another night in the backcountry: Besides a little snack food, we had nothing left to eat. Like pitiable waifs in a Dickens novel, we faced the grim reality of going to bed very hungry and of a long, stomach-growling walk the next morning before that hunger would be sated.

Somehow this did not trouble us enough to immediately abandon the climb. Maybe we had a bad case of peak fever, or our decision-making ability was obscured by the lingering full feeling from that morning's breakfast. I don't recall exactly why, but we continued upward.

Just below the summit, we encountered two other climbers. Our short conversation quickly came around to our lack of food. One of them generously offered, "We have plenty of food, more than we can eat. You can have a couple of dinners. Just come to our campsite after you get down."

Saved! we thought. They pointed to a patch of green in the cirque far below—their campsite was in those trees. Out of curiosity, I asked whether they'd had any problems with the black bears that had stolen food from several other campers in the area. "We heard about the bears," one of them said, "so we put our food in our tent to keep it safe."

Penny and I shot quick glances at each other, thinking the same thing: We won't be the only hungry climbers tonight.

Well, good fortune smiled on us. The bears prowling the cirque did not find and shred our saviors' tent and devour all their food, as we'd feared. We found their campsite undisturbed, and they gave us the dinners they'd promised.

And that would not be the last time Penny and I would finish a climb later than anticipated, or fail to bring enough food on a backcountry trip.

What, you expected a happy ending and a valuable lesson instilled?

Lugging the Chuck Wagon

I have since learned that, as much as any other aspect of your backcountry trip, your food should be thought out and planned in advance. Food is nutrition and strength, and not having enough is a serious mistake. But it's also weight on your back. The longer your trip, the higher the percentage of total weight you're carrying is in food. You certainly don't want to run out of food—and always err on the side of having plenty rather than not enough. But having far too much unnecessarily increases your burden without a benefit.

Plan your meals in detail. Decide what you're going to eat for breakfast, lunch, dinner, and on the trail, and consume the food over the course of your trip according to your plan. Beyond that, having an extra meal, perhaps in the form of a dehydrated dinner that adds little weight to your load, is good insurance in case you don't get out of the backcountry according to schedule. The more remote and committing your trip, the more "insurance" food you might bring.

An extra chocolate bar or two or some enjoyable snack that provides a source of quick energy is a good idea for the same reason, and something you'll probably eat anyway. I usually measure out a prescribed amount of gorp per day, then throw in a little extra. Gorp, or "good old raisins and peanuts," can consist of almost anything you like—my own favorite combo is raisins, granola, chopped dates, unsalted peanuts, and peanut M&Ms. Leave some nonperishable food in your vehicle for when you return to it—just in case you return a lot later and hungrier than you planned.

Experience will give you a better idea of just how much you will eat in the backcountry. But a pretty good rule of thumb is to figure that on a weekend trip in which you're exerting yourself for several hours a day, your appetite will increase at least 25 percent above normal. You can also estimate food consumption in pounds or calories—the average backpacker will consume two to two and a half pounds of mostly dried or dehydrated food per day, or between 3,500 and 5,000 calories daily. Naturally, the more physically demanding your trip, the more food you will need. And your appetite usually grows the longer you're out there—your appetite on day five will exceed what it was on day two.

On longer trips, at some point most fit people find their caloric needs roughly doubling. **Long-distance hikers** who are out for weeks or months sometimes far exceed their food budget because they failed to anticipate this enormous leap in their body's demand for fuel. My wife and I have spent two and three months at a time traveling around the West, hiking and climbing almost every day, and always amazed ourselves at how much we could eat.

Basically, your fat reserves become so diminished that your body constantly needs a carbohydrate booster. On Vermont's Long Trail, I found myself "hitting the wall" at some point almost every day, feeling a sudden, overwhelming exhaustion and lethargy. I'd sit down, eat an energy bar or some gorp, drink some water, then within minutes feel a burst of energy and start motoring up the trail again. To borrow a comment I heard from one AMC leader, "Lunch starts immediately after breakfast and ends at dinner." Keep food, especially carbohydrates, readily accessible and eat in moderate amounts all day long.

You can carry only so much food, of course. Trips of more than seven to ten days will require a **resupply of food** and stove fuel, among other things. That may be as easy as walking a mile or two off the trail to the nearest town or store—as is often the case along the Appalachian Trail—or it may require assistance from someone bringing supplies in to you. Backpackers on the Pacific Crest Trail or Continental Divide Trail have far fewer resupply opportunities, and have no choice but to carry more food between points of resupply.

I would caution that it's hard to know what it's like to carry a pack loaded with food for seven to ten days until you've done it. Choose foods, like oatmeal, that provide a high amount of calories per pound. For the same reasons that you don't carry more of anything than you need, always look into resupplying at some point on a trip of more than five or six days; in less remote parts of the country, this is often possible. Backpacking for nine days through Maine's 100-Mile Wilderness a few years back, we resupplied on day five. Not having to start the trip with food for nine days undoubtedly made the miles easier on us.

Chow Time

The word "leftovers" is about as foreign to my backcountry vocabulary as terms like "traffic" or "stress." I finish food. When I'm sharing a meal, I'm the one whose eyes dart nervously back and forth between my companions and what's left in the pot before I casually inquire, "Anybody else want some of that?" I rarely feel unable to eat more.

Here's an honest confession: While traversing Maine's Saddleback Range on my own a few years ago, I came upon a single, unbroken, fresh Ritz cracker sitting atop a bare rock. I knew that a family I'd shared a campsite with the night before was not far ahead and probably had dropped it there. No, I didn't eat it. But I did stare at it for nearly a full minute before deciding against it.

But I have met members of that curious breed of backcountry traveler who are sometimes unable to consume all of the food they prepare. I've even hiked with some of them—and hope to again. Unfortunately, though, when these people are not accompanied by a tapeworm-afflicted glutton with a hollow leg, they get stuck with—what's the word again?—oh yeah, leftovers. Leftovers aren't much fun to eat in the backcountry, are less fun to pack out, and too often get scattered in the woods or buried in the ground, neither of which is the proper means of disposal (see more on that in chapter 7).

the menu

Widely accepted nutritional guidelines suggest that a healthy diet is made up half of carbohydrates, 30 percent of fats, and 20 percent of proteins. Below are some basic foods that travel well in the backcountry in each category.

Carbohydrates, which provide quick sources of fuel, include pasta, rice, cereal, dried fruit, bagels or bread, fig bars, chocolate bars, snack bars, fresh vegetables that keep well (like carrots), and energy bars.

Fats contain about twice the calories per pound than carbos or protein and provide the slow-burning fuel that keeps you warm through the night and moving long after your last meal or snack. Fats are found in cheese, chocolate, soups, canned meat or fish, pepperoni, sausage, and nuts.

Proteins are necessary to cell health, and are found in cheese, beans, nuts, and grains like oatmeal, crackers, breads, and bagels.

Don't prepare a meal in the backcountry as you would at home, without regard to whether you'll have leftovers. If you're really not sure how much you'll eat at dinnertime, prepare the meal in waves: First, cook only as much as you're certain you will eat. When that's eaten, you can decide whether to have more, and how much more.

Backcountry Cuisine

While many backcountry travelers tend to think of the lack of refrigeration as the primary limitation on their culinary options, the only real limitations are your imagination and how much you're willing to carry. As I discussed in chapter 1, how much weight you're willing to bear in food may depend on the nature and length of your

Lightweight cooking gear makes gourmet meals a possibility on the trail...

trip—and some foods are much lighter than others. But one conclusion I've reached over the years is that one of my life's greatest pleasures—good food—should not be divorced from another of my great pleasures, the outdoors.

There are two basic schools of backcountry dining. The first, which I will call the **Minimalist** School, relies on freeze-dried meals that generally require only adding boiling water and letting the combination set or simmer for several minutes. Their advantages are light weight, little bulk, and easy preparation, making them the preferred choice for long and/or gear-intensive trips, or when cold or trip logistics make complex meal preparation undesirable. Some packaged dinners come with instructions for preparation at high altitude, but expect altitude to affect preparation time even if the packaging makes no reference to it. Temperatures below freezing may have the same effect.

The innovations in these packaged backcountry meals continue to impress me—I've had many that are quite tasty. They run the

...but you don't always need to break out the camp stove. A simple snack of gorp can provide sufficient energy. (Capitol Reef National Park, UT)

gamut from breakfast foods to dinners and desserts. Several companies market meals directly to the backcountry consumer; you'll see them in most outdoor-gear stores. They tend to be more expensive, especially given that a meal whose package indicates it serves two may be enough for only one hungry person. Supermarkets also carry pasta- and rice-based meals and soups that are cooked in boiling water, and they are often less expensive and pretty good—although some are pretty bad. One way to lessen your expense, as well as avoid leftovers, is to share one packaged dinner and supplement it with a soup and/or appetizers like cheese and crackers.

The second approach to backcountry cuisine I will call the **Imaginative** School. You first enter this school when you begin improvising on the packaged meals described above by adding things like spices, garlic, dried or dehydrated vegetables or fruits, canned fish or chicken, bouillon cubes, and Tabasco or a similar flavoring sauce. If weight is no issue, you can feast on real pasta and sauce, smoked salmon, tortillas and ingredients for burritos—this list could go on almost indefinitely. (Before leaving home, repackage these foods into reusable, lightweight packaging like zip-lock plastic bags and sealable plastic containers.) And with existing choices in lightweight cookware, you can now bake and fry any number of foods in the backcountry.

I tend to prefer meals that are tasty and fairly simple. If you're really intrigued by the possibilities, there are entire books devoted to backcountry cooking. While this approach becomes less practical on longer outings because of weight, it's a great way to "spice up" weekend trips. When backpacking for five or six days, you might alternate imaginative meals with more-lightweight packaged meals.

Some vegetables, like carrots and potatoes, keep well on the trail. Their drawback is that they're fairly heavy. Fresh fruits do not last very long in a pack, and are quite heavy and bulky because of their high water content. But **dehydrating fruits and vegetables** greatly expands the variety of foods available to you in the backcountry. Suddenly peaches, pears, apples, bananas, strawberries, and cherries can be thrown into your gorp or eaten straight. You can toss dehydrated onion and peppers into any dish. Dehydrating can be accomplished at home, if you live in a dry climate, by slicing fruits and vegetables and laying them out on a cookie pan either in a window that gets lots of sun, or in an oven set very low with the door ajar. But the easiest and most effective method is to invest in a food dehydrator.

In **cold temperatures** more food options become available. In many mountain ranges during the warmer months, days get warm and the sun is hot. But that warm period of time is confined to a few hours in the middle of the day. Nights conveniently drop down to around the temperature of a refrigerator, or below freezing, while mornings and evenings are cool. Perishables like cheese and pepperoni keep longer, especially if you insulate them in a fleece jacket or the like inside your pack during the warmest part of the day, and keep them out of direct sunlight. In spring and fall or at high altitudes, you can often count on almost twenty-four-hour refrigeration outdoors, enabling treats like cheesecake and pie (carried in an airtight plastic container).

There is also the science and art of identifying and **eating edible wild plants,** to which many books are devoted. As a way of feeding yourself in most North American backcountry areas, it's not very practical. If you want to explore this, exercise appropriate caution and educate yourself—eating the wrong thing can induce serious illness and in rare instances cause death.

Children and Food

We've all seen how kids start a hike: running ahead, ignoring your advice about pacing themselves. Children burn up a lot of energy in the backcountry, and they will let you know when they're hungry. Give them nutritious snacks frequently to replenish their energy stores. The advice above applies to children as well as adults, but most importantly, bring along plenty of food that you know they will like and eat. Don't experiment with new foods in the backcountry.

chapter
six

ON THE TRAIL

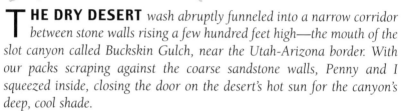

THE DRY DESERT wash abruptly funneled into a narrow corridor between stone walls rising a few hundred feet high—the mouth of the slot canyon called Buckskin Gulch, near the Utah-Arizona border. With our packs scraping against the coarse sandstone walls, Penny and I squeezed inside, closing the door on the desert's hot sun for the canyon's deep, cool shade.

The canyon alternately widened enough to drop an office building into it, then narrowed to barely more than shoulder width. In places, the cliffs rose vertical and sheer, devoid of features. But where water had hurled itself into bends in the canyon, it chiseled out great arches in the stone, some of them fifty feet tall and twice as wide. Everywhere, black water streaks ran down the red walls.

For the first ten miles the hiking was flat and easy. We walked casually, stopping frequently—thinking that, aside from having to carry enough water for two days and twenty miles, it was the easiest backpacking trip we'd ever taken. Then we reached the spot labeled on our map as the "Cesspool."

Undulating, overhanging canyon walls blotted out the sky, and the air grew cold and clammy, like a cave. Rounding a bend, we stopped before a muddy pit several feet across, spanning the four or five feet of ground between the walls, its depth a mystery. We frowned at the utterly uninviting pool, knowing it must be the "possible quicksand" our guidebook had briefly mentioned.

Not to worry, the book had reassured, the quicksand was rarely more than knee-deep. Nonetheless, flickering across the big screens in our minds were images from bad B-movies of hapless adventurers writhing and bellowing vainly for help as a pool of something that resembled molten milk chocolate swallowed them whole.

We changed from boots into sandals. Then, with me probing ahead with a walking stick, and Penny right on my heels, one hand on my shoulder, we slowly waded in.

It was shockingly cold. Broken sticks floated beneath the surface of the thick muck like chopped vegetables in a stew, trying to trip us up. Two steps in I sank to midthigh, but my feet found a firm bottom, so I kept inching forward. When I paused, the muck seemed to harden around my legs. Each step felt like plowing through a vat of honey.

We reached the opposite side of the pit and clambered out—our feet emerging with tremendous sucking sounds—relieved to have survived the Cesspool with no worse than having our legs plastered with the quick-drying goop. Or so we thought.

Just around the next bend, we stopped before a second pit—then a third around the next turn. Within a stretch of 100 meters or less, we forded several of them. Finally, the canyon widened and we hiked again on flat beach sand, with the Cesspool behind us. But two miles beyond it awaited a far more formidable obstacle: the Rock Jam.

Boulders the size of RVs piled up in a mind-boggling heap from canyon wall to canyon wall, two stories high. The ruins suggested a cataclysm of geology that we couldn't begin to imagine. We gaped at it, awestruck, before dropping our packs to search for a way through the debris. The sky above the four-hundred-foot-high walls had grown a deep blue—evening approached, and in the canyon the light grew dimmer and the air sharply cooler.

I scrambled around on the boulders, following openings that all ended abruptly at sheer drops of up to twenty feet. At one short cliff, I looked down at a ladder of shallow toeholds chiseled into the soft sandstone, and wondered how many hundreds of years had passed since they were put there by the ancient people who once roamed these canyons. I certainly couldn't imagine trying to descend them.

Then Penny's muffled voice called from someplace unseen: "I found a passageway underneath." We crawled under an enormous boulder, pushing our backpacks ahead of us on the sand, and emerged on the other side of the Rock Jam. Then we hiked another mile down Buckskin Gulch before finding a high shelf of ground where we could pitch our tent for the night. It was nearly dark as we stood in an ankle-deep, trickling creek, washing the encrusted muck of the Cesspool off of our legs.

We need a rich vocabulary to describe the tremendous diversity of experiences encompassed by the term "hiking." Just on public lands within the United States, those experiences can include following a well-marked trail along an open alpine ridge or through a dense forest; trying to follow an indistinct trail through the woods or a mountain pass; navigating cross-country in open tundra, desert, or woods; walking a sandy beach or canyon bottom; bushwhacking through thick willows or subalpine spruce; route-finding across a treeless mountainside of broken, sliding shale; and fording a river or creek in the mountains or the bowels of a canyon.

Going into those encounters with a sound knowledge of how to deal with them will make them safer and more enjoyable, and lessen your impact on the land. The aim of this chapter is to impart some of those varied skills to you.

Loving the Backcountry to Death

I started up the Falling Waters Trail almost hopping with excitement. It was one of my first hikes, an eight-mile loop over the rugged chain of alpine peaks known as Franconia Ridge, one of the most popular hiking destinations in New Hampshire's White Mountains. That day hardened my growing conviction that I wanted to spend as much time as I could in the mountains.

One of the first things to catch my eye—before we ascended above the trees to endless vistas, even before we reached the first of several waterfalls and cascades—was the unusual appearance of the trees along the trail. With several inches or more of their roots exposed, they seemed almost to spring from the ground. I'd never seen anything like it. And somehow—despite the hordes of fellow hikers all around us, despite having just left a parking lot with a hundred or more cars in it—I saw it as an indication that the trees there in the mountains were "wilder" than those I'd grown up around.

Maybe I can blame my naïveté partly on youth, but I suspect it's mirrored in many novice hikers who still flock to Franconia Ridge every year. As I did, many may fail to realize that the trees are suffering from erosion exacerbated by too many feet.

For a few decades now, our most popular backcountry areas have been overwhelmed by the sheer numbers of us who seek to enjoy them, and the problem continues to worsen. If we are going to maintain them for the enjoyment of future generations, we have to keep educating newcomers to the outdoors on the gospel of low-impact travel. We can all lessen our impact on the trail and backcountry while hiking; the box below outlines some basic guidelines. For more-detailed guidelines, contact Leave No Trace Inc., P.O. Box 997, Boulder, CO 80306; 303-442-8222 or 800-332-4100; www.lnt.org. (See chapter 7 for tips on low-impact camping.)

Even with these guidelines, of course, you'll have to make subjective judgments in the backcountry, and your own experience may lead you to a different decision than another person would make. These judgment calls are not always black and white, good and evil. But educating ourselves about good practices, and making decisions from a basis of knowledge, is the best way to be a careful and conscientious user of the backcountry.

"leave no trace" guidelines

- Stay on the trail, especially in sensitive areas or where the trail is marked off with stone borders.

- Do not shortcut switchbacks—it hastens erosion and often consumes more of your energy than staying on the trail.

- Be alert. Sometimes a bend in a trail may be easily overlooked, and all the hikers who miss the turn help stomp out a false trail. If the path suddenly narrows and becomes less distinct, you have probably wandered onto a false trail. If you see sticks or brush lying in the trail, they may have been placed there by a trail maintainer trying to keep you off a rogue or closed trail; stop and look around for the real trail.

- Unless you need heavy boots with rugged soles because you're carrying a large pack, hike in lightweight boots, which dig up the trail less.

"leave no trace" guidelines

❖ Do not walk around mud puddles; it widens trails or creates unsightly parallel ditches. During the mud season, avoid trails that tend to be wet. Respect trail closings and restrictions—some trails are closed during mud season; others lie on private land that could be closed to the public if trail users don't respect restrictions.

❖ Clear leaves, mud, sticks, and other debris from drainages to prevent water backing up onto the trail.

❖ If you're in an area where wandering off-trail is not prohibited, stick to durable ground like sand, rock, snow, dry grass, and pine needles. In the desert, hike in washes whenever possible, and learn to identify and avoid cryptobiotic crust, also known as cryptogram, which has the appearance of soil but is actually composed of microorganisms and loose sand and provides the foundation for much plant life in the high desert. In the mountains, avoid fragile alpine vegetation.

❖ When off-trail hiking on vegetation or soil is unavoidable, disperse your group's impact by spreading out rather than walking single file.

❖ Don't always take the popular hikes. Seek out lesser-known trails to divert traffic from heavily used trails.

❖ Leave natural and cultural artifacts, such as bones, pottery, or petrified wood, intact where you find them.

❖ Consult the appropriate land-management agency for its recommendations on low-impact practices.

❖ Support your local or regional trail-maintenance organization. Volunteer for trail maintenance.

Walking Lightly

Walk lightly. That may sound like meaningless advice, but it is possible to walk in a way that's easier on the trail—and on you.

Watch a good rock climber scaling vertical rock. She eyeballs each foothold before actually committing the foot to it, then watches the foot attach itself to the hold the way a baseball batter watches the bat connect with the ball. Watch a climber hike a trail, and you will see that same efficiency of movement. Each step is deliberate, the foot placed where it's not going to slip.

She probably does it out of unconscious habit, because she has learned that careful hiking protects her from turning an ankle and conserves the energy she would otherwise expend catching herself after all those trips and slips. But by avoiding those slips, she also churns up less dirt and stones and mud on the trail, and avoids stepping on delicate mosses or trailside plants. She makes less of an impact. It may seem insignificant, but all those exposed tree roots and trenched-out trails in the backcountry weren't caused by one hiker. If everyone walked more lightly, the backcountry would be a healthier place.

Walking lightly also eases the stress on your feet—which, except for your brain, are your most important body part in the backcountry. Someone walking a city sidewalk strides briskly along, landing on his heels. That's fine for walking a flat sidewalk, but a rocky mountain trail would eventually start working some soreness and perhaps a nice blister into your heels. Landing more flat-footed distributes the impact over the entire sole of the foot and helps prevent hot spots that lead to blisters. It also centers your body weight more directly above your foot, reducing the chance of a slip going uphill or down.

Another trick the rock climber uses on the cliff is to take short steps. This helps keep her weight more directly over her feet, reducing the chance of that foot slipping off the rock face. The same principle applies to hiking a trail, especially when descending. Taking smaller steps and creating your own short switchbacks within the trail treadway as you walk downhill—so that your boots land at an angle to the slope rather than pointing straight down it—reduce your chances of a slip. They also reduce the impact on your joints and muscles because your knees bend less deeply.

Hike at a comfortable pace. Take deep, regular breaths rather than moving at a pace that causes you to hyperventilate and tire

Thousands of boots have created a hardened trail along Bigelow Mountain, ME. Try to walk as lightly as possible in the backcountry.

more quickly, increasing the likelihood of a falling injury (this becomes increasingly important at altitude; see chapter 10). Don't force slower members of a group to hike faster than they are comfortably able. Using one or two trekking poles greatly reduces the impact on leg joints and muscles and your back, going downhill and up, helping prevent sore knees and injury.

Adhering to these pointers does not mean you'll start seeing glaciers and slugs pass you on the trail. The most experienced and careful hikers not only avoid blisters and ankle sprains while leaving fainter footprints, but they can often cover ground pretty darn quickly. They also burn up less energy by avoiding the myriad slips and trips that drain us physically—not to mention mentally. Think about how to walk in the backcountry, and soon the better walking habits come without thought.

Navigating

A light snow fell briefly as my friend Doug and I packed up our camp in the Presidential Range–Dry River Wilderness of New Hampshire's White Mountains. But deep snow obscured the Isolation Trail. We scoured the area where our map indicated the trail should be—bushwhacking through trees blown down in giant piles like uncooked linguini, and post-holing to our thighs in soft, wet snow.

Finally, we stumbled upon the trail and followed it to a junction marked with signs. And we stood there baffled at what the signs told us: basically, that we were not at all where we thought we were. Confused, we pulled out a map. We kept looking back and forth between the map and the trail signs, but we still couldn't comprehend what all the evidence clearly indicated.

After a few minutes, I noticed a strange familiarity to our surroundings. I muttered sheepishly, "Doug, this is where we camped last night." Doug looked around, recognized the tracks leading to our campsite off the trail, then closed his eyes and grimaced.

We took a compass reading and bushwhacked downhill toward a tributary of the Dry River, which our map indicated the trail eventually paralleled. Our plan did reunite us with the trail—but not before we spent a couple of hours zigzagging around tangles of vegetation and downed trees, falling into spruce traps (defined in chapter 11), and post-holing to our hips in the soft snow.

At one point, both of us sweating and panting hard, I turned to Doug and we both started laughing—at ourselves. I said this episode would at least make for a good story, and he responded, "Yeah. Whenever I read stories like that I say, 'I'm glad I'm not those guys.'"

We all know that the ability to find your way is fundamental to backcountry travel. And most of us have taken a wrong turn, lost a trail, or—as in my adventure with Doug—embraced such intransigent assumptions about where we were that we failed to see the obvious. There are several skills you can use to navigate through the backcountry. Your situation will dictate which combination of those skills is needed.

The simplest and most common means of navigation is **charting your course on a map** and following trails. If you know with certainty your beginning point on the map, if the map is accurate, and if you're following obvious, well-marked trails in a place where trail junctions feature signs that show trail names or numbers just as they appear on your map, finding your way is relatively easy. You may need a compass to orient your map (see Using a Compass below) and to confirm your direction of travel at some trail junctions. But often you only have to follow the signs and turn at trail junctions in the direction shown on your map, just as you follow a road map. Some trails, including the Appalachian Trail and many maintained by the AMC, are sufficiently well marked and signed that this basic skill is all you need to go hiking. Many national parks have similarly well marked trails.

Maps designed for nonmotorized backcountry travel generally show trails and roads; public-land boundaries and facilities like ranger stations and camping areas; and land forms, waterways, and water bodies and their common names. They show the lay of the land through contour lines, which connect points that lie at the same elevation and which give a map its resemblance to a giant, complex fingerprint. Elevations are marked for some contour lines on a map, in either feet or meters, and the map indicates in its legend what the constant interval is between all adjacent contour lines so that you can figure out the elevation of any point on any contour line.

A map always should show the direction of true north and magnetic north. Along its edges will be markings that indicate the nearest whole-number lines of longitude and latitude for that area, measured in degrees and subdivided incrementally by minutes (sixty minutes to each degree of longitude or latitude). Colors may be used to indicate wooded and nonwooded areas or other relevant zones such as alpine areas or public-lands boundaries. The legend explains a map's markings and displays on a linear scale how many actual miles and/or kilometers are represented by one inch on the map, so that you can measure distance. (One kilometer equals 0.6214 miles; one mile equals 1.6093 kilometers.) The legend also may indicate the year the map was printed or revised, or that information may appear in the map's border. If it's an old map, it may not be entirely accurate. (See more on that in the section below on when the trail becomes indistinct.)

Maps in a large scale like 1:24,000, with contour lines that show elevation changes in intervals of anywhere from 20 to 50 feet—such as standard United States Geological Survey (USGS) 7.5-minute topographic quad maps—provide the detail necessary for traveling off-trail and are more than sufficient for hiking on trails.

Sometimes cairns are the only indication of the trail. (Capitol Reef National Park, UT)

But maps on a scale as small as around 1:95,000, with contour intervals of 100 feet—like the AMC's White Mountains maps—are adequate and often preferable for hiking on trails. Many maps designed for hiking trails are on a small scale because that allows them to cover a larger area, reducing the number of maps you have to carry. The inconvenience of USGS quads is that you may need several maps to cover the area of your trek. Some USGS quads are also years or decades old, and may not show the current location of trails or all the trails in an area. Computer-based map programs now offer the advantage of creating a customized map at home, but these are more expensive than traditional paper or waterproof maps and aren't always easy to print out to a convenient size.

Using a compass—that is, being able to orient a map and determine your direction of travel using the map and compass—is a skill every backcountry traveler should master, at least on a basic level. Learning more-advanced skills with a compass and map allows you to navigate in remote places where trails are indistinct or nonexistent or when visibility is limited.

First note the **components of the compass**. The magnetic needle has a red or orange end and a white or black end. The red or orange end points to magnetic north—a geographic spot on the Earth that is actually below the North Pole. All you really need to know about magnetic north is that it lies in a different direction from true north, and that the degree of difference between magnetic north and true north varies depending on your position on the Earth. For example, if you're standing on New Hampshire's Mount Washington, magnetic north lies 17° west of true north. In the Grand Canyon, magnetic north is about 13° east of true north.

The term for the measure of difference between true north and magnetic north is **declination.** The declination for Mount Washington is 17° west, and for the Grand Canyon it's 13° east. A good backcountry map will indicate the declination for that area, as well as the direction of true north and magnetic north, which you need in order to orient the map (below).

The compass has a rotating, circular faceplate, also referred to as a graduated dial or rotating graduated dial. It is marked off in degrees—360° in a full circle—and typically marked to indicate at least the four basic compass points—north, east, south, and west—which correspond, respectively, with the degree measures zero/360, 90, 180, and 270. The larger the faceplate, the more precise is the

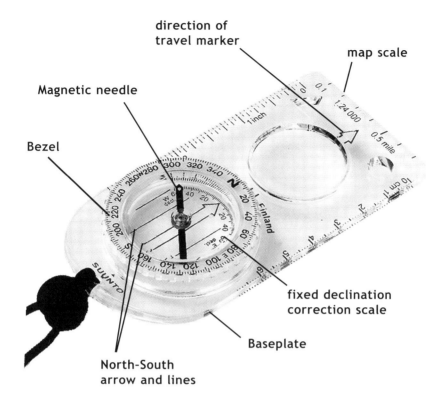

Anatomy of a compass. (© Suunto)

compass for advanced uses like traveling off-trail. That rotating faceplate and the compass base plate—which does not rotate—both have at least one line with a direction arrow. The faceplate lines are often referred to as north-south lines, and the base–plate line or arrow as a direction-of-travel arrow, or simply a direction arrow.

Knowing how to **orient your map** is fundamental to figuring out where you want to go and what physical features of the land you're seeing, and it gives you a refined sense of location. It's very simple. Lay your map out flat and place your compass on it, holding the compass firmly in place. Align the long edge of the compass, or the direction arrow on the compass base plate, with the line indicating the direction of magnetic north on the map. Rotate the compass face plate until its north-south lines and arrow are pointing in the same direction as the base plate's direction arrow (and in the same direction as the map's magnetic-north line). Then rotate the compass and map together until you "box" the red half of the needle into the face plate arrow. Your map is now oriented, and any landscape feature within sight can be identified because its actual direction in relation to you corresponds with its direction from your position on the map. You also know in which compass direction any trail leads.

You can use the compass to **plot a course** between any two points on the map. The ability to follow a compass bearing is a necessary skill for any off-trail travel, including activities like mountaineering, bushwhacking, and backcountry skiing, or to find your way through a whiteout when visibility is zero—an extremely difficult situation in which to navigate even with good compass skills.

Place the compass on the map so that the base plate's long edge connects your current position with the place you want to reach, and its direction arrow points to the destination. Then rotate the faceplate until the red half of the needle is boxed into the north-south arrow on the faceplate and the needle and arrow are pointing in the same direction; in other words, the north-south arrow on the faceplate is pointing to magnetic north. You can now put the map away, hold the compass horizontally in your palm, and walk in the direction indicated by the base-plate direction arrow—taking care not to turn the face plate and keeping the north-south arrow on the faceplate always pointing to magnetic north.

Whenever possible, use natural features as aids. Identify a rock, tree, or other feature in line with your compass course, walk to it, then identify another feature in your compass line, walk to it, as so on. In limited visibility where no natural features stand out, substitute your partner(s) for rocks, having them walk along your compass line until they are nearly beyond sight while you stand still holding the compass; then you walk up to them, send them ahead again, and so on.

When you **take a compass bearing,** the direction arrow also aligns with a degree measure on the faceplate, another way of plotting a course cross-country. If you have instructions to "take a bearing of 60°" from a certain point and walk in that direction, rotate the faceplate until its 60° mark points in the same direction as the base-plate direction arrow. Then, with the compass held horizontally in your palm, turn your body until you box the red part of the needle into the faceplate arrow—so that the needle and faceplate arrow are both pointing to magnetic north. Now walk in the direction indicated by the base-plate direction arrow, again keeping the north-south arrow on the faceplate always pointing to magnetic north.

Terrain often will prevent you from walking in a straight line, of course. When you have to go around a cliff or other obstacle, take a bearing on the new direction of travel required by the obstacle. Say it's 320°: Count the number of paces you take in that direction to circumvent the obstacle—say, ninety paces. Turn again to walk in your original direction of travel—say it's the 60° bearing used as an example above—and walk in that direction until you are beyond the obstacle. You are now walking parallel to your original course, but could miss your destination because you're not precisely on course. To return to your original course, you have to reverse the ninety paces you walked on a bearing of 320°; in other words, take a bearing in the opposite direction of 320°, which is 140°, walk ninety paces in that direction, then return again to your bearing of 60°, and you are back on course.

Be aware that any magnetized objects—including certain rocks and other compasses, metal objects in your pockets, or your belt buckle—can throw off a compass needle, but the compass will function properly as soon as it's moved away from the magnetized object.

An **altimeter**, which provides a reading of your altitude above sea level, is a valuable navigation tool at any altitude, whether in dense forest or open terrain. It's helpful to backpackers, if not critical, and an important piece of gear for mountaineers. Knowing your altitude helps pinpoint your location on a map. Remember, though, that altimeters are affected by changes in temperature and barometric pressure (see Weather section below), and even when frequently calibrated they can give inaccurate readings.

A **GPS** unit receives signals from global positioning system satellites orbiting the Earth to provide its user with his or her precise coordinates of latitude and longitude anywhere on the planet, in any weather. The system was originally developed by the U.S. Department of Defense but is now used for purposes as varied as courier services, wildlife research, and backcountry rescues. It was even used during the construction of the tunnel beneath the English Channel linking Dover, England, to Calais, France, to make sure the two construction crews digging simultaneously from opposite sides actually met in the middle. Different models of GPS units are accurate to within various margins or error; many units sold commercially are accurate to within 300 feet.

Knowing your latitude and longitude coordinates, of course, is no more useful for backcountry navigation than knowing your weight unless you have a detailed map and can use the coordinates to figure out your position on the map, then plot your course from that position. Understand also that GPS units, while probably destined to enjoy growing popularity among backcountry travelers, do have their shortcomings. Batteries can fail, particularly in the cold. Mountain ridges, canyon walls, and other terrain features can inhibit reception of a satellite signal, rendering the unit ineffective. Master the basics of compass and map before turning to a GPS.

When the trail becomes indistinct and hard to follow—which happens in remote or infrequently maintained areas—you have to become more attentive to stay with it (see chapter 11 for advice on following a snow-covered trail). First of all, trails rarely terminate abruptly or transform from a broad, well-traveled path to something much less distinct; that's often a sign you have wandered off the trail. Backtrack to the last point where you're certain you were on the trail and look for a marker or the most obvious treadway. Look behind you for a blaze or marker indicating the trail's opposite direction to confirm you're on the trail.

Sometimes a large tree blown down in a storm will obscure a trail, making it seem to suddenly disappear. Hikers get turned in the wrong direction by the blowdown, starting a rogue path that others who follow help widen. It usually peters out before long. If a trail ends abruptly, backtrack and look for a large blowdown; the real trail may be hiding right behind it.

Even the most faint, unmarked path can be followed with careful attention to it. Most trails show signs of wear in the treadway: packed earth, bare rocks in an environment where rocks off the trail are moss covered, and less ground vegetation than beside the trail. Keep in mind that a trail usually follows the most logical course between two points—contouring rather than making unnecessary climbs or descents, for instance. In forest, besides a worn treadway, the other sign of a trail is its corridor through the trees, which is usually at least three or four feet wide. Heavily overgrown trail may be detectable only at ground level. Three of us once followed an unofficial bushwhackers' trail in Washington's North Cascades that was so overgrown with willows we couldn't see it at all—but our feet could feel the narrow treadway of packed earth where nothing grew.

In some places, a map will not show all existing trails, and trail junctions are not all marked. In Idaho's Seven Devils Mountains, two friends and I had trouble determining our exact location for a few hours because of a lack of signs and a map that did not show every trail. Desert parks can be laced with rogue trails because they last forever in the dry environment.

Use your map to identify landmarks like creeks, drainages, cliffs, peaks, and other natural features, or a distinctive sharp bend in the trail to help pinpoint your location. A guidebook may show a photo of some peak or cliff to help you identify it. Use your compass to determine what direction the trail leads, then consult your map to see where along its course the trail points in that direction (the larger the map scale, the more precise this technique). The compass also can indicate whether a certain landmark is what you think it is: if the peak you're staring at lies to the east, and the map shows the peak you're looking for lying to the north, either you're not looking at the peak you want or you're not standing where you thought you were.

Keep track of the time: if you know your approximate hiking pace, and what time you were at the last point at which you knew your location, you can at least roughly estimate how far you've traveled from there.

Most importantly, where a trail is very indistinct, proceed slowly enough that if you wander off of it, you realize your mistake before going too far to relocate it.

Canyon hiking presents unique difficulties, even on trails. Desert soils tend to retain any footprint for a very long time—including footprints that lead in the wrong direction. When you're in the canyon, high walls prevent a long view of the terrain. Whether in the canyon or on the desert tableland above one, the myriad twisting cliffs, washes, and side canyons can look endless. Consult your map as frequently as necessary, and use any distinct feature to help pinpoint your location—count the number of side canyons you pass, for instance, and note the location of a trail junction or a feature like a natural bridge that's marked on the map.

Also, remember that hiking in a canyon is typically the opposite of hiking a mountain: In a canyon you go down first, then up. Save yourself for the hike out. And don't assume the hike down will be easy. When you begin a hike with a long downhill, leg muscles

Consult your map frequently to stay on track.
(Sawtooth Mountains, ID)

that haven't had a chance to warm up take a greater pounding and are more likely to cramp or stiffen than when you start down a mountain after a long climb up. From spring through fall, midday can get dangerously hot for hiking, so get on the trail in the cool of early morning, rest in a shaded area during the hottest hours of the day, then finish your hiking later in the day.

Getting lost or separated from others happens to everyone. If handled well, the outcome can be no worse than a disagreement over who's at fault. First of all, remain calm and take a look around. If little time has passed since you last saw your companions, they can't be too far away and may be within earshot, so try shouting for them.

If they have wandered beyond earshot, and you are not sure where they went or which way is your ultimate destination, then sit down, have a snack and a drink, and wait for the members of the party who know their way around to come back for you. If they return to that point and find you gone, they may have no idea which way you went, which makes finding you much more difficult. If you wandered in a different direction from your partners and can find your way, backtrack to the point at which you were last together. Stay on trails whenever possible—you're more likely to encounter other people, and trails are usually the most efficient route to follow.

At some point, of course, if no one finds you and waiting longer is not a good option—because, for example, you're unprepared for nightfall—you need to assume control of the situation. If you remember where you came from and help is a reasonable distance away in that direction (either a trailhead or a campsite), then backtrack that way. If you have a map, figure out the shortest route to a road, campsite, or trailhead and take it. Stay on trails whenever possible—you're more likely to encounter other people. Leave an arrow and your name in the dirt or snow, or with stones, to indicate your direction of travel to anyone who reaches that spot while searching for you. In an open area, make that marker large enough, and in sufficiently sharp contrast with the ground, to be seen from the air.

If you lose the trail entirely and foresee little chance of anyone finding you, following a creek downstream or walking downhill will eventually lead to a road if you're in a relatively populous region like the Northeast. (Where there is no creek to follow, maintain a straight line of travel by constantly sighting three objects, like trees or rocks, that are in line in your vision; walk from the first to the second, then sight a fourth object that's in line with the second and third, walk to the third, sight a fifth in line with the third and fourth, and so on.) But remember, this may be a disastrous tactic in remote areas. If you are many hours or days from the nearest road or town, the smartest strategy is to stay put; if someone knows approximately where you are (see Be Flexible, chapter 1), you will eventually be found.

Weather

To the old saying that the only two certainties in life are death and taxes I would add a third certainty for backcountry travelers: bad weather. Spend enough time outdoors and you are going to have days of cold, wet misery. There's no avoiding it.

Weather, of course, is the existing temperature, precipitation, and wind at a given moment, while climate is the average long-term weather patterns in a particular area.

Familiarize yourself with the climate of a backcountry region, including how climate is affected by elevation, for the season in which you are traveling. Local backcountry users, land managers, and guidebooks are good sources for that information. Knowledge of the seasonal climate will help you make informed choices about when to travel and what clothing and gear to bring along.

Check the local weather forecast for the period of time you will be in the backcountry. Understand that forecasts are based on models of past weather patterns, and the ability of those models to predict weather accurately declines the farther you look into the future. In some localities, the accuracy rate of forecasts may drop significantly beyond twenty-four hours; the AMC's Pinkham Notch Visitor Center in New Hampshire's White Mountains, for instance, provides only a twenty-four-hour forecast for nearby summits. In other places, such as the desert Southwest in dry months, forecasts for three days or more are fairly reliable.

Know the direction of prevailing winds locally, so you'll know which direction the weather comes from. Most weather in North America moves west to east, but things like mountain ranges, oceans and large lakes, and hurricanes all make a mockery of that rule. Be aware of peaks or canyon walls that may block your view of approaching storms until the last moment.

Keep an eye on the sky. High, wispy cirrus clouds—sometimes called "mare's tails" for their appearance—announce a storm front arriving within a day. Lenticular clouds, which resemble an upside-down bowl and form over the tops of high peaks, indicate very strong winds. A falling cloud ceiling is obviously a sign of rapidly approaching bad weather. Precipitation can be visible from a distance as a dark veil dropping over the land or dropping from the belly of a cloud. (From a campsite at 11,000 feet in Wyoming's Wind River Range, six of us once watched a thunderstorm erase from sight one mountain ridge after another as it rolled toward us. When the veil was just about upon us, we fled to our tents as high winds and two inches of hail buffeted our nylon walls.) Higher elevations are synonymous with high winds and a greater chance of encountering storms; descending to lower elevations often takes you out of the severe weather.

An altimeter can help forecast weather, because it's affected by barometric pressure. If your altimeter reading goes up when you have not changed altitude—for instance, you may notice a significant change overnight—that means the barometric pressure has dropped and foul weather is on the way. Similarly, if your altimeter reading drops when you have not changed altitude, the barometric pressure is rising and the weather is likely to improve. The altimeter is certainly not a foolproof seer of weather, though, and can be affected by temperature (including your body heat). Altimeters should be calibrated whenever you reach a known elevation, such as a summit or a trailhead.

In short, take foul weather very seriously. Either be prepared to stick it out with the proper gear and clothing, or find a way to escape it. Bad decisions made in the face of worsening weather have precipitated many injuries and fatalities. See chapter 3 for suggestions on clothing choices for climates in different regions of the country.

River Crossings

Streaming with perspiration, my friend Keith and I pushed and kicked through chest-high brush on the tundra of Alaska's Denali National Park, vegetation so dense in places that we couldn't see the ground. The mashed carcasses of mosquitoes plastered our faces and forearms. Mosquitoes flew into my eyes, ears, nose, and mouth. I spat some out, swallowed others.

We sang up a pitiable racket to announce ourselves to the real man-eaters we suspected lurked in the thicket all around us. We were in grizzly country, and leery of stumbling upon one of those burly fellows hunkered down low in the brush looking for food—one of those awkward social encounters best avoided.

Just when we thought we had developed a refined understanding of all there was to fear and loathe in the Alaskan wilderness, we staggered out of the brush onto the bank of the Thorofare River—and stared at what lay before us. Swollen with a day's melt-off from the mountains, the Thorofare was a raging channel twenty to thirty feet wide and no telling how deep; like most Alaskan rivers, it was a flat gray color from the fine silt, or "glacial flour," that's actually rock pulverized by glacial movement. The water was also maybe four degrees warmer than freezing.

We walked the riverbank upstream and down, studying the current and lobbing rocks into it to try to gauge the depth. But the churning waters just seemed to gulp down the rocks like M&Ms. Finally we picked a spot where the water looked more shallow and the current less threatening, and waded into the icy bath, braced against each other as our feet groped over rocks we couldn't see. At midstream, we dropped into a hole where the water rose nearly to our hips. I could feel my pulse in my ears. We dashed the last few steps out of the river onto the opposite bank, shivering with cold and frayed nerves, and burst out laughing.

Whatever your level of disdain for biting insects, or your terror of grizzlies, river crossings pose one of the gravest and most common dangers in the backcountry. As experienced paddlers know, a river is an unforgiving medium. Misjudging a current can quickly result in serious injury or drowning.

In late spring and early summer, when runoff from melting snow swells river levels, vast areas of the North American backcountry may be rendered inaccessible. I was in Yosemite during the record-high water of June 1995, when you couldn't hike most of the park's trails beyond their first creek crossing. A well-planned trip (see chapter 1) into an area where you may encounter river crossings avoids these potential disappointments. Consult your map and note the crossings along your chosen route, then ask the management agency about water levels. If there's a chance of problems, postpone your trip or choose a safer route. In bigger mountains, creeks and rivers that are easily forded in August or September sometimes remain impassable well into July.

Here are some guidelines for safe river crossings:

- If it doesn't appear safe, don't attempt it. Better to end your trip disappointed than dead. You don't necessarily have to see foaming whitewater for the current to be dangerous, especially where big rocks complicate the flow. A good rule of thumb is to assume the crossing will be harder than it looks, and leave yourself the option of backing out of the crossing if the current seems too dangerous.

- Consider alternatives to crossing a fast and deep current. Check your map. Does the trail soon cross back over the river again to the side you're on? If so, you might be able to bushwhack along that riverbank to the point where the trail crosses back. Be sure, of course, not to bushwhack in an environmentally sensitive area where land managers discourage wandering off-trail.

- Explore the area. There may be a log bridge in the vicinity, or a line of stones you can hop across the river. Beware of logs and stones that are wet or look smoothly buffed by water—they can be treacherously slick. If your map indicates a tributary entering the river a short distance upstream, bushwhack along your bank until you're above that confluence; fording two smaller currents is easier than fording the bigger current they become once they merge.

- Remember that creeks and rivers that originate in glaciers or snowfields are highest in late afternoon and lowest in early morning, because daytime sun and warmth accelerate melt-off while the cold of night slows it down. Plan your crossings for early morning.

If you decide the current is safe enough to ford:

- Look for a spot where the river is wide and shallow, or braided in multiple channels. Particularly in deeper water—i.e., above your knees in a swift flow—beware of big boulders, which can make a current do squirrely, unpredictable things.

- Be alert to any hazards downstream: a waterfall or cascade, big rocks, or a tree with branches that has toppled into the river perpendicular to the current. The latter is called a "strainer," and it's easy to get pinned underwater against it by the current. A standing wave in the river indicates deep water and a submerged boulder; avoid it.

- If you don't have trekking poles or walking sticks, find a pair of sturdy dead branches on the ground (obviously, don't cut live branches). They will provide needed support balancing in the current.

- Remove your socks and boots and tie them securely to your pack, or tie the laces together and drape the boots around your neck, to keep them dry on the crossing. Change into sandals or old sneakers—rocky creek bottoms can cut bare feet or make you stumble. Make sure anything of value, like a camera, is sealed in plastic or watertight bags and packed at the top inside your pack; if you packed smartly, your dry clothes already are in zip-lock plastic bags.

- If the current poses any risk of sweeping you away in the event that you fall—and remember, it doesn't have to be very deep or white to do that—loosen all of your pack straps and unfasten your hip belt and chest strap. You have to be able to get the pack off quickly if you go down—if you think walking with a pack is difficult, you're going to hate swimming with one on. But if the current is shallow and slow enough that there's no real risk of drowning—i.e., the greatest risk is that you will fall and get wet but be able to pick yourself back up again—keep the pack buckled on snugly. A shifting backpack can make you more wobbly.

- While crossing the river, focus your gaze straight ahead. Staring at the swirling current at your feet can be dizzying and unhinge your balance. Don't worry, your brain will remember where to step, even if you're not looking directly at your feet. Cross at a slight downstream angle. Probe ahead with those walking sticks, set each securely and make sure you're comfortably balanced on one foot before lifting the other. Fording a swift current should be a slow, methodical procedure. If the situation calls for it, wade as a pair or a group, braced against one another.

- In glacial rivers, such as those found in Alaska, silt prevents you seeing below the river's surface. Read the surface for clues. Avoid standing waves (see above). Cross where there are small,

Poles or a sturdy staff make river crossings safer. (Hells Canyon Wilderness, OR)

closely spaced ripples, which indicate shallow water and a smooth bottom. Throw big rocks into the water; a hollow ker-ploop sound indicates deep water that's potentially dangerous. If the rock moves downstream before sinking, or if submerged rocks can be heard rolling downstream, avoid crossing there.

♦ If you do fall, don't panic. If your pack hinders you at all from getting up, get the pack off. Hold on to your pack if you can, but if you can't, forget about it. A backpack often contains enough air to float—though it certainly won't keep you afloat—so you or your companions may be able to retrieve it downstream eventually. Try to get back to your feet or swim to safety. If the current carries you away, try to float face up, keeping your feet raised and pointed downstream, both to protect yourself from collisions with rocks and to avoid getting your feet pinned beneath rocks on the river bottom. If your feet become entrapped on the bottom, your upper body may be forced under by the current. Remember that once you're safely on shore again, you may have to quickly get into dry clothing to avoid hypothermia (see chapter 10).

A related hazard worth touching on briefly is **tidal waters.** High and low tides can affect backcountry travel on the seashore, on very large lakes, and in places with tidal rivers. I once sat and waited about an hour for the tide to drop enough for me to negotiate a rocky section of Washington's Olympic coast—and I certainly made a point of pitching my tent well above the high-tide mark on that trip. Guidebooks and land managers can inform you about any concerns regarding tide, and tide schedules for virtually any locale are available through area land managers and maritime agencies.

Venturing Off-Trail

To some hikers and backpackers, the term "off-trail" conjures nightmarish visions of steep, loose talus and scree sliding beneath their boots; of bushwhacking through dense, leg-whipping spruce or willows; and of taking careful steps across long, exposed snow slopes. But to those seeking the enhanced challenge, the term "off-trail" conjures enticing visions of steep, loose talus and scree sliding beneath their boots; bushwhacking through dense, leg-whipping spruce or willows; and....

OK, you get the point. However you look at it, anytime you leave the trail behind, life becomes more difficult. But to some people, leaving the trail is merely a further extension of the original objective of leaving civilization behind. Leaving the trail is often synonymous with leaving the crowds behind. From the Appalachian Mountains to the Rockies, Cascades, the Sierra, and countless other places, the only route to certain peaks is off-trail.

Hiking off-trail safely, though, requires a combination of good navigation skills (see Navigating section above) and the ability to move over varied, difficult, often hazardous terrain. Traveling off-trail incorporates basic skills used in mountaineering, but real mountaineering entails risks that many hikers and backpackers lack the experience to recognize and evaluate. If you want to delve into mountaineering, get instruction and read books on it (*Mountaineering: The Freedom of the Hills* from the Mountaineers is widely considered the bible for technical climbers). The line separating off-trail scrambling from technical climbing is fuzzy, but in general anywhere you face the potential for a long fall or the hazard of rock fall, avalanche, or crevasses is technical ground.

The first rule of traveling off-trail is **never to do it unnecessarily;** use any available trail if it's going in the right direction, whether a faint path stomped out by other bushwhackers or climbers, or a game trail. Once you step off-trail, you greatly increase the amount of energy you expend per mile or meter and you typically cut your speed at least in half. Follow the easiest, most open terrain to your destination, even if it means not taking the most direct line. Wherever possible, contour—or follow the same elevation—rather than unnecessarily climbing or descending. Think about conserving energy.

Don't strike out blindly. Use your map and compass to identify your position, and chart a course over the easiest and most open terrain to your destination. In dense forest or anyplace you cannot see your route clearly, take frequent compass bearings to maintain the proper course, and watch for natural landmarks. In open terrain, eyeball the route from below before you start out, look around frequently to orient yourself as you follow the route, and eyeball it again from high points or summits. If you're returning the same way, turn around frequently and memorize the terrain, or make notes on it, so you can find your way back. Plot your progress on your map. An altimeter is invaluable in helping you pinpoint your location on a map.

In some situations, you may want to mark the route for your return with rock cairns in open terrain, wands planted in snow, or colored crepe paper tied to trees—but avoid doing that unless absolutely necessary, and always remove any markers on your return. If you find any such markers left by others, consider them potentially helpful but don't assume they lead in the direction you want to go; use the other techniques described here to confirm your course.

In dense forests, such as those in the Northeast and Northwest, protect yourself from cuts and wounds caused by sharp branches, as well as from poison ivy, with **long pants and sleeves.** In really dense vegetation your clothes may get badly torn, so you might not want to wear those expensive technical duds. Guard your eyes, and be careful not to release a branch that will whip someone behind you. Try to go around pockets of dense, subalpine conifer forest, which from a distance often has a darker green color than more-open deciduous forest. Use clothing in desert climates—right down to thick socks—to protect yourself from thorny plants and poison ivy.

Talus and scree are the sloping, fan-shaped piles of rock that accumulate over the eons at the base of cliffs, rocky peaks, and old rock-slide paths. Talus usually refers to consistently large rocks, scree to smaller stones. Assume that any rock you step on or lean against on such a slope could shift under your weight, and test it first. Avoid, or exercise extreme caution on, talus that shows signs of recent rock fall; such signs include an absence of larger, older vegetation, or vertical swaths of rock that are much cleaner and lighter in color than surrounding rock. Similarly a clean, vertical scar of lighter-colored rock on a cliff overhead is a sign of a recent rock fall and a strong warning not to walk beneath it. When hiking on scree, low gaiters save you from constantly removing your boots to dump out stones.

Depending on its condition, **snow** can provide an ideal route up or down, or can be too icy or soft. Never attempt to climb, traverse, or descend steep snow without the proper mountaineering gear and the knowledge of how to use it (see below). Beware of snow undercut by running water or by heat radiating off of rocks or trees—your snow bridge may look secure but be dangerously thin. Remember that in the warmer months, snow in the mountains often firms up nicely overnight for walking on in crampons, but gets very mushy during the day, so traveling at night or in the early morning is often easiest and safest.

Progress can be plodding when you're checking every rock to see whether it's loose or constantly surveying your route. But don't rush—it only increases the chances of injury or getting lost. When walking uphill, conserve energy by employing the **mountaineer's rest step:** Pause briefly after each step, during which you lock the knee of your lower leg to briefly bear your weight on bones rather than muscles, and relax the bent upper leg. The higher the altitude, the more you'll need that rest step and the more deep breaths you will need to take between each step.

In the mountains, particularly in early summer, backpackers can encounter snow at higher elevations that obliterates the trail and forces them to figure out the route themselves. Sometimes the best response is simply to turn back rather than get lost or attempt risky terrain. If you judge the terrain safe, you can employ some basic **mountaineering skills and gear.** In soft snow crampons are often more hindrance than help, but they are mandatory gear on hard snow or ice. Make sure before you head out that your crampons fit securely to your boots and that you know how to put the crampons on. Crampons are most effective when all or most of their points contact the snow or ice. Take aggressive steps, with your feet at an angle to the slope rather than straight up or down it, to help your crampons find better purchase.

On any snow slope where the risk of a long slide exists, always carry an ice ax. Walk with the ax head in the hand on your uphill side, with the adze (the flat, hammerlike end) facing forward and the pick facing backward, planting the spike end of the ax into the snow for balance and to employ as an anchor. If you slip, try to get both hands on the ax head and fall onto it, burying the shaft in the snow to act as an anchor.

If that fails, you must know how to use the ax to **self-arrest** your fall. The self-arrest is difficult to accomplish, especially given how hard it is to keep a clear head as you slide out of control down a mountain. But often, unless you self-arrest immediately, you will quickly accelerate to a speed at which self-arrest is impossible.

There are four basic self-arrest methods, each used in one of the four ways someone typically falls on a slope: head uphill and face down; head uphill and face up; head downhill and face down; head downhill and face up. The objective in each method is to roll so that you end up face down, head uphill, with the ax shaft held diagonally across your chest and the pick planted in the snow just above one shoulder, braking your fall.

When sliding on your back, always roll onto your stomach in the direction of the ax head, not toward the spike; otherwise, the spike will become planted in the snow before you have completed the roll onto your stomach, and your self-arrest will fail. Planting the spike and using the shaft as a rudder during a controlled slide in a seated position—known as a sitting glissade—is a way of controlling your speed, but it will not halt an out-of-control slide.

Proper self-arrest technique is difficult to learn from a book. Get a lesson from someone who knows how to do it, and practice each method on a snow slope where you have a safe run-out zone before you face a situation where you actually have to arrest quickly to save your life.

Lace your boots to adjust fit or support for different situations. Laces can loosen up over the course of the day, so before starting a long descent, snug them up tightly for maximum ankle support and to keep your toes from jamming. Hiking on- or off-trail in stiff leather or plastic mountaineering boots can be difficult because the sole doesn't flex with the ball of your foot. Loosen the upper laces to allow your ankle more freedom of movement, while keeping the laces snug over the top of your foot.

> # loading your pack for various terrain
>
> Chapter 2 described how to load a backpack for traveling on the trail. Here are tips for packing the load when you venture off-trail, whether into a slot canyon, squeezing between glacial erratic boulders, or bushwhacking through dense forest.
>
> ❖ Make sure nothing on your pack extends higher than your head, to avoiding catching it on a rock or branch.
>
> ❖ Do not attach anything to the outside of the pack that can snag on branches or be damaged by sharp objects like branches or rock. If you cannot fit your inflatable pad inside the pack, strap it vertically to the backside of the pack, where it's most protected, and put it in a stuff sack or a chair kit with a tough nylon backing.
>
> ❖ The more difficult the scrambling, the more helpful it is to lower your pack's center of balance. Put the heavy items in the middle of the pack, close to and at or below your shoulder blades. When backcountry skiing in steep terrain, place heavy items near the bottom of the pack.
>
> ❖ Adjust the hip belt to bear most of the load without restricting leg motion. Shoulder straps should allow full range of arm motion. Compression straps should be tight enough to prevent contents from shifting.

Traveling at Night

Hiking a trail under a bright moon or a sky shot through with stars is one of the most exciting ways to experience the backcountry, and one of the most difficult and potentially troublesome. Doing it safely requires a little extra caution.

First of all, attempt it only if you're on a trail that's obvious or that you know well, or if you have well-developed skills at following a trail (see the Navigating section above). Time your night hiking for the full moon and a clear sky. Always have at least two bright, reliable light sources and extra batteries that you have checked beforehand. A headlamp allows you two free hands. If the temperature is near or below freezing, lithium batteries will perform better than standard nickel cadmium (nicad) batteries.

Distances seem much greater in the dark. Calculate how far you've gone by watching the time and using your map-reading and navigation skills. Move slowly, watching closely for the trail with every step, and anticipate that you will not cover ground as quickly or hike as far as you would by daylight. Dress in layers to avoid overheating or getting cold (see chapter 3).

Consider all the potential implications of hiking your chosen trail at night—whether there are water crossings that may be too dangerous, or sections where the trail may be hard to discern; or whether there could be ice; or the moonlight will be obscured by dense forest, a mountain ridge, or a canyon wall. Think about your options, such as alternative campsites, in case things don't go as planned. Remember that many animals are more active at night, and hiking can be dangerous in bear or mountain-lion country.

Going Solo

A few days into a two-week solo hike on Vermont's Long Trail, I came to a spot where the trail skirts the top of a cliff about twenty feet high, with a view partly obscured by trees. It was late October, cold and windy. I'd seen only a couple of other hikers all day, and I wouldn't see another person until the next day.

I set my pack down and scrambled around the ledges above the cliff, seeking the best angle for a photo of the valley below. I'd rock-climbed and scrambled peaks in much more exposed situations; I felt perfectly comfortable while taking care to be cautious. So it came as quite a surprise suddenly to slip and start sliding out of control on my butt toward the twenty-foot drop.

In the first instant, I reached to my right to a big crack I'd noticed a moment earlier and sunk my hand into it, catching myself. I then rose carefully to my feet and easily scrambled back up to safety—but my heart didn't stop pounding for a few minutes.

That Long Trail hike also was marked by several days of cold rain which left every rock and root along the trail slick and created mud bogs knee-deep in spots. I took more hard falls than I could count, and I considered myself just plain lucky to walk away from the worst of them. Many evenings, I hiked up to an empty shelter, stripped off my soaked clothing, rubbed myself dry as best I could in the cold, clammy air, then pulled on my one set of dry clothes and crawled into my sleeping bag until I stopped shivering. The next morning, I'd put the wet clothes back on and hit the trail again.

I've traveled solo through the backcountry a number of times, but never did I face so many reminders of the risks of being alone as during that Long Trail trek. There's no escaping the fact that hiking solo magnifies the risks. Some people stand by a rule of never heading out alone, and that decision clearly enhances their safety. But I like the amplified sense of adventure that going solo evokes, and I believe it can be done in a way that maximizes safety, provided you have the right experience.

I used to live near New Hampshire's Mount Cardigan and ran up it many times for the exercise. I never thought of what I was doing as a "solo hike," although I would take a different perspective hiking to Cardigan's exposed summit in winter. Most of us will never climb Mount Everest even with oxygen and a support team, but the alpinist Reinhold Messner did it alone without oxygen. We all have to define our own limits for what is safe to attempt solo, and your past experience should dictate those limits.

Be honest with yourself about your physical ability and experience. Traveling solo into the backcountry is not an endeavor for non-experts. You should possess a refined understanding of the environment you are entering and its dangers, and know how to move safely through that environment whether you're with someone or not. This does not mean you already should have hiked that particular summit or trail; nor does it imply that having hiked it before prepares you to do it alone. But you should have enough familiarity with the type of environment you will enter that nothing takes you by surprise, that you know what potential circumstances may arise and how to handle them. Surprises invite trouble.

Even an expert, though, accepts greater risk by traveling alone and has to take steps to tip the scales of risk back in his favor. How you prepare depends on too many variables—including your trip's length and destination, and you—to spell out specific recommendations. But things I might do when going solo that I might not do when with others include carrying overnight gear on a day hike (sleeping bag, pad, stove, etc.), along with extra food and water. You might consider taking along a cellular phone—although there's no assurance it will work, cell phones have speeded up response time in many rescues.

I take extra precautions when alone, avoiding situations that present even the slightest chance of a debilitating injury. I'm more likely to turn around in the face of uncertain weather than I might be with someone else. I make decisions based on worst-case scenarios.

Going solo—especially when you decide to bushwhack—requires extra care. (North Cascades, WA)

Some solo travelers adhere to an ethic of self-reliance so rigidly that they refuse even to notify someone at home of where they're going and when they'll be back. But I think going solo is risky enough. I always leave my precise itinerary with someone who will miss me if I'm not back on time, who will know the proper authorities to contact and how to describe where I've gone, and who won't panic and call for a search if I'm only an hour or two late.

Older People and Children

There's no reason healthy people can't enjoy the backcountry at any age, but the old and the very young may require a little more sensitivity to their needs and stamina. Don't ask them to carry a load or maintain a pace that exceeds their comfort. Set appropriate objectives regarding distance, elevation, terrain, etc. Be aware of changes in their energy level, and rest whenever necessary. Children often require frequent, short breaks. Keep them from getting bored by choosing trails that offer frequent rewards like swimming holes, waterfalls, or good views, and by bringing along fun snacks.

Infants can ride in baby backpacks once they're old enough to hold up their own head. Remember that a child in a pack is not working as hard as you are while hiking; he will cool off more quickly. Check his hands and body frequently to make sure he's warm.

Children overheat faster than adults, because their internal cooling systems are not as developed. They also get cold faster, because a child usually has a higher ratio of body surface area to body mass than an adult, which translates to faster loss of core body heat. They need extra clothing layers sooner than adults when the temperature drops or the wind kicks up. They also need more time to acclimate to heat than adults.

Children sunburn more easily than adults and need to be protected from sunlight. (See chapter 10 for advice on preventing sunburn in children. See chapter 4 for advice on children and water, and chapter 5 for advice on children and food.)

Sharing the Trail

There's a lot of hostility in the backcountry these days. Hikers don't like mountain-bikers or hunters, horse packers and backpackers scowl at each other, and no one knows what to think about cell phones. In some places, self-powered backcountry travelers encounter all-terrain vehicles, dirt bikes, and snowmobiles. The animosity doesn't arise merely from different choices of transportation—there's a clash of cultures taking place. The growing numbers of users of all kinds only make the problem worse, each group blaming another for trail erosion and conflicts.

This Balkanization of backcountry users is unfortunate, because many of us are out there for the same reasons. Many of us also participate in more than one activity. The strategy some majority groups are pursuing of attempting to ban minority groups can only backfire. It won't, in the long run, keep people off trails or help realize the goals of preserving the resource and the experience we all seek. In some places, designating trails for different user groups to avoid conflicts is an appropriate solution; in other places, different users have to learn to live together. But we all need to work together toward mutually beneficial goals and demonstrate due respect for each other on the trail.

There are some generally accepted **rules of the trail.** All users should yield to horses by stepping aside—everyone to the same side of the trail—and remaining still and quiet while the horses pass. Spooking horses can be dangerous to their riders and to bystanders. Likewise, horseback riders and anyone with stock animals should, whenever possible, avoid situations where their animals are forced to push past hikers on very narrow trails. Mountain-bikers should yield to hikers. Nonhunters should wear blaze orange or an equally bright, conspicuous color during hunting season.

Beyond those safety guidelines, let courtesy rule all encounters. If there's a need for one party to yield the trail, be the one who's big enough to step aside. Keep in mind that other people sharing the summit or alpine lake with you may not have come all that way to listen to your banshee screams or loud conversation. In many backcountry areas, backpackers, climbers, and paddlers can expect to encounter people carrying guns. Fortunately, most of them are responsible hunters and not interested in shooting you, so don't treat them as if they don't belong out there. If you've enjoyed a summit to yourself in a remote area and notice another party coming along, move on so that they might enjoy as much solitude as you had.

Be aware of any restrictions on **group size,** and obey them. Large groups have a disproportionate impact on backcountry campsites and on the experience of other people, particularly when it comes to noise. Even if there is no regulation, keep your group size to no more than ten people, and preferably no more than eight (see more in the Sharing the Backcountry section of chapter 7). In regions where a dense population squeezes into limited backcountry, these goals can be difficult to achieve, but they nonetheless represent a standard to strive for rather than accepting a presumption that our trails and summits must all be crowded and noisy.

Advances in **communications technology** have found their way into the backcountry, and we can only expect this trend to accelerate. But using these things properly and discreetly can preserve the quality and character of the experience most of us seek in the backcountry.

Cellular phones are increasingly common pieces of backcountry gear. Some people carry them for safety and take them out only to report an emergency. Having been involved in backcountry accidents, I can't say that's a bad idea. But recognize that cell phones do not always work—batteries die (especially in the cold), or you may not get a signal. Don't count on a cell phone to save you.

The ethical dilemma over cell phones arises when their owners use them in the backcountry to carry on casual conversations, or to check in at work. Many backcountry travelers go out there precisely to get away from things like phones, and find it annoying to hear someone nearby chatting into a box about the beautiful view, or trouble-shooting a problem at the office.

Some public lands, like Maine's flagship Baxter State Park, prohibit such use of cell phones. It's a good policy. Keep them hidden inside a pack until an emergency arises—and then, do not rush to call for help before determining whether an injured party can walk out under his or her own power. Search-and-rescue operations are time-consuming and labor-intensive affairs which potentially put rescuers at risk, and they should never be instigated for a broken wrist or hikers who don't feel like finding their own way out. If you feel a need to call home or the office for a nonemergency, do so beyond sight and earshot of other people.

Computers and personal electronic devices are increasingly portable. They too are considered by many to be an intrusion on the tranquillity of the backcountry. Leave them at the trailhead.

Dogs seem to be an increasing source of friction in the backcountry. While dog owners like to hit the trail with their pet, too many are not respecting rules, and some public-lands managers are considering prohibitions against dogs. Many public lands, including the U.S. national parks, now prohibit dogs because they chase wildlife, can be aggressive toward people, and heavily used areas get overrun with dog droppings. If you have a dog and take it on hikes, respect any rules regarding them. Keep it under physical control whenever other people are approaching. Not everyone enjoys your pet as much as you do.

There are **other ethical issues** pertaining to the backcountry. Some critics, for instance, bemoan the recent, albeit limited, popularity of so-called "fast-packing," the practice of traveling very light and very fast through the backcountry. These and other issues boil down to aesthetic tastes, to people simply seeking different experiences, and are better left to individual choice.

I'll close this chapter with one thought about what I'll call **"outdoor know-it-alls."** These are the people who stop complete strangers on the trail and suggest they are not attired in the proper technical clothing, or who roll their eyes and cluck their distaste over what they perceive as an epidemic of incompetence in the backcountry, or who simply bore you into a catatonic state with their endless discourse about having hiked New England's hundred highest summits or all the Colorado 14ers. They seem driven primarily by a need to let everyone else know how remarkably informed and experienced they are in all matters of the outdoors, and they are supremely annoying. If you encounter an outdoor know-it-all, the appropriate reaction is to discourage his blustering conceit by ignoring him.

chapter
seven

MAKING CAMP

MY FIRST WAKING THOUGHT *that November morning in New Hampshire's White Mountains was really nothing more than a vague, amorphous sense of wetness. Staring blankly at the tent ceiling in the dim light, blinking myself to consciousness, I could smell the dampness. It hung so heavily in the air I thought I could taste it. Somewhat disturbingly, though, a suspicion began to form that I could feel it.*

Shifting slightly in my sleeping bag as my brain lumbered stiffly toward wakefulness, I noted on some low cognitive level that, yes, my bag did seem a bit boggy. After a pause sufficient for that awareness and all it implied to register, I reached a wary hand outside my bag and groped blindly for the tent floor. My fingers sank to the second knuckles in water—very cold water, water that had in the very recent past (the previous evening, in fact) existed in a form that floated tents much more effectively: snow.

The sound of rain percussing most vigorously on the tent provided the final sensory data I needed to conclude that the morning was about to turn extremely ugly.

Our trip had begun two nights before. It was later in the season than most reasonable people care to traipse into mountains that are notorious for their cruel meteorological whim. But we started out after dark hiking through a comfortably cool Zealand Notch beneath a clear sky and a gloriously obese moon that shone brightly enough, it seemed, to read the newspaper classifieds or perform organ-transplant surgery. The mercury bloated up nearly to freezing as we lounged around our campsite that first night. The mountain gods smiled upon our adventurous spirit—for about twenty-four hours.

Late in the afternoon of the second day, as we hiked up Mount Willey, the sky dropped and darkened rapidly. Clouds raced past us as if fleeing the very weather they carried. A sharply cold wind pinched at our faces, and snow began to fly horizontally—even blowing incongruously upward at times. We found a patch of hardened campsite amid the dense subalpine spruce forest. It was covered with snow and ice and didn't look much bigger than a game board at first glance, but we managed to pitch a tent for Keith and me, and extend a tarp off the front of it under which Mike could lay out his bivy sack.

As the snow piled up and wind buffeted our shelter, we cooked up a leisurely dinner and played some cards before turning in—never thinking the temperature might rise just enough overnight to turn our site into a small pond. But that's what we awoke to find ourselves half-immersed in. And as I anticipated in the prescient fogginess of those first moments of wakefulness, the morning did turn quite ugly.

In a wind-driven rain, we broke down camp as quickly as possible and hiked four hours back to our car, the rain never relenting for a moment. It soaked through every layer of clothing I wore and left my pack so thoroughly waterlogged its weight may have doubled. I periodically removed my Gore-tex overmitts and dumped the water from them. For the first time in my life, it occurred to me that our distant ancestors' decision to wriggle out of the ocean and take up a new life on dry land was based primarily on comfort. Being wet for an extended period of time, I decided, was not very pleasant.

We all have tales of campsites that transformed into places of wretched suffering. But the image of the perfect backcountry campsite—with its stirring view, embracing solitude, and maybe a killer sunset to frost the cake—is a big part of the lure of the backcountry. We're always looking for the perfect spot to pitch our tent. Some basic skills and a careful eye can ensure that your campsite does not become a place of suffering—and does not suffer from your visit.

Selecting a Site

When choosing a spot to pitch your tent, take a good look around at all the things that may affect your comfort or safety. The spot with the best view—in a mountain saddle, or col, for instance, or on any exposed high ground—may be pounded by winds, which can render your night chilly and sleepless. On the other hand, in some regions you may want a site with a breeze to keep biting insects down (avoid standing water, where insects are usually thickest). Avoid the lowest part of a basin or valley because the coldest air tends to pool there overnight. If nights are cold, look for a spot that receives early-morning sun.

Clear the tent area of stones, but don't pull up roots. Examine the ground for signs of water flow, usually indicated by patterns in dirt, leaves, and needles or by soggy ground. Avoid anyplace where water will flow or pool if it rains. Gravel, sand, and a solid bed of leaves or needles all drain well. In the desert, camp in a wash only if there's absolutely no chance of rain; even if the sky overhead is clear, rain upstream can trigger a flash flood that reaches you.

If you're tenting on snow, stomp out a flat platform for your tent. Regular aluminum or plastic tent stakes will pull out of snow; you need snow stakes, which are wider and often have holes which help keep the stakes securely planted. In lieu of snow stakes, tie guy lines to skis, poles, sticks, rocks, or even well-packed snowballs, bury the object under a few inches of snow, then stomp on the snow to pack it down. It will soon freeze into a very secure foundation, but unless you get rain on it and a freeze afterward, it won't be difficult to dig up when you're ready to leave. (Stand poles or skis upright in the snow rather than burying them completely, or they may be hard to dig up the next morning.)

Lie down before pitching the tent to see whether the ground tilts, so you can put your head uphill; avoid any more than a slight angle if you can, or you'll be sliding either down toward the foot of your tent or onto your partner. If your tent has a low end, pitch it into the wind.

In bear country, pitch your tent upwind from where you cook and store your food. Try to camp in the open, where you and the bear will have ample advance notice of one another, to preclude any surprise encounters. Check any potential campsite and its environs for signs of bear activity, like tracks, scat, broadly spaced claw marks in the bark of a tree, or a dead log that's been shredded by a bear looking for a meal of bugs. When possible, check with the management agency on whether certain campsites have problems with regular visits from bears. (See more on protecting food and yourself from bears and other animals in chapter 8.)

With a little effort, you can usually find a suitable camping spot.
(Grand Teton National Park, WY)

You can usually count on designated camping areas on public lands to be safe from rock fall. But especially in the West, backpackers are wise to know how to recognize that hazard nonetheless, and such knowledge is a prerequisite for climbers and off-trail scramblers. In mountains or near a cliff, look for signs of recent rock fall, such as a vertical scar of cleaner rock on the cliff above, or rocks sitting incongruously atop a thick blanket of snow below a cliff. Avoid setting up a tent in the fallout zone, or pitch the tent in the protective lee of a large boulder.

Avalanches are hardly ever a concern for three-season backpackers who stick to trails, and the science of evaluating avalanche hazard is too complex to cover here. If you're heading into big mountains in a season when heavy snow can fall—including late spring and early summer—ask the management agency about avalanche hazard, and avoid anyplace the hazard exists.

A more common hazard for backpackers is a tent being struck by falling trees or branches. Usually, you can avoid them with a careful eye. Look up into the canopy over your site to ensure there are no dead limbs that have been broken off and are snagged in live branches, waiting for a good gust to send them earthward. Avoid close proximity to dead trees that appear ready to topple, whether they're rotting with age or were destroyed by fire but remain standing.

Roughing It Comfortably

If lugging a heavy pack up a trail presents a unique set of hardships, spending the night outside can present difficulties of its own. Nights get cold. You're dirty and tired. It may rain or snow or hail or sleet or get windy, or do all of the above. Good skills, though, can mitigate the discomforts of backcountry camping and help you concentrate on its many rewards.

First of all, do whatever is necessary to be comfortable. That begins with the pre-trip decisions you make on what gear, clothing, food, and other things to bring. Remember, this is supposed to be fun.

Keep your sleeping bag dry by lining your sleeping bag stuff sack with a plastic trash bag, and having a waterproof backpack cover (see chapter 2) in case of heavy precipitation. Treat your sleeping bag as your last refuge from the cold: protect it from getting wet, and carry a bag that's adequate for the temperatures you will encounter. Don't bring wet clothes into the tent. At night, lay your sleeping bag out at least an hour before bedtime, to let its insulation loft. Every morning, unzip the bag and lay it out atop your tent or on a dry rock to air out in the sun, to prevent the buildup of moisture (from your body) inside the bag that can render it less effective.

One of the first things I do upon arriving at a campsite is wash by wiping myself down from head to toe with a bandanna dipped in water. Getting the dried perspiration off your skin will keep you warmer and more comfortable as the temperature drops. While there are many so-called "biodegradable" soaps on the market today, none of them is good for the environment or really necessary. Alcohol-treated antibacterial cloth wipes, however, are lightweight, can be packed out with your trash, and do the job of getting your hands and face fairly clean. Washing your hands with them also lets you handle food in a sanitary manner. Never bathe or use any kind of soap in a water source.

Keep an **extra change of clothing** dry by packing the clothes in waterproof plastic zip-lock bags and not wearing your "camp clothes" on the trail (wear the same trail clothes over again—you're just going to sweat and get dirty again anyway). Change into those dry clothes after washing, right down to your underwear, because the clothes you sweated in that day, even if just barely damp, will conduct heat out of your body. A warm hat should be one of the first extra garments you put on—if the hat doesn't feel too warm, it's helping to keep your body from cooling down. Put on extra warm layers when you begin to feel a chill, not after you're shivering.

Take active measures to **avoid getting cold.** Get up and walk around. Sit on a foam pad, in a camp chair (portable kits are available for many inflatable pads), or on your empty pack to insulate yourself from the cold ground. Or sit on a log instead of a cold rock. Eat and drink plenty. Your body needs extra calories and to be well hydrated to keep you warm (see chapters 4 and 5). Stretch in camp to avoid sore muscles the next morning; static stretching also helps warm you up. If soreness begins, consider taking an over-the-counter anti-inflammatory like ibuprofen.

Make sure your **ground cloth** does not protrude out from the edges of your tent, where it can collect rain which may pool underneath your tent floor. Use guy lines to stake out your rainfly, both for stability in strong winds and to keep rain from hitting the tent. If you've chosen your campsite well (see above), you should be protected from any cold wind or a small flood.

Tent and stove makers generally recommend against **cooking in a tent or vestibule** because of inherent risks. But in a storm, deep cold, or high winds, it may become necessary. Use extreme caution if you attempt it, and make sure your stove does not flare up. Double-check that the rainfly and vestibule are secure, so that a gust of wind doesn't blow your fly or door into your lit stove.

Be sure the stove is on a stable platform; snow melts beneath a hot stove, so use a folding metal stove base, old license plate, or something similar. Light the stove near the open tent door or outside the tent if possible, so you can toss it outside quickly if it flares; that's also a better place to do your cooking. Ventilate the tent or vestibule well to prevent the buildup of carbon monoxide, which is colorless, odorless, and lethal and has killed many people who've cooked inside a tent. Carbon monoxide is a greater threat inside a tent because it's a heavy gas that settles at ground level and becomes trapped by the nylon floor of a tent.

Don as much clothing as necessary to be **warm in your sleeping bag**—although not so many layers that you are too uncomfortable to sleep. I almost always wear one or two pairs of synthetic socks, because feet get cold first. I'll often wear a synthetic jersey or turtleneck, and long underwear when needed. A hat is one of the first clothing items I wear to bed, even with a mummy bag's hood closed up. If I'm really cold, I'll add a layer of fleece and gloves. If I'm still cool, I'll stuff dry extra clothing into the foot of my bag and around me inside it, for insulation and to reduce the volume of air my body has to warm up. And I'll fill a bottle with hot water, seal it tightly, and sleep with it for the warmth and a drink during the night. (See chapter 11 for more on staying warm in winter.)

What's outside your bag affects your warmth too. **Add extra insulation** between you and the cold ground by spreading out your jacket or an emergency space blanket beneath your sleeping pad. Pack extra clothing between you and the tent walls as insulation. Push your pad up against your tentmate's to keep cold air from rising up between the two. But don't lay extra clothing atop your bag; it can compress the bag's down or synthetic fill, reducing its loft and ability to trap heat. Any fabric atop your bag that does not breathe will also trap the moisture from your body that your bag releases overnight, and leave your bag soggy come morning.

Tents have mesh or uncoated nylon walls that breathe, but their nylon rainfly is typically coated to make it waterproof and does not breathe. So you have to ventilate the tent in order to prevent the buildup of **condensation** inside, especially in the cold. Condensation occurs because you exhale moisture in your breath overnight, and it can actually become so heavy inside a tent that it begins to rain from the ceiling. Condensation buildup also forces you to either take the time to dry the tent out, or pack and sleep in a wet tent the next night.

How well a tent ventilates varies among models (see chapter 2). You may have to open windows or leave the rainfly door partly open to allow enough circulation of air to prevent condensation buildup. Experiment with what works for your tent in different conditions. In a storm, of course, you may have to close up the tent completely, but the resulting condensation is still probably not as bad as allowing rain or snow inside. (For tips on tenting atop snow, see chapter 11.)

The hardest thing about sleeping outside can be the moment you unzip a warm bag to face **the cold morning air.** Before unzipping, pull the clothes you intend to wear into your bag to warm them, and dress inside your bag—a rigorous exercise that generates lots of heat. Do some sit-ups in your bag. If you're not wearing a warm hat already, put it on first. If you awaken cold during the night, take a drink and eat a high-calorie snack, like a chocolate bar. Peeing in the middle of the night is rarely enjoyable in the cold, but get up and do it—holding it may just keep you awake, and your body wastes energy keeping that fluid warm. If you really dread it, keep a pee bottle handy for such emergencies—and make sure it's clearly labeled to avoid confusion.

Bring along something to read, a deck of mini cards, binoculars, a field guide to birds—things to occupy your free time in camp. But don't forget that the backcountry presents an opportunity to escape the hustle of everyday life, when all of our time is filled with duties and responsibilities. Kick back, enjoy the view, daydream, explore the vicinity of your campsite, talk to your companions.

Finally, maintain a positive attitude; anticipate the bad aspects of camping out before they become too bad, then take steps to counter them.

Low-Impact Camping

Most popular backcountry areas in the United States show signs of overuse. From the Appalachian Trail to the Pacific Crest Trail, Maine's Mahoosuc Range to Colorado's Front Range, Washington's Alpine Lakes Wilderness to New Hampshire's Pemigewasset Wilderness, Idaho's Sawtooth Lake to Wyoming's Big Sandy Lake, you will find expanding areas of soil compacted so hard that nothing grows, creek and river banks and lake shores eroding and denuded of vegetation, and water sources fouled by human waste.

Even places considered remote and wild have not been exempt from the abuse: One study conducted during the 1990s found that campsites used by kayakers in Alaska's Prince William Sound have seen nearly total loss of vegetation, in forested areas as well as on grassy gravel bars.

The problem is one of sheer volume. The Outdoor Recreation Coalition of America, an industry trade group, estimates there are 2 million kayakers, 7 million cross-country skiers, 7.5 million rock climbers, 9 million mountain climbers, 14 million canoeists, 47 million hikers, 57 million bicyclists, 58 million fishermen, and 62 million people who enjoy viewing wildlife.

Other studies offer more optimistic conclusions, most importantly that effects from heavy use can be minimized by employing low-impact camping techniques and confining campsite activities to established sites in popular areas.

Some of us have been traveling in the outdoors long enough to have seen a favorite spot become denuded by overuse; others need to be convinced of the merits of low-impact practices. Consider how many people are using the backcountry, how their sheer numbers can cause harm, and how you would like these places to look in 10, 50, or 100 years.

It's much easier to learn better habits than to repair an eroded riverbank or meadow. Start by thinking about how your actions affect the environment where you're camping, and how to minimize that impact, and learn the following guidelines. For more-detailed guidelines, contact Leave No Trace Inc., P.O. Box 997, Boulder, CO 80306; 303-442-8222 or 800-332-4100; www.lnt.org.

- Know the area and what to expect regarding weather, travel conditions, popularity, regulations, and customs before heading out (see chapter 1). Consider an alternative to a popular destination.
- Repackage food into reusable containers and bags to decrease the amount of refuse brought into wildlands.
- Gear such as backpacking stoves, free-standing tents, and collapsible water carriers help reduce your impact on a campsite.
- In popular areas, concentrate use in established campsites and shelters. Be prepared to camp in case a shelter is full when you arrive. Limit tents, kitchen areas, and walking to "hardened" areas that are already bare from previous use.
- In remote areas, spread use and avoid creating paths in camp. Camp only on durable ground like sand, rock, snow, dry grass, and pine needles.
- In the mountains, do not camp in meadows or on delicate alpine vegetation.

Whenever possible, camp in established sites to avoiding creating more hardened campsites. (Elk Mountains, CO)

- In the desert, learn how to identify and avoid camping or walking on cryptobiotic crust, or cryptogram, which has the appearance of soil but is actually composed of microorganisms and loose sand and provides the foundation for much plant life in the high desert.

- On river- or sea-kayaking trips, camp on nonvegetated gravel bars, beaches, or sandbars or in established sites without spreading beyond the site's perimeter; otherwise, camp at least 100 feet from the river and 200 feet from side streams and springs. Avoid areas with nesting seabirds from early April through mid-August, and seals from mid-May through mid-June. Leave pets at home.

- Avoid campsites where impact is just beginning. Never trench around your tent.

- Wear soft-soled shoes around camp, and watch where you walk to avoid crushing vegetation.

When you're kayak- or canoe-camping, be sure to dispose of waste 200 yards away from the shoreline. (Lake Umbagog, ME/NH)

- Camp and wash cook pots at least 200 feet from trails and water sources in the mountains, and at least 300 feet from trails and water in the desert. Avoid using soap—keep the backcountry free of chemicals. In bear country, either consolidate cooking waste water in sump holes, or scatter it after straining out food scraps.

- Kitchen floor tarps make cleanup easy. Plan meals so you don't have leftovers (see chapter 5), or pack them out. Strain cooking water and dishwater and put food scraps from it with your garbage.

- Before leaving, "naturalize" the site by replacing rocks or sticks that were moved and brushing out footprints or a matted area. Leave no trace of your presence.

- Carry out all trash and food scraps—never burn or bury them.

Campfires

There was a time when sitting around a campfire was the archetypal wilderness experience, considered as natural as, well, drinking water straight from a stream or cutting live pine boughs for a bed. Those latter practices fell into disuse when people realized there are too many of us out there to be doing things like that. Now it's time to rethink the campfire.

On many public lands, campfires are already prohibited or restricted during dry seasons if not year-round. They can pose the threat of brush or forest fire. Their legacy is a plague of unsightly black scars on the earth and rings of burnt rocks in backcountry areas across America. Regular use of campfires in popular areas results in the ground in the vicinity becoming unnaturally stripped of deadwood, and sometimes in live trees and branches being improperly and illegally cut for fires.

In most parts of the desert Southwest, in particular, building a campfire is simply impractical and insensitive. It consumes what little deadwood lies on the ground, which is important to the local ecology, and for that reason alone campfires are often prohibited or restricted on public lands. If no regulations exist and you feel a desire for fire, let the availability of dead and downed wood determine whether you build one. Small campfires may be possible in

Consider a low impact alternative, such as a cooking stove, to a campfire.

washes, canyons, or arroyos where substantial driftwood has been deposited by periodic flooding. Forested areas of the Southwest may also contain adequate wood for small fires.

Certainly, no three-season travelers should place themselves in a position to need a fire. Carry enough spare clothing to keep yourself warm, and cook with a lightweight stove (see chapter 2). A campfire is not a very efficient means of cooking anyway.

Before building a campfire, consider whether you want to leave so significant an impact on the land—especially in a popular area, where even a healthy forest usually cannot produce enough deadwood to fuel fires for every group of backcountry travelers. Instead of staring into a fire, enjoy the moonlight or the star-riddled sky.

In remote areas where campfires are legal and sensible, use either a fire pan or a mound fire, neither of which leaves any trace of the fire afterward. A fire pan—more practical for river trips than for backpacking—is a metal tray with sides at least three inches high to contain wood and ashes. Metal oil drain pans and backyard barbecue grills work well. Line it with several inches of inorganic soil, or prop it up on small rocks to protect the ground from heat.

A mound fire is a platform or mound of mineral soil, which contains little or no decomposing organic material, built as a fire pad and later easily disguised. First locate a naturally occurring source of mineral soil, sand, or gravel, such as the hole left by a tree's roots when it falls or large stream courses where sand or fine gravel has been deposited along the banks. Use pots or a stuff sack to carry the dirt to the fire site. Build a circular, flat-topped fire platform, six to eight inches thick and about two feet across, with the mineral soil. A tarp or ground cloth should be laid beneath the soil to facilitate cleanup. The thickness of the mound is critical for insulating the tarp and ground beneath from the heat. Once the fire is out and cold, the leftover ashes can be scattered and the mineral soil returned to its source, which you can "brush up" to eliminate signs that it was disturbed.

Below are widely accepted guidelines for building campfires propounded by the organization Leave No Trace.

leave-no-trace guidelines for campfires

- Know current regulations and weather conditions. During dry periods, fires may be dangerous or prohibited. In the Northeast and other popular areas, campfires are generally discouraged and often prohibited.
- Where they are legal, use existing fire pits.
- Gather firewood away from camp so the vicinity does not look unnaturally barren. Walk five or ten minutes away, then start picking up wood as you walk so that no single place becomes denuded.
- Collect and burn only dead and downed wood. Do not break dead branches off any woody shrubs or trees, alive or dead. Broken branch stubs and scars are obvious, long-lasting impacts.
- Use small wood (wrist size or smaller), which burns hot and easily reduces to ash.

When Nature Calls

When my mom first took up hiking, in her forties, its most unappealing aspect to her was the idea of relieving oneself outdoors. So she endeavored to avoid it at all cost, an effort which she elevated to an art form through calculated consumption of water and timely visits to trailhead outhouses and hut bathrooms (we did our first hikes in New Hampshire's White Mountains). She demonstrated a control over her bladder I always thought worthy of coverage in leading medical journals. But, of course, her method eventually proved futile, and she gave in to the mild inconvenience of necessity.

While her motivation, I suspect, was strictly personal, my mom's objective—had it been successful—might have provided a model for saving the backcountry from one of its most pernicious impacts: human waste. If only we could all just hold it until we get home again. But that's not a realistic option, of course. Besides being uncomfortable, it can lead to urinary tract infections, fecal impaction, and severe gastrointestinal distress. Not drinking enough fluids can precipitate a host of medical problems. Instead, we need methods for disposing of human waste and its all-to-frequent companion—the "white flag," toilet paper—in ways that do not leave the backcountry looking like a neglected gas-station restroom.

On a trip of more than a day, it's wise to consult with the land-management agency for its recommendations or regulations regarding human waste; some places have site-specific rules or guidelines. For instance, in the heavily used Enchantment Basin of Washington's Alpine Lakes Wilderness, hikers are asked to urinate only in the existing pit toilets, or in a hole dug in the sand, then to bury it, because the resident mountain goats have become habituated to licking up human urine for its salt. On some popular rivers, paddlers are advised to dump dishwater and urinate directly into the river, because moving water can disperse high volumes of both fluids better than the land.

Use pit toilets and other backcountry facilities wherever they exist—they are there to reduce human impact on the land. In the absence of such facilities, urinate at least 200 feet from water sources in forests and at least 300 feet from water in the desert. The cat hole (explained below) remains the most ecological practice for disposing of solid waste. Commercial river outfitters and other large organized river trips should pack out solid human waste, as many now do in heavily traveled river corridors such as the Colorado River through the Grand Canyon.

Pit toilet in Glacier National Park, MT. Disposing of human waste in the backcountry is a vital part of low-impact camping.

Regarding used toilet paper, the only really responsible thing to do today is pack it out, period. The common practice of burning and/or burying it is rarely successful—toilet paper gets damp—and results in animals digging it up, or "white flags" rudely left fluttering in the breeze. Burning paper also creates the risk of fire, especially in a dry environment. Pack it out in doubled, sealable plastic bags. Or forgo TP altogether for excellent natural alternatives like sticks, snow, leaves, or smooth stones, which can be buried in the cat hole afterward.

The following are guidelines for use of cat holes put forward by the organization Leave No Trace:

- Carry a small, lightweight garden trowel for digging a cat hole to bury human waste.
- Cat holes should be widely dispersed. Go for a short walk to find an appropriate site away from camp. Better yet, use a remote location during the day that other visitors are not likely to accidentally discover. Where the ground is snow covered, seek dry ground near trees for cat hole sites. Human

Making Camp 159

waste buried in snow does not decompose and may be exposed when the snow melts.

- To promote decomposition, locate cat holes in organic soil (topsoil) rather than sandy mineral soils. Dig a hole four to eight inches deep and four to six inches in diameter. After use, mix soil into the cat hole with a stick, fill in the hole, and disguise it with natural materials. Do not deposit human waste under rocks, which inhibit the moisture and heat that aid decomposition.

- In the desert, locate cat holes at least 300 feet from water, trails, and camp, and disperse them widely. Avoid areas where water visibly flows, such as sandy washes, even if they are dry at the moment. Select a site that will maximize exposure to solar radiation, such as south-facing slopes and ridge tops, in order to aid decomposition. Because the sun's heat will penetrate several inches into desert soils, it can kill pathogens if the feces are buried properly.

- The desert cat hole should be four to six inches deep and four to six inches in diameter.

- If members of your group are unable to utilize cat holes effectively (for example, young children), choose a route or campsite where outhouses are available. Where possible, urinate on rocks or sand to prevent animals digging up the urine for its salt.

Sharing the Backcountry

Head into any mountains in close proximity to a sizable population of college students, and you may have an experience similar to one some friends and I had in the Carter-Moriah Range of New Hampshire's White Mountains a few years ago. We arrived at a shelter after dark to find it occupied by a dozen college students on an orientation program. We pitched our tents nearby and turned in early, but there would be no early sleeping that evening. The students talked and laughed loudly late into the night—until I walked up to them and politely explained that we were trying to rest up for the next day's hike. This revelation they accepted with all due sheepishness, and quieted down considerably—for about ten minutes.

I think it's wonderful to introduce young people to the outdoors, and to use an outdoor trip to help students adapt to a new school environment and make friends. And some college orientation programs deserve credit for having begun to work with public-lands managers to direct their groups to less used areas. I tell the story merely to illustrate how the size of your group can affect the backcountry experience of other people.

This is important. We strive to practice the highest ethics concerning our impact on the land, but we don't always think about how our behavior will affect other backcountry users.

The organization Leave No Trace advises keeping **group size** to ten or fewer, and splitting up during the day into smaller groups to reduce your noise and visibility impact. Federally designated Wilderness areas generally set a group limit at ten persons. I would argue that ten is still too many—too many voices, too much bustle of activity, too much of a physical presence and impact on the land. We should start voluntarily trying to limit group sizes to eight people. Also, large groups should carry their own tents rather than taking over shelters in popular regions.

No matter what the size of your group, respect the fact that there are probably **other people** out there with you. Camp in a place out of sight and earshot of other campers when possible, and keep noise at a minimum. If you come upon others already camping in a spot where you had intended to spend the night, work from an assumption that they would prefer solitude unless they indicate otherwise, and move on to a different site (except in places where this is not feasible, like popular backcountry campsites and shelters).

Many backcountry areas prohibit **dogs** or have regulations regarding them. Know and follow the rules. Keep your dog under physical control around other campers, who may have an allergy or simply not wish to be visited by your dog. Before deciding whether to bring a noisy or rambunctious dog into the backcountry, consider how the pet might affect the wilderness experience of other people and disturb wildlife. All things considered, it's often best to leave a pet at home. (See Sharing the Trail in chapter 6.)

chapter
seven

BLOODSUCKERS, SLITHERING THINGS, AND OPPORTUNISTIC CARNIVORES

WE GATHERED QUIETLY *as if for a religious service, lined up side by side, gazing westward. Behind us lay our tents and other gear; downwind was the spot we'd cooked dinner a short while earlier that evening. Our small group of friends had backpacked several miles into the backcountry of Yosemite National Park that hot summer day, parking for the night on a flat, open hilltop with an expansive view of forest and distant peaks that left us feeling rather pleased with our efforts.*

So, with bellies contentedly full and eyelids beginning to droop, we stood transfixed. The sun thickened and flared at the edge of farthest land, bloating with a last-hurrah intensity as if to inform us with Schwarzeneggerian dispassion, "Ahll be bok." It was the type of scene depicted in outdoors magazines and gear ads with captions that offer some pithy message like, "No traffic, no messages, no phone, no kidding." And we were enjoying it completely.

Our friend Mike turned and started for his tent—but never made it. As the rest of us continued staring with dopey dreaminess at the slow-

ly cooling lava of western sky, we heard him blurt the sort of words that stagger from the mouth when the brain's sentence-forming cells are addled by alarm:

"Whoa. Hey, look what we got here!"

Not mistaking his tone to suggest that an ice cream truck was pulling up to sell us soft-serve vanilla cones, we all spun around to see Mike backpedaling toward us, and a black bear flanked by two cubs strolling into our campsite.

As anyone who's read beyond the Goldilocks chronicles in the study of *Ursus americanus* behavior understands, startling a mother bear with cubs at short range is about as healthy as practicing your breaststroke in the cooling tanks at Chernobyl. To put it in the dramatic parlance of early twentieth-century explorers: Our situation was pregnant with danger.

We instinctively reacted as seasoned veterans of wilderness travel do when confronted with imminent peril: We yanked our hands from our pockets, stiffened, and babbled inanities like, "Hey!" "Oh!" "What the...?!" "Sh—!" "Bear!" (the last remark intended to put the varmints on notice that we were no fools and knew exactly what they were).

Our prompt, calculated response succeeded. Mother and cubs—clearly as surprised to see us when they crested the hilltop as we were to see them—spun on their heels and bolted back down the slope.

We dashed across the campsite to observe their retreat. Within seconds, the bears were a couple hundred yards below us on the open hillside. But they had fled in two different directions. Mom and one cub were still bounding away to the south, while to the east the other cub had stopped running when he realized he'd become separated in flight from his family.

If an encounter with ill-mannered humans had upset this cub, it was nothing compared to the emotional trauma of finding itself suddenly orphaned. The cub raised a little black snout to the air and let out a sound which could be described only as crying. Mom slammed on her brakes, spun in the direction of the sound, and launched herself toward her lost child with cub number two fast at her heels.

Reunification calmed the bear family instantly. With dusk layering thickly over the land, the three melted into the forest as if the excitement of the past minute had never happened. I think we humans all nearly wept.

Ethics of Human–Animal Encounters

Chance encounters with wildlife are one of the special treats possible when traveling in the backcountry. But even as growing numbers of people describe themselves as environmentalists, our relationship with wild animals remains one beset with ironies. We fear some species and consider others an annoyance, and still others we revere with an admiration bordering on worship. Yet on many fronts we pose the greatest threat to many animals. We have to understand our impact on the habitat and behavior of wildlife in order to minimize that impact. Reducing your chances of a negative encounter with a wild animal is not only safer for you, it's safer and better for the animal.

Animals become habituated to human food—thus becoming "problem animals" in the eyes of land managers—usually because of poor handling of food by people both in the backcountry and in frontcountry campgrounds. The inevitable consequence of that is the sort of problem now plaguing Yosemite Valley, where in recent years black bears have learned to associate certain models of automobile

Wildlife can become acclimated to human activity: this goat is looking for a handout from hikers in Enchantment Basin, WA.

with food and break into them, causing hundreds of thousands of dollars in property damage annually. Easy access to human food can prompt wildlife to change their feeding habits, ultimately reducing their chances of survival. Animals, particularly bears, can become aggressive in pursuit of human food, which leads to them being destroyed by land managers or relocated to a remote area where they may or may not survive.

Wild animals are generally better off when we do not disturb them. Observe and photograph wildlife from an unobtrusive distance; binoculars and long telephoto lenses (300mm or longer) give you a close look without the need to get too close. Never approach a wild animal, and certainly don't offer one food, or leave food where an animal can get at it. Report any encounter with a large predator like a bear or mountain lion to the land manager. If an animal changes its behavior as a reaction to your presence—including running away, looking in your direction, or ceasing to forage—you're too close. Similarly, if you've come between a female and her young, move away from them.

Avoiding Animal Problems

Bears are a major concern among backcountry travelers. **Black bears** are most common, with a range covering most substantial areas of forest and mountains in North America. Adults weigh between 200 and 600 pounds, with females being much smaller than males. They are opportunistic carnivores—their diet consists mainly of insects and larvae, berries, and vegetable matter, but they will eat fish, carrion, and garbage, and have been known to kill the young of deer, caribou, and elk.

Encounters with black bears are usually brief, resulting in the bear fleeing before you can even get a good look. But never assume that a black bear will be unaggressive. Many experts believe that bears, like people, make decisions based on past experience: if a particular bear associates humans with a tasty treat, it could be aggressive.

In bear country, never leave a pack or food unattended. Cook at least 100 feet downwind from your tent site when possible and store your food at least 100 feet from your tent and cooking area. Bring nothing with a scent into your tent, including food, clothing that smells of food, even toothpaste.

A common method for keeping food out of reach of bears and other animals is **bear-bagging**. With a rock tied to one end of at least fifty feet of 3mm nylon cord, toss the cord over a tree branch that's sturdy and at least twelve feet off the ground. Hoist a nylon stuff sack containing your food to at least eight feet above the ground, four feet below the branch, and six feet from the tree trunk. Tie off the other end of the cord to another tree.

A perhaps safer bear-bagging method is to counterbalance two food sacks. Tie one sack to an end of the cord and hoist it up to the branch. Tie the second food sack (preferably somewhat lighter than the first) to the other strand of the cord so that at least eight to ten feet of cord separate the two sacks. Using a stick or pole, push the second sack upward until the first sack drops down beside the second, and both are at least eight feet off the ground, four feet below the branch, and six feet from the trunk.

Store anything with a scent in the bag, including food, toothpaste, and tampons. When done properly, bear-bagging can be effective, but it may only delay the bear's acquisition of your food. Black bears are excellent tree climbers. If you hear a black bear going for your food, make noise to scare it off.

Managers of certain public lands, like Yosemite National Park, recommend or require that backcountry travelers use **bear canisters** because bear-bagging has proven ineffective at keeping bears from food. Canisters are made of hard plastic and have screw-on lids which bears cannot open. They are indispensable in treeless regions like the Alaskan tundra. They weigh a few pounds, can be purchased or rented in some places, and can hold up to four or five days' food for one person.

Some public lands also provide tall bear poles at campsites from which to hang food.

Grizzly bears, or brown bear, pose much greater risks. They are numerous in Alaska and western Canada but endangered in the mainland U.S., living only in parts of the Montana Rockies and Wyoming's northwest corner, with small populations in northern Idaho and Washington's North Cascades. Adults can weigh several hundred pounds and stand more than seven feet tall. They can sprint faster than 30 MPH over a short distance.

Bear proofing protects your food and the bears, who endanger themselves and humans when they become dependent on hikers' food. (Yosemite backcountry, CA)

Besides the precautions listed above for black bears, below are widely accepted guidelines for traveling in grizzly country:

- Get advice on bears from the management agency and obey all regulations.

- Most maulings occur when a hiker surprises a bear. Sing, talk, or make other loud noises to let bears know you're around. There's no consensus on whether a bell jangling on a pack warns a grizzly of your approach; some experts say it merely mimics natural sounds like birdsong.

- Be especially careful in dense brush where visibility is low, in berry patches, wherever you see bear tracks or scat, and along rivers, where bears cannot hear you over the noise of the water.

- If you come across fresh grizzly scat, consider turning back.

- Be aware of wind direction to recognize when you are traveling upwind and a bear may not be able to smell you before you get too close. Strong winds can drown out any sound you make.

- Travel in a group and stick together.

- Never intentionally approach a bear (which is illegal in some parks).

- Avoid traveling at night, or the early morning and evening, when bears are most active.

- During the day, you are less likely to encounter a bear on a popular trail, and more likely to encounter one off-trail.

- Some experts recommend carrying pepper spray, though it may not deter an attack and could be difficult to use effectively under duress. Portable air horns, available at marine supply shops, have been known to deter bears.

- Avoid bear cubs; mothers will violently defend them.

- Distance yourself from any carcass you may come upon—it could be a bear's meal.

- It's best not to run trails in bear country, especially alone.

Don't disturb wildlife. This foraging grizzly was photographed with a zoom lens camera without interrupting its feeding activity. (Denali National Park, AK)

- Don't take a dog—it puts the dog at risk, and dogs have been known to lure a bear back to their owner.

- Never run from a bear; you cannot outrun it, and fleeing may prompt it to give chase. Never abandon your pack.

- If the bear is unaware of you, detour quickly and quietly away. If the bear notices you but does not seem aggressive, back away slowly, speaking in a low, calm voice while waving your arms slowly above your head. Bears that stand up on their hind legs are merely trying to identify you. But a grizzly snapping its jaws or making a low coughing sound is issuing a warning.

- Grizzlies occasionally make bluff charges, even coming within ten feet before stopping or veering off. Stand your ground without making eye contact or acting aggressively. If the grizzly attacks, play dead: Fall to the ground on your stomach, lying spread-eagle to prevent the bear from turning you over. Your pack might protect your back.

Mountain lions live throughout much of the rural West and have been sighted in New England and upstate New York, although it's uncertain whether there's a permanent population in the Northeast. A small number of endangered Florida panthers live in the Everglades. Mountain lions range in size from 75 to 200 pounds, with males larger than females. Their primary food is deer and elk, so anyplace in the West where you find healthy populations of either species, presume there are lions around. They prefer mountainous regions over flatlands.

Most of us will never see a mountain lion in the wild. They are reclusive and avoid humans. Rarely do encounters result in injury to a human. But follow these precautions:

- Obtain information about lions from land managers and obey all regulations.

- Travel in a group, and keep small children nearby.

- Do not let pets run unleashed.

- Minimize your travel at dawn and dusk, when lions are most active.

- Never approach a mountain lion. Slowly back away, maintaining eye contact. Never run away.

- A mountain lion more than fifty yards distant may watch or follow humans out of curiosity, a slight risk to adults but considerable risk to unaccompanied children. Move away while keeping an eye on the lion.

- A lion drawing closer than fifty yards and staring, hiding, crouching, and stalking may be preparing to attack. Make noise, wave your arms, and try to make yourself appear larger. Have everyone group together. Pick up small children.

- Pick up a rock or stick and defend yourself if a lion attacks.

Snakes occasionally bite humans in self-defense, although they are much more likely to flee an approaching human. Bites from poisonous snakes like rattlesnakes, copperheads, water moccasins, and coral snakes number about 7,000 per year, most in summer and in the Southeast and Southwest. Most bites have occurred when someone attempted to pick up a snake. A snake may release no venom when it bites, or enough to kill a human, although deaths are very rare and most involve children or the elderly.

Know when you are in snake country. Wear long pants and boots. Do not place your hands or step anywhere without looking first. Tapping a walking stick warns snakes of your approach, giving them a chance to flee. If you hear a rattle, freeze, locate the snake with your eyes without moving your head, then slowly back away.

Symptoms of a poisonous snakebite may include bleeding, blurred vision, burning sensation, dizziness, excessive sweating, fever, increased thirst, loss of muscle coordination, nausea and vomiting, numbness and tingling, rapid pulse and respiration rate, skin discoloration, and swelling. Keep the victim calm and still, and keep the affected area below heart level to slow the flow of venom. Wash the bite. Remove any rings or constricting items in case of swelling. Splint a bitten extremity. Hydrate the victim and get medical help.

Scorpions are numerous in deserts like those in the Southwest and are most active at night. Their sting usually causes pain similar to a bee sting and rarely causes illness, although certain species have been known to kill humans, typically small children and elderly.

Most stings result from accidental contact. Watch for scorpions at night, especially when lifting objects off the ground, and do not walk barefoot. Sleep in a shelter like a tent and keep it zipped up.

Animals often use hiking trails for the same reason we do: it's easier than fighting the underbrush. (Yosemite backcountry, CA)

Shake out things like boots or clothing before putting them on, or a sleeping bag that's been outside. Apply a cool compress to a bite for the pain and monitor the victim. If he becomes ill, get help. Avoid taking ibuprofen or any medication that thins the blood.

Other large animals, like **moose and bison**, rarely pose any kind of threat to people unless they are approached, although bull moose can be aggressive during the autumn rut, or mating season. A good rule of thumb is to avoid approaching any critter that outweighs you by several hundred pounds. Moose and deer pose a greater threat to motorists at night in rural areas: Collisions with deer often damage vehicles and may injure the occupants, and collisions with moose frequently prove fatal to the people in the car. Drive a little more slowly at night and use your high beams. **Wolves**, which live in isolated areas of the lower 48, and coyotes, which are widespread, are not considered a threat to humans and rarely even show interest in us.

Some **smaller animals**, from raccoons and squirrels to rodents like mice and kangaroo rats, pose threats to humans ranging from their interest in your food to rabies. Always hang your food beyond the reach of animals—many, including the ubiquitous squirrel, will chew through a pack for food. If possible, hang your pack to keep animals from chewing on straps for the salt left by your perspiration. If someone is bitten by a wild animal, clean the wound as thoroughly as possible and evacuate the victim immediately to a medical facility.

Insects

In wet seasons in most mountain regions of North America, you will at some point have to deal with **biting insects like mosquitoes, black flies, no-see-ums,** and various other annoying bugs. They usually are thickest from spring into midsummer, depending on latitude and altitude, and dissipate by mid- or late summer. They are more numerous for longer periods of time in wet mountains like those in the Northeast and Northwest than in dry mountains like the Rockies. Most are thickest in early morning and early evening, although some will hound you all day long.

Find out before your trip whether insects are heavy. Sometimes you simply have to grin and bear it. But use clothing to the extent possible to protect yourself against insects: long sleeves, pants—a couple of layers if necessary, and a hat with a bandanna hanging from it to protect your head and neck. In hot weather, wet down those layers of clothing to keep cool. Mosquito netting draped over a hat has probably preserved the sanity of many a backcountry traveler in heavy mosquito country like Alaska. If the bugs are heavy, pick a campsite with a good breeze. In Alaska's Denali National Park, we ate every meal facing into the wind because the mosquito clouds were less annoying behind us than in our faces.

Carry and use insect repellent anywhere you anticipate high concentrations of biting insects. Many contain the chemical DEET, which often comes in a high concentration and should be applied sparingly—squirt a few drops into the palms of your hands, then rub your palms over exposed skin and hair. Wash your hands afterward to avoid getting DEET in your eyes or food. Use it very conservatively on children, and apply it to them yourself to keep it off their hands. If you're concerned about using a chemical repellent, look for one of the products that contain natural ingredients like citronella to ward off insects.

Children tend to scratch itchy bites and are more susceptible to infection than adults because they don't keep themselves as clean. Use hydrocortisone cream on a bite to reduce the itch. Wash any bite that has been scratched open with soap and water and cover it with an adhesive bandage.

Ticks are a concern because they transmit diseases such as Lyme disease, Rocky Mountain spotted fever, tularemia, and Colorado tick fever. Again, clothing is the best protection, including long pants tucked into thick socks. Examine one another's flesh and clothing for ticks during and after a hike—bearing in mind that some ticks are as small as the period at the end of this sentence. Be thorough: I've discovered ticks on my socks and car floor only after driving home.

Remove a tick right away, because some will not pass along a disease until hours after they latch onto skin. Don't use petroleum jelly or a hot match. Pull the tick off gently with tweezers, being careful not to crush it. Clean the small wound afterward with alcohol. You could save the tick in a sealed container (without touching it) to have it tested later for disease. If you experience a rash, fever, and flulike symptoms after a backcountry trip—even weeks afterward—see a doctor and get tested for the aforementioned diseases.

Nasty Flora

Poison ivy, poison oak, and poison sumac flourish in climates as diverse as the wet Northeast and Northwest and the desert Southwest. An individual's reaction to direct contact with these plants depends on how allergic that person is, but often consists of a red, itchy rash. Poison ivy and poison oak are usually identifiable by their clusters of three leaves, while poison sumac has several leaves arranged symmetrically along either side of its stalk and one at the end of the stalk. The plants' appearance can vary between regions.

Immediately wash any skin that makes contact with a poisonous plant, and wash any clothing or objects similarly exposed, because they can retain the poisonous urushiol oil for years. Make sure children know how to identify any poisonous plants and avoid them. Hydrocortisone cream helps reduce swelling and itching. If a victim develops blisters or his eyes swell shut, see a doctor.

Beyond the poisonous species of flora, there are many **thorn-bearing plants,** particularly in desert regions. They are painful to encounter, can be difficult and painful to remove from your skin, and sometimes leave thorns embedded in clothing or skin. Wear long sleeves and pants and/or thick socks pulled up over your calves, and watch where you're walking.

Other "Opportunistic Carnivores"

Despite a few highly publicized incidents, violence by people against people is extremely rare in the backcountry. You are statistically safer hiking a trail than driving to work. More common, though certainly not epidemic, is vandalism and theft against vehicles parked at trailheads.

If possible, park where there is a constant flow of people rather than in a secluded area. Ask permission to park at a nearby business or home and walk or get a ride to the trailhead. Lock your vehicle and leave nothing visible in it; stash everything in the trunk. If you can't avoid leaving some stuff visible in the cabin of the vehicle, make it look unappealing: I've scattered dirty laundry, especially undergarments, inside my car as an antitheft device, and so far it's worked.

Resources

Bear Attacks: Their Cause and Avoidance by Stephen Herrero (Lyons Press).

Bear Aware: Hiking and Camping in Bear Country by Bill Schneider (Falcon).

Medicine for the Backcountry by Buck Tilton and Frank Hubbell (ICS Books).

Mountain Lion Alert: Safety Tips for Yourself, Your Children, Your Pets, and Your Livestock in Lion Country by Steve Torres (Falcon).

Tracking and the Art of Seeing by Paul Rezendes (Harper Resource).

chapter
nine

LEADERSHIP AND DECISION-MAKING

LIGHTNING FLASHED *all around us as we clung to a cliff high up 10,560-foot Symmetry Spire, in Wyoming's Grand Tetons. Thunder rent the air with a sound like atoms splitting, a sound I could feel in my ribs. I stood on a ledge about the width of my foot as rain streamed down the rock, drumming on my helmet; soaking my clothing, climbing shoes, and gear; and pelting my eyes as I gazed up into a narrow chimney of stone, trying to figure out how to push myself through it. Some 80 feet below, out of sight, my friend Gerry stood on another ledge belaying the rope linking us, probably wondering why that rope hadn't moved in a few minutes.*

A strange noise rang in the air behind me. I spun around, but saw nothing. When I turned back to the cliff I heard it again, and felt suddenly ill realizing what it was: the ice ax on my pack humming like a tuning fork in the electrified air. First the rock had become dangerously slick; now I had become a lightning rod.

It was probably the only time in years of traveling through the mountains that I thought about dying as a real and imminent possibility.

The thunderhead had zoomed up on us like a speeding car in the passing lane only about fifteen minutes earlier. Just 100 feet or so from the top of our route, we had decided to go up rather than rappel hundreds of feet back down the ridge we'd just climbed. We knew that a short rappel off the other side of Symmetry Spire would land us at the top of a gully, where we could start hiking back down—a much easier, safer, and faster retreat than a lengthy rappel. I'd started up the final hundred feet under a Gatling-gun volley of hail, which had the one redeeming value of not making the rock wet. But the rain soon followed.

Keeping my back—and the ax—to the cliff seemed to ground it and stop the humming, so I stood frozen in that position for several minutes. After the worst of the thunderhead passed and my ax stopped humming when I faced the cliff, I thrashed up the chimney to the top of the ridge and belayed Gerry up.

But there was more mountain above us, and I glared at it with irritation. In my anxiousness to finish the most difficult part of the climb, I hadn't thought about the long, if easy, scramble separating the top of the ridge from the summit. Now, after the impromptu concerto from my ax, and with the sky still spitting and snarling, the thought of going any higher brought a taste of bile to my mouth.

So we did what seemed to make the most sense: We sat down for a break. In a light rain, we gulped down energy bars and water and surveyed our surroundings. And in those few minutes of collecting our thoughts, I noticed something we'd overlooked at first—a small notch in the ridge where we could rappel easily into the gully. Moments later, we stood on dirt, still soaked but smiling, happy to be below the lightning zone and changing into boots for our long hike down.

Those smiles soon changed to expressions of horror and disbelief. Picking our way carefully down the gully, we noticed a spot of color farther below. As we drew closer, we realized we were looking at the body of one of the three climbers who had been below us on the ridge. They had apparently decided to rappel down when the storm rolled in. We'd lost sight of them, and had simply been too preoccupied with our own troubles to think about them.

I approached the body on the slim chance that he might be alive, but after touching a frigid wrist I reeled backward, trembling from the sight. A rope lay in tangles about him, and a rappel device was still attached to his harness, evidence that he'd fallen when a rappel anchor pulled loose. From his twisted, broken remains, I knew he'd fallen a long way.

Gerry and I spoke with the two survivors the next day and got their story. In the anxiety of trying to escape the storm, their companion may have rushed in setting up one rappel anchor. The block of stone he had trusted as the foundation of his anchor dislodged when he leaned back to rappel, sending him and it to the bottom of the cliff.

I don't tell that story to criticize its victims or their decisions. They've been through a terrible tragedy with which I can empathize. Things are far from black and white in circumstances like that, and everyone makes decisions based on their own experience. Our decision to go up rather than rappel the ridge could have proven disastrous. But I think the single best move we made up there was pausing for a few minutes to think through our predicament, while perhaps the only mistake committed by the man who died was rushing himself. Sadly, he paid an awfully big price for a small lapse of concentration.

Think Things Through

Part of the challenge of the backcountry is that things go wrong, and part of the reward is using your knowledge and skills to surmount problems. No book can give you the answers to the infinitude of woes that can arise out there; besides, the response that works for one person based on her skills and experience won't necessarily be wisest for another person whose experience is more limited or simply entirely different. No matter how far technology advances, or how much humans change the face of the wilderness, problems will always crop up and individuals will have to deal with them as best they can, on their own.

Decision-making gets very cloudy very quickly in a tense situation. Events can seem to spiral out of control before you have a chance to react. Sometimes a quick response is necessitated by circumstances. But more often, rushing into action without thinking things through leads to bigger problems. The best solutions usually emerge after careful thought.

When an emergency arises, or some kind of trouble brews—a storm, an injury, the realization that you are far off course, or maybe the failure of an important piece of gear—remain calm, step back, and assess the situation. Take a broad perspective—we tend to focus myopically on the source of the problem and not always see the big picture. For example, in our adventure on Symmetry Spire, I was so focused at first on how to climb the last bit of mountain still above us that I failed to see we didn't have to climb anymore at all: There was another escape route. Think outside the box.

Rationally consider and discuss all possible options and variables and weigh their pros and cons and potential consequences against each other. Don't settle on the first course of action that comes to mind—it may not be the best. Obviously you don't want to stand around conducting a committee meeting in the face of any immediate threat to life or limb. But in many backcountry emergencies, there is time to stop and spend fifteen minutes figuring out what to do. (Chapter 10 addresses specific injuries and ailments.)

Ask yourself which options pose the least risk to all members of the party; heroic efforts make great movie scripts, but an unnecessarily risky move that fails only aggravates the situation and increases risk for all members of the party when there's suddenly another injured person. For instance, don't try to be a hero by offering all your warm clothing to the injured person—your hypothermia will only worsen matters.

Make use of the collective intellectual energy of your entire group, even if experience levels vary greatly. The most-experienced

Turning back from the summit of Mt. Washington, NH, due to impenetrable fog. Always put safety first, no matter how far you've traveled to reach the summit.

members are probably best able to evaluate options but should not ignore the concerns or ideas of others, and the least–experienced members should not just kick back and assume the experienced people will figure everything out. This isn't just to make everyone feel good. Any solution has to work for everyone, or it won't work, and that solution will be dictated as much by the novice members of the group as by the veterans.

Don't suddenly forget all of your survival skills (such as those discussed in this book's other chapters). Miles into the backcountry, emergencies are not mopped up and over with in minutes. They drag on for hours, sometimes days. All members of the party still have to eat, drink, stay warm, go to the bathroom, etc. Forgetting your own needs doesn't make you a hero, it simply increases the group's risk by raising the potential for another member—you—to join the ranks of those needing help.

Anticipate and Head Off Problems

As I wrote above, no book can give you the answers to the many problems that can arise out there. But use this book to supplement your own skills and experience in helping you anticipate what can go wrong and how to avoid those problems. Avoiding trouble is the best strategy in the backcountry, where the seriousness of any injury or problem automatically magnifies because of your distance from advanced medical care; a dry, heated shelter; etc.

Victims in backcountry accidents often recall the events as happening quickly, and certainly the actual moment of the accident often does occur in an instant. But a regular reader of accident reports like the American Alpine Club's annual *Accidents in North American Mountaineering*, or the report in each issue of the AMC's journal *Appalachia*, or incident reports from national parks will see that many accidents are attributable at least in part to human error—they have their origin in one or more decisions or actions by the victims that helped precipitate the accident by increasing risk.

A few examples from a recent issue of *Appalachia* illustrate my point: A hiker on a high mountain ridge suddenly exhibits flu symptoms, including dehydration and vomiting, and her companions allow her to hike down by herself; she subsequently falls, breaking her leg. A hiker heading down from the summit of Mount Washington at 6:00 P.M. becomes disoriented by darkness, takes the wrong trail, then ends up losing that trail and trying to find his way by the light of a candle stuck onto the end of a stick. A man on his first hike in the White Mountains falls to his death attempting to descend the steep and very rugged headwall of Tuckerman Ravine.

In each case, decisions made by the parties were a major contributing factor in the accidents. And none of us should take comfort in the assumption that all of these people were inexperienced or reckless. That's a dangerous attitude, because what we're really telling ourselves is, "That couldn't happen to me." Accidents happen to experienced people too—read the reports if you want proof of that—and they arise from decisions that may have seemed perfectly safe and sensible at the time. The moral is never to get overconfident or let your guard down.

Check your gear one last time before you head out on the trail.

Think of mercury in a thermometer as a metaphor for risk and your decisions and actions causing the mercury to go up or down—increasing or decreasing your relative risk. You cannot control the many variables of backcountry travel, but you can significantly control your exposure to those variables, from the first preparations for a trip to its final steps. When you understand the inherent hazards of any outing and environment, you are more aware of them while in the backcountry and better able to anticipate and avoid problems.

The decisions and actions to which I refer run the gamut of every subject covered in this book, from pre-trip preparation, clothing, and gear to your trail and camping skills, knowledge of wilderness first aid, etc. I'm not suggesting you can't go into the backcountry without an encyclopedic knowledge of all of these areas, or that you should pass each moment out there quaking in fear. Simply be aware. Don't overextend yourself or any companion either physically, emotionally, or in terms of their abilities or how well equipped they are for a particular activity. Recognize when you're inviting an uncomfortable level of risk, and adjust your plans accordingly.

Remember the adage, "The mountains will always be there." Too many accidents happen because people didn't turn back when they should have. And there's no telling how many accidents were avoided because people were well prepared and made the right decisions.

Know When to Take Charge

Leadership in backcountry situations typically takes one of two forms: a designated leader on an organized trip, whether as a volunteer for a club or a paid commercial guide; or, more informally, a more experienced person in a group of friends or family.

The **designated leader on an organized trip** has tremendous responsibilities—in fact, courts have consistently recognized the role as implying legal liability for the leader's decisions and actions, and for the organization's or commercial outfitter's training of the leader. The degree of legal liability usually depends on such factors as whether the leader is paid or a volunteer and whether the trip participants are paying clients, and the legalities are far too complex to explore here. But the point is this: Society and trip participants presume that the participants are placing their safety in the hands of the designated leader of an organized trip.

Trip leaders and guides should receive training in leadership, the appropriate advanced skills for their activity, and in wilderness medicine (the last involves three levels of training; see chapter 10). Trip participants are wise to inquire about the training and experience of their leaders rather than assume a volunteer leader or professional guide has the appropriate background.

The advice offered in the sections above applies to trip leaders and guides as well. But it becomes more imperative for them to adequately screen participants, whom the leaders often do not know beforehand, to determine whether they have the proper experience, equipment (including clothing), and physical training for the planned trip. Similarly, leaders need to pay close attention to the physical and emotional condition of trip participants at all times, and react early enough to head off problems.

For their part, participants should not head out on an organized trip without a full understanding of what will be demanded of them, the ability and willingness to meet those demands, and proper preparation. And participants should not hide any developing problems from leaders—whether blisters, fear, mounting exhaustion, an injury, or worse—because that only allows the problem to worsen. A key component to any safe and enjoyable outing is communication.

Informal trips taken by friends or family naturally entail a more relaxed relationship between the participants, who may or may not have varied skills and experience. Still, there's often one person assuming the bulk of trip-planning duties, and it's usually someone the others can count on to know how to plan it. That person may know his companions well, but he should nonetheless involve them in the planning to the extent necessary for them to understand the level of commitment expected of them and ensure they are comfortable with it, especially if the activity requires any specialized skills, like paddling or rock climbing.

In the backcountry, friends often will turn to the most experienced member or members of the group for guidance on questions small and large. The experienced person should assume some responsibility for the comfort, safety, and enjoyment of less experienced companions. But as any good manager knows, everyone draws more satisfaction from an activity or decision when they feel they've contributed to the outcome. Involve everyone in decisions. If a major issue arises, like an injury, members of a group typically turn to the most experienced person for leadership, and that person needs to be confident enough to assume that responsibility without letting it corrupt his or her thought processes. Don't let others' faith in you overinflate your own sense of your abilities.

A **backcountry emergency** demands, first and foremost, cooperation and cohesion among everyone. It's better to step back and let someone else take charge than to let disagreement over how to handle a situation erupt into discord and chaos. Preferably, everyone involved respects one another's skills, and the group combines their various talents toward an optimal outcome to the emergency. Smooth communication becomes vital.

Let someone with the proper background assume the role of field marshal, delegating responsibilities while overseeing everything, rather than having several people acting independently without knowing what others are doing. Wilderness-medicine programs often teach that it is best to decide before a trip who will be in charge in a medical emergency; but the reality is that many of us don't take that step. If the decision has to be made in the field, make it quickly and without rancor.

If you encounter a person or group with an apparent problem, stop and inquire politely whether they need help, but don't assume they do—unless, of course, they're unable to respond and it's obvious they need help. They may have their situation completely under control, and any attempt to intercede may only lead to discord and bigger problems. Never involve yourself unless your involvement will improve the situation.

If a stranger requests help, you should always do anything within your power to provide it, without assuming unnecessary risk for the group or any member. As I wrote above, never make the situation worse—for example, by risking injury to another person, or risking further injury to the victim—through some failed heroic effort. The more you know about backcountry rescue and wilderness medicine, you more help you can provide. But the best you may be able to do is make the person comfortable and go for help.

Someone who needs help may be unable to request it, or may not be in the right state of mind—perhaps due to hypothermia or a serious injury—to comprehend that he needs help. You may have to convince the person that he does need help. Still, if challenging someone's combativeness or refusal of help only makes the situation worse, don't do it. Use your best judgment. If the best you can do is move on and notify authorities that the person may need help, that's what you should do.

Maintain a Positive Attitude

Picture this hypothetical scenario: You come upon someone lying on the ground, obviously injured but conscious. He's pretty bloody, alone, and scared, and he's been calling for help. You walk up to him, introduce yourself, ask him what happened, then reassure him, "We're going to make you comfortable, and we're going to get help for you." Now, imagine the same scenario, except that when you walk up and look at his bloodied face, you cry out, "Oh, my God!"

Which reaction on your part will better help that victim to relax?

It's a bit of a cliché, but maintaining a positive attitude in difficult situations and calm in an emergency can only help matters, while a negative attitude or panic can easily make a bad situation worse. By reassuring the victim in this hypothetical situation, for instance, you just might allow him to relax enough for his pulse and respiration rates to return to normal, rather than being elevated by anxiety. That alone is a positive development, because elevated pulse and respiration rates suggest other possible problems and make your evaluation of his condition that much more difficult.

As I've tried to emphasize throughout this chapter: keeping a cool head is the key to resolving any backcountry emergency.

chapter
ten

WILDERNESS FIRST AID

I'M NOT GOING TO RELATE *some gruesome personal story about tragedy in the backcountry. Suffice to say that I have twice touched death in the outdoors—the first time was a close, longtime friend—and on a third occasion came upon a man who had taken a long fall down a mountainside and was very fortunate to suffer nothing worse than broken bones and minor blood loss.*

All three accidents occurred in rock-climbing or mountaineering situations, which entail greater risk than an activity like backpacking on a trail. But hikers and other outdoor enthusiasts shouldn't take comfort in that. Accidents can happen in seemingly benign situations, and they happen to the experienced as well as the inexperienced. The ones I've seen have not diminished my passion for the outdoors, but they have clarified for me the grave seriousness of an accident when you're miles, hours, or days from help, and the importance of prevention and caution.

Educate yourself on how to avoid trouble, and remain alert to potential hazards while in the backcountry. (See chapter 9 for advice on leadership and decision-making.) Prevention can't be overemphasized. While someone suffering life-threatening injuries at home might be transported in minutes to an emergency room and saved, the same injuries in the backcountry usually prove fatal.

All that said, I want to reiterate what I've tried to emphasize throughout this book: Traveling in the backcountry is supposed to be fun.

Remaining alert to possible hazards does not mean spending every waking moment in terror. It means understanding the environment you're in and recognizing your own needs and those of your companions. It's part of the bigger picture of an awareness of yourself and your surroundings that enhances your enjoyment and feeling of self-sufficiency. Having fun and being safe are complementary objectives.

You Can't Dial 911

Well, actually, in some backcountry areas in populous regions of the country, given modern communications technology, you *can* dial 911. But don't get taken in by all those cell phone ads promising security. Many mountains ranges and canyons are still too remote, or their topography too rugged, to receive a cell signal (a fact for which, I submit, we should be grateful, though we may not fully appreciate it until the day when it's no longer true). And even if you can put through a cell phone call for help from a trail or summit, in most places that help will not reach you for hours, quite possibly a day or more.

This physical separation from civilization and protracted response time to emergencies are what distinguish wilderness medicine from street medicine. It's a distinction many backcountry travelers fail to comprehend. In the wilderness-medicine courses I've taken, I've seen how slowly even experienced backcountry travelers come around to the understanding that help is not around the corner when you're out there.

In a typical urban setting, mere minutes elapse between the moment an accident occurs and the arrival of the injured at a hospital emergency room. In the backcountry, someone often has to hike miles down a trail to the nearest phone to alert authorities. Then rescuers and gear have to be assembled and organized, and rescuers may have no way to reach the accident scene but on foot—helicopters are not always readily available, nor can they land anywhere or in any conditions. Rescuers may have trouble pinpointing your location, or be hampered by weather or terrain in reaching you.

It's not unusual for rescuers to learn of an accident as night approaches and have to wait until daybreak to respond. In fact, one of the ironies of wilderness medicine is that the patient may be literally minutes by air from an emergency room, but on a cliff face,

Help is often a long time away in the backcountry. Take a first-aid course and learn to be self sufficient. (Mt. Bond, NH)

mountainside, or deep in a canyon from which an evacuation takes hours or days.

When some friends and I came upon a man in the Tetons who had taken a long slide down a snow couloir and landed on rocks, breaking some bones, he'd already been lying there, alone, for at least an hour. We assessed his condition and helped make him comfortable, then some of us went for help. Grand Teton National Park has an elite mountain-rescue team, with a helicopter which was able to drop rescuers a short distance from the injured man, enabling a much faster response than would be possible in many North American mountain ranges. Nonetheless, some four hours passed between his fall and his helicopter evacuation to a hospital.

In a backcountry emergency, an injured person's companions, or whoever happens to find him, have to stabilize and care for the patient for an extended period of time. What they do for an injured person in the hours between the accident and his arrival at a hospital may determine whether he survives or dies, recovers fully or has permanent injuries.

How Much Should You Know?

You can no better say how much training in wilderness medicine is appropriate for traveling safely in the backcountry than you can predict whether you'll encounter an emergency. But your specific activities and responsibilities come into play as you decide the level of training and knowledge you want to achieve.

Consider, for instance, the objective level of risk inherent in your activity—whether it's hiking, wilderness backpacking, whitewater kayaking, mountaineering, or something else—how frequently and where you practice it, and the real hazards of that place. You may want to take into account your role as a formal or informal leader, whether a volunteer trip leader for a club or simply one of the more-experienced persons in a group of friends. Some organizations prescribe minimum training levels for leaders or guides, and if you're a paying client on a guided trip, that's one important thing to inquire about.

We all pick up wilderness-medicine fundamentals through experience and from companions: how to avoid and treat blisters, how to prevent hypothermia, why you should avoid too much sun, what poison ivy looks like. It's a good way to learn and a process that should never stop. A broader knowledge base can be culled from books; this chapter provides an introduction to wilderness medicine, and other books are devoted entirely to the subject. But the best and most intensive way to learn it is to take a course with an organization that offers certification in the various levels of wilderness-medicine training (see the Resources and Training section at the end of this chapter).

There are three levels of training and certification:

- Wilderness first aid (WFA) is a 16-hour program that can be taken over a weekend. It provides a solid foundation of training in how to assess a patient's injuries and what important information to communicate to rescuers or medical professionals. It also covers a spectrum of injuries and ailments, including those explained below. Given the cost and time commitment for more-extensive training, WFA certification is the level most often sought by recreational backcountry travelers. Some organizations also offer an advanced wilderness first-aid program that takes about 32–36 hours.

- Wilderness first responder is a 72- to 80-hour program providing more in-depth training in backcountry medicine, geared more toward professional guides and outdoor leaders.

- Wilderness emergency medical technician training involves at least 150 to 160 hours and is designed for professional search-and-rescue team members, backcountry rangers, outdoor leaders, and others who routinely provide emergency care in remote settings.

Reacting to an Emergency

Short of a charging bear, there's probably nothing in the backcountry that can destabilize a person or a group like witnessing or happening upon a serious accident. The normal reaction is disbelief and confusion—uninjured companions may begin crying, screaming, or cursing angrily, or may simply stare dumbly as if they can't figure out what's happening. Chaos can result, and rash, improper handling of the injured can cause more-serious injuries. Someone with a clear head must take charge and rein everyone in by calmly explaining that an orderly and cooperative effort is required to handle the situation effectively. (See more on leadership and decision-making in chapter 9.)

In any group, one person is often the designated leader or is recognized by the others as the most experienced decision-maker, and must take charge. But even in a group comprised of people of equal background, it's important that **one person direct a response to an injury** to ensure the efficient coordination of everyone's efforts. It's a good idea to designate that leader before the trip. That person can delegate responsibilities to the others. If there is more than one injured person, optimally one person coordinates the evaluation of each patient, and one field marshal of sorts oversees the entire response.

If there are more injured than uninjured, or if you are the only person on hand to care for several injured, then difficult decisions must be made to determine who is in the most immediate need of help—and who may be beyond help.

The first rule is never to do anything that creates more injured people. **Survey the scene** for immediate hazards, such as an exposed slope or potential rock fall or avalanche. Don't all dash toward an injured person—you could end up duplicating his accident. Although moving an injured person can risk injury to his spinal cord (see below), sometimes circumstances—say, the injured person is in a rushing, freezing creek—demand that you move him to a safer location before doing anything else, to protect the injured as well as the uninjured. On the other hand, moving the patient may not be advised, but you might have to secure the patient and everyone else with anchors on a cliff or a steep snow slope. Employ all of your outdoor skills in surveying the scene.

If you decide to move a patient immediately, for the patient's and everyone else's safety, employ a technique known as BEAMing the patient, or "**b**ody **e**levation **a**nd **m**ovement." Gather enough able persons to surround the patient, with everyone getting their hands under him and particular care paid to the head and neck (see the section on injury to the spinal cord below). On a three count, everyone lifts the patient in such a way as to maintain his body in the same position he was in on the ground. Carry him in this manner to safe ground and set him down gently in the same position. This presents a good opportunity to get a sleeping pad beneath him as insulation against the ground.

Take a head count. All of the injured may not be immediately visible. Make sure your entire group is present. If you've come upon an injured party of strangers and one or more of them can answer questions, find out how many people are supposed to be there.

In anything you do, decisions may not be clear-cut, but inaction and indecision can worsen matters. As you go through the information in this chapter, or any other resources, bear in mind that in the field you may have to improvise on these procedures. If someone is calling for help and you see blood spurting from his femoral artery, you're not going to check his airway—if he can speak, he has an open airway—you're going to apply pressure to the wound. You simply have to use your best judgment.

Patient Assessment

Even when you witness an accident, the extent of the victim's injuries may not necessarily be apparent. Come upon an injured person, and the problem may be a complete mystery. Either way, you need to examine the patient. The patient assessment is best conducted by one person to ensure that nothing is overlooked.

It is critical that someone take detailed written notes as you evaluate an injured person's condition, including recording the time of all notes and changes in the patient's condition. When it comes time to communicate the patient's condition to emergency-medicine professionals—whether rescuers, EMTs, or someone in a hospital emergency room—this information will prove vital in helping them make important decisions like what rescue and medical gear to bring and how to treat the patient. (See the box below with the SOAP note form.)

The **primary survey** of a patient covers immediate threats to life, and should be completed right away, although the patient's behavior may eliminate the need for some or all of this survey. Remember this procedure as your ABCs.

- **A**irway. Check that the person is moving air in and out of his lungs. Place your hand in front of his mouth to feel for breath. Noisy breathing indicates obstructed breathing. Any facial injury raises the possibility of an airway blockage. If he's not breathing, look into his mouth to see whether anything is obstructing his airway, and remove it. To open someone's mouth, employ a modified chin thrust: Place your hands on the mandible, or jaw hinge, and push downward. Sweep his mouth with your finger. (The modified chin thrust is taught in CPR classes; see below.)

- **B**reathing. Ask a conscious person whether he is having difficulty breathing. See whether an unconscious person's chest is rising and falling in a normal rhythm. An abnormal rhythm may or may not be obvious; an adult normally takes twelve to twenty-four breaths per minute. Anyone not breathing should be given rescue breathing, which is taught in CPR classes.

- Circulation. Feel for a pulse in the carotid artery of the neck, or in the wrist. Listen to the chest for a heartbeat. Check for severe bleeding, bearing in mind that it can be hidden in layers of clothing, or beneath the injured person. Severe bleeding virtually always can be stopped with direct pressure to, and elevation of, the wound. A victim with no pulse should be given cardiopulmonary resuscitation. CPR can be learned in inexpensive, one-day or two-evening courses in many communities. Contact your local YMCA, American Red Cross, American Heart Association, or civic organization, or try a fire department, college, or hospital.

The **secondary survey** is a full examination of the patient to determine what is wrong. By this point, if possible, get a sleeping pad beneath him for comfort and insulation from the cold ground to guard against hypothermia. To avoid moving him, roll him gently onto one side—keeping his neck and back stable (see below)—and lay the pad beneath him, folded in half lengthwise. Roll him back the other way, unfold the pad, then lie him flat on it. In that most accident victims are not found lying flat on their backs, you first have to decide whether it is safe to move him onto his back, which is an easier position in which to examine him. Moving a patient may create a serious risk of causing or exacerbating a spinal-cord injury (see below).

Determining the so-called **mechanism of injury**—or how the accident happened—can tell you a lot right away about the patient's potential injuries. Did he fall? If so, how far, and what did he land on? A conscious and coherent patient may be able to tell you exactly what happened and to identify his injury; then again, he may not necessarily be aware of all of his injuries. If the person is unconscious, look around for evidence of what happened.

If anything suggests the potential for **injury to the spinal cord**—including a serious fall or loss of consciousness—the protocol is to presume spinal injury until you can confirm otherwise and stabilize the patient's neck and spine to prevent movement. No patient with a potential spinal-cord injury should be moved before the neck and spine are stabilized, unless the victim and/or rescuers are faced with an immediate threat to life. Stabilization of the neck and spine is accomplished initially by giving one rescuer the sole responsibility of kneeling by the patient's head and gently cradling his head and neck in the rescuer's hands, to prevent any movement of the neck. Later, you may have to immobilize the patient's neck and spine using clothing, a piece cut from a foam pad and folded in half lengthwise for rigidity, or other improvised materials wrapped around the patient's neck and secured in place with tape, cravats (see below), or whatever you have available.

Talking to the injured also immediately provides you with some vital information: whether his airway is clear, whether he is breathing without trouble, whether his respiratory rate is elevated, his emotional condition and comfort level (hot? cold? thirsty? lying on a rock?), and his level of consciousness. Any degree of diminished consciousness indicates a possible **head injury,** which can be life-threatening. A head-injured patient needs evacuation to a hospital as soon as possible.

Emergency medical personnel measure someone's level of consciousness on a scale you can remember with the acronym AVPU. The levels are: **a**lert and oriented times three, that is, he can tell you his name, where he is, and what day it is; responsive to **v**erbal stimuli, meaning the victim responds physically or verbally to your questions or comments, though he may not be coherent; or responsive only to **p**ain such as a skin prick. Otherwise, the patient is **u**nresponsive.

Examine the patient from head to toe, palpating with your hands—that is, gently and carefully pressing to feel for broken bones, unnatural rigidity in the abdomen, or a reaction of pain. A rigid abdomen may indicate internal bleeding, a serious condition which can lead to shock (see below) and death. Look for external bleeding, removing or cutting away clothing where necessary. Run your fingers along the spine to feel for a break, if you can do so without moving a patient with a potential spinal-cord injury. Compress the ribs from both sides, feeling for breaks or soft spots. Palpate the shoulders and arms, hipbones, and legs.

Check for sensation in the feet and fingers, the lack of which can indicate nerve damage, spinal-cord injury, or circulation being cut off by a broken bone or swelling. Note the skin color and temperature and whether it's dry, moist, or clammy. Check for normal capillary refill by squeezing their fingertips and toes between your thumb and forefinger for several seconds; if the digit does not return to a healthy pink color within two seconds after you release it, circulation is being impaired. Monitor vital signs—level of consciousness, heart and respiratory rates—every five minutes until the patient is stable, then at regular intervals. Avoid unnecessary movement of the patient.

Record a SAMPLE history to relay to emergency medical professionals. It should contain the following information:

- **S**ymptoms—chief complaints, injuries, physical maladies
- **A**llergies—the patient's problem may be tied to something ingested, a medication he's taking, or environmental conditions (such as anaphylaxis caused by bee stings; see below)
- **M**edications—both prescription and non-prescription drugs of any kind
- **P**ast history—any past trauma, injury, surgery, or chronic medical problems, or a current pregnancy

♦ Last food and fluids—how recently they've eaten and drank, how much, and what
♦ Events—what led to the accident

Record all the information you obtain about the patient on a SOAP note, a standard way of communicating a patient's condition that is widely recognized by emergency-medicine professionals. A good SOAP note brought to a rescue team or communicated to a hospital emergency room will better help those people prepare for the patient. The box below is a basic SOAP note which you can copy and bring into the backcountry.

---

soap note

Subjective analysis (patient's age, sex, SAMPLE history):

Objective analysis (vital signs, results of patient exam, time):

Assessment (diagnosis of potential problems):

Plan (how you intend to deal with the patient's problems, and your long-term plan—e.g., getting the patient to help or waiting for help to arrive):

Backcountry Ailments: Avoidance, Symptoms, and Treatment

Dehydration is the most common problem among backcountry travelers (see more on this in chapter 4). Avoidance is simple: drink plenty of fluids. Symptoms include reduced urine output, an increasingly dark color to the urine, and a dry mouth. Treat it by consuming fluids steadily over a long enough period of time to rehydrate—it may take hours—and to rest out of the sun if you're feeling weak, woozy, or nauseous.

Heat exhaustion occurs in people who are not acclimatized to heat or hot sun, and is brought on by salt and water loss through perspiration. Avoidance entails consuming plenty of fluids and being aware of your condition, or that of your companions, particularly if traveling in a region much hotter and sunnier than where you live. Wear a baseball cap or wide-brimmed hat. Symptoms can include pale, cool, clammy skin; dizziness, nausea, and possible vomiting; slightly increased pulse and respiration rates; and possibly heightened anxiety or confusion. Treatment with rest in a cool place and plenty of fluids should bring some improvement in how the person feels even within an hour or two and full recovery within a day.

Heatstroke is far more serious than heat exhaustion—the patient could lapse into a coma and die without immediate care. Avoidance is the same as for heat exhaustion, and be vigilant about any sign of heat exhaustion worsening. Symptoms include skin that is red and hot and which could be dry or wet, and a diminished level of consciousness manifested in confusion, disorientation, extreme agitation, even hallucinations. Treatment requires immediate removal from heat and sun, cooling by soaking the body in water and fanning, massaging limbs vigorously, and transport to a hospital as soon as possible.

Sunburn is another common problem, especially at high altitudes and in dry, sunny western climates. Avoidance can be difficult, particularly where there is persistent snow cover, but includes using clothing to cover as much skin as possible, and frequently reapplying sunblock with a high SPF rating to any exposed skin—a tan helps prevent burning but does not protect against UV rays. Get a sunblock that guards against ultraviolet A and ultraviolet B rays and is waterproof. Wear a wide-brimmed hat or baseball cap and full-coverage sunglasses, the latter to protect your eyes from the internal

Guard yourself from the sun to avoid sunstroke, heat exhaustion, and dehydration. (Canyon Lands National Park, UT)

burning that can cause temporary snow blindness (see more in the Climate and Clothing section of chapter 3). Symptoms include red, dry, peeling, and blistered skin. Treatment includes avoiding the sun, drinking plenty of water, and optionally applying a moisturizing lotion for comfort.

It's important to protect children from excessive sun exposure—80 percent of skin damage from the sun, including that which leads to skin cancers, happens before age twenty, although it usually does not manifest itself for thirty years. Dress children in tightly woven clothing and use sunscreen on any uncovered skin. Keep infants out of the sun as much as possible, and be conservative using sunscreen on them. Test it on a small area of skin to see whether the baby has a reaction. Treat a child's sunburn immediately with cold compresses, moisturizing lotion, and acetaminophen for the pain. Adults and children should wear sunglasses to reduce the chance of cataracts later in life and to protect the sensitive eyelids of children.

Hypothermia is defined as a drop in the core body temperature due to the body losing heat faster than it produces heat. It can be brought on in temperatures well above freezing and in circumstances that seem relatively benign. Avoidance begins with consuming sufficient food and fluids. Be aware of any sustained cooling felt by you or your companions or any symptoms of hypothermia. Recognize and dress appropriately for environmental conditions that can cause hypothermia, such as becoming wet (from perspiration, precipitation, or immersion in water), exposure to wind, or a falling temperature (see chapter 3).

Symptoms develop with escalating seriousness and include a cold or numb feeling in the extremities, diminished physical coordination and alertness, confusion, apathy with regard to helping oneself, disorientation, and shivering. Severe hypothermia is characterized by slurred speech, convulsive shivering which eventually ceases, then the apparent absence of a pulse or breathing and a blue skin color. There's a saying in medicine that "you're not dead until you're warm and dead." Someone may be icy cold to the touch and appear dead but actually be suffering severe hypothermia; that person can be revived. A possible hypothermia victim should never be presumed dead until resuscitation attempts and rewarming fail.

Treatment depends on the degree to which hypothermia has advanced. If it's caught early, someone can recover quickly simply by eating, drinking, and getting into dry, warm clothing or a sleeping

Avoid hypothermia by dressing for the weather on the summit—not in the valley below. (Mt. Jefferson, NH)

bag and shelter if necessary. A severely hypothermic person has lost the ability to produce adequate body heat and needs to be stabilized. Handle the person gently, remove any damp clothing, and get him into dry clothes.

Then place the patient in a hypothermia wrap: Lay out a tarp, tent rainfly, or anything wind- and waterproof. Lay a sleeping pad for insulation from the ground atop it. Lay the patient in a sleeping bag atop the pad. Place warm water bottles or chemical heat packs in the patient's hands and/or around the torso, neck, and groin (chemical heat packs can pose a threat of burn injury if used improperly; follow instructions). Zip up the sleeping bag, leaving just a hole for the patient to breathe, then wrap the windproof layer over the top of the patient, ensuring that he's completely enclosed within this cocoon except for his breathing hole. Then get help.

Frostbite is the cooling or freezing of skin tissue which occurs when circulation is cut off to that part of the body. It occurs most commonly when the brain stops sending blood to an already cold body part in order to protect the vital organs from receiving cooled blood. It can also be caused by a physical obstruction to circulation, like a compound bone fracture. It usually occurs in temperatures below freezing, though not exclusively, and is preceded by hypothermia. Avoidance measures are the same as for hypothermia, with particular attention paid to the feet, hands, face, and ears, which are most easily frostbitten. Also, be careful not to impede circulation by tying boots or wrapping a bandage too tightly.

Symptoms of superficial frostbite, which is less serious, include numbness, pale color, cold but pliable skin, and sharp pain when the skin thaws. Superficial frostbite can be treated in the backcountry and heals completely. Deep frostbite is very serious and usually leads to loss of the body part. It is characterized by skin that is numb, cold, white, and frozen solid, and which eventually blackens.

Treat superficial frostbite by rewarming through contact with warm skin—for instance, stuffing hands in your armpits or placing cold feet against your partner's warm stomach. Do not massage cold skin because that can damage cells. If a blister forms after the skin is rewarmed, do not pop it. Keep the area warm and get medical attention. Deep frostbite requires evacuation to a hospital. Insulate the patient to prevent further freezing of skin, but do not attempt to rewarm a solidly frozen body part while in the backcountry—that would leave the patient in extreme pain and risk refreezing the area.

Blisters—we've all had them. They are a minor burn caused by friction on hardened skin like heels and palms, are more likely to occur on skin that's wet and warm (like a foot in a boot), and can be debilitating. Avoidance is very important—the worse blisters get, the more of a problem they become, and one person immobilized by blisters can affect the entire party.

Cool your feet whenever possible to help avoid blisters. You can use duct tape to protect sensitive areas prone to blistering.

The first line of defense is taking care of your feet. Start each backcountry day with dry socks, preferably a wicking liner sock beneath a heavier sock of a wool-and-synthetic blend. Make sure your boots fit (see chapter 2), are laced properly, and are broken in if they require it.

Feet perspire in boots, so whenever you stop for a short rest, sit down, pull off your boots and socks, and let them and your feet dry out—even if only for a few minutes. Wash your feet at the end of the day. If you feel any hot spot developing, do something about it before it progresses into a blister. Hands can blister from repetitive work like shoveling, or even from using a walking stick. Wear gloves to protect them.

Symptoms are familiar to us all—a patch of skin grows tender and red. Treatment depends on how early you catch it. A slightly red or tender hot spot can be protected from developing into a blister with an adhesive bandage, tape (even duct tape), or a square of moleskin. If a blister has formed, clean the area around it thoroughly to avoid infection. Sterilize a needle or knife in a flame, then pop and drain the blister to promote faster healing. Put an antiseptic ointment on the spot, then cut a piece of moleskin or Second Skin (which have a soft side and a sticky side with a peel-off backing) large enough to overlap the blistered area. Cut a hole as large as the blister out of the center of the moleskin, then place the moleskin over the blister so that the blister is visible through the hole. If done properly, you should be able to walk without aggravating the blister.

Soft-tissue injuries and bleeding run a gamut of wounds of varied seriousness, including bruises, scrapes, lacerations or cuts, avulsions (a.k.a. "flappers," for the way a flap of skin is torn back like a door), punctures, amputations, and impaled objects. Avoidance is obvious—be careful out there—but these accidents occasionally happen. As I've stressed elsewhere, know what you're getting into and don't overextend yourself. Symptoms may not be immediately obvious, especially in the cold; sometimes a sign of blood on clothing is the first indication of the injury.

Treatment depends on the injury. A bruise or swelling should be treated with RICE—**r**est, **i**ce, **c**ompression, and **e**levation above the heart—to reduce swelling. With any bleeding injury, the first priority is to control bleeding. Direct, flat pressure virtually always works; never use a tourniquet. Anyplace where pressure could dangerously impede circulation, such as in the neck, try pinching off the wound to stem bleeding. If there is a danger that pressure could force broken bone into tender, vital tissue like that on the skull or ribs, apply very light pressure, and if that fails pack the wound with sterile gauze or clean bandages to help promote clotting.

Any open wound must be cleaned by irrigating with sterile water to prevent infection, then bandaged and checked regularly. Change the dressing at least once or twice a day. You should evacuate for stitches when a cut is gaping, is on the face, hands, or over a joint, or there is damage to a blood vessel, ligament, or tendon.

With an avulsion, if the flap of skin isn't too badly torn, you can put it back into place after cleaning and before bandaging. With a puncture wound, some bleeding is beneficial to help flush clean the wound before bandaging. An amputation obviously requires evacuation; wrap the amputated part in a moist, sterile dressing, seal it in a plastic bag, and keep it cold. Impaled objects are also serious for the threat of infection and injury to an internal organ. Usually it's best to stabilize rather than remove the object, then evacuate the victim. Check periodically to ensure that any bandage is not cutting off circulation. In cases of significant blood loss, look for signs of shock.

Shock is a medical term for the inability of the circulatory system to supply the cells and organs of the body with oxygenated blood. It can lead quickly to death if the patient is not evacuated to a hospital. It has three basic causes: severe bleeding—external or internal—or fluid loss through advanced dehydration, vomiting, diarrhea, or excessive perspiring (hypovolemic, or volume, shock); decreased blood flow due to heart failure (cardiogenic shock); or damage to the blood vessels from a nervous-system failure or injury, body-wide infection, or allergic reaction, inhibiting blood flow (neurogenic, a.k.a. vasogenic, or septic, shock).

Avoidance entails simply being prepared, making wise decisions—and being lucky. Unfortunately, accidents happen. Symptoms may escalate as the patient's condition worsens, beginning with anxiety; restlessness; nausea and possible vomiting; rapid and shallow breathing; rapid and weak pulse; and pale, cool, and clammy skin, then progressing to an ashen color, disorientation, unconsciousness, and a steadily weakening pulse and respirations that slowly fade away.

Treatment includes maintaining an open airway, treating the underlying cause if possible (such as bleeding), keeping the patient flat with legs elevated (with the exception of a heart-attack victim, who may be more comfortable sitting upright), monitoring vital signs, and maintaining the victim's body temperature. Give the patient small amounts of water and food only if he is able to ingest it on his own without vomiting. Evacuate to a hospital as quickly as possible.

Sprains are the overstretching or tearing of ligaments that support the bones around a joint like the ankle, and **strains** are painful tears in muscle tissue. Avoidance is hard—these injuries tend to happen abruptly and without warning.

I've trained myself to use one little trick to protect my ankles, which have become so floppy from so many sprains over the years that I commonly roll one or both of them on hikes. As soon as I feel an ankle roll, I shift my weight to my other leg and bend that knee deeply. I can't stop the ankle from rolling, but, by taking my weight off it, even a bad twist results in no more than a brief, sharp pain, and I'm walking again without pain moments later.

Someone rarely has trouble recognizing a bad sprain—it's quite painful, especially at the moment it occurs, and the victim often cries out. Discoloration and swelling quickly follow. Symptoms of a muscle strain can be immediate sharp or burning pain, or a pain that builds over time—back strains, for example, may not be noticeable until hours after the incident.

Prompt treatment of a sprain will affect how quickly it heals and can mean the difference between it healing completely within weeks or bothering the victim for months. Use RICE—**r**est, **i**ce, **c**ompression, and **e**levation above the heart. Get crushed ice or a chemical ice pack on the injury immediately. In the backcountry, improvise with whatever is available, including snow; immersing the injury in cold water; wrapping it in a wet T-shirt; or digging into the earth for cool soil to pack around it.

Compress it by wrapping it in an elastic bandage, like an Ace bandage, but check below the injury periodically to ensure circulation is not cut off (e.g., make sure his toes aren't getting cold or numb). Let the pain dictate whether the victim tries walking on the injury. After the swelling and pain subside, exercise the joint to promote rapid healing by doing things like pretending to write the alphabet with your foot.

There are two schools of thought on treating muscle strains. One advocates treating any pain that comes on suddenly by icing for brief spells for the first twenty-four to forty-eight hours, then using heat, while using heat exclusively on strains that develop more slowly. The other theory advocates using ice on any strain because it tends to penetrate more deeply than heat.

In my vast personal experience with pulled and torn muscles, I've had the most success speeding up the healing process by using ice exclusively (on the advice of a good friend who's a sports-medicine physician), as frequently as three times a day, for about fifteen minutes at a time. An anti-inflammatory like ibuprofen also promotes healing, and you can take up to four 200 mg tablets three times a day for a short period of time if it does not bother your stomach. For intransigent muscle strains, see a doctor or physical therapist.

Fractures and dislocations include the range of broken bones and joint injuries. Avoidance, again, is not guaranteed even when you're careful, but bear in mind that these injuries often occur when someone is attempting something beyond his abilities or being inattentive, and they often happen late in the day when the victim is tired. Symptoms may include a cracking sound at the moment of the accident, pain, discoloration, swelling, muscles spasms around the injury, the feeling of broken bone scraping together (called crepitus) when you palpate the area, deformity or unnatural angulation of the injured area, or broken bone protruding from the skin.

A rule of thumb for distinguishing a sprained ankle from a fracture is that if you can bear weight on it immediately after the injury, it's probably not broken. Mechanism of injury is a good indicator too: If the victim suffers a hard fall or collision, there's obvious potential for a broken bone.

Treatment in the backcountry generally involves RICE—**r**est, **i**ce, **c**ompression, and **e**levation above the heart—returning the joint or bone to a natural position if possible, then immobilizing the injury with a splint or sling. This skill takes some practice, is best learned in a hands-on wilderness-medicine course, and requires improvisation in the field.

Returning the joint or bone to a natural position may require employing traction-in-line, or gently pulling the limb straight outward until the two broken sections of bone are in line again. If pulling traction-in-line increases pain significantly, or if there is resistance, stop. A splint must be rigid and roughly the length of the bone that is broken; a protruding splint can hit or get caught on things while the victim is in transport, causing him quite a lot of pain. Use whatever is available for a splint—a sturdy stick; a SAM splint (see The First-aid Kit below); or a ski, trekking, or tent pole.

Place the splint along the broken bone. Pad the limb and splint generously, using whatever you have: extra clothing, pieces cut from a foam pad, whatever—but be sure to pack it evenly around the limb. Secure the padding and splint with strips of cloth or something similar—preferably strips an inch or so wide, as opposed to narrow nylon cord, which can be uncomfortable. Your splint must immobilize the joints above and below the fracture in a natural, comfortable position—for example, a slight bend in the knee, the foot at roughly 90° to the leg, elbow bent at 90°, the fingers curled comfortably around rolled-up socks.

In a compound fracture, where the broken bone protrudes from the skin, the open wound must be cleaned to prevent infection (see the soft-tissue injuries section above). Frequently check that circulation is not cut off to the extremities by splints and bandages; adequate circulation is indicated by fingers and toes showing a natural color and feeling warm to the touch.

A **broken femur**, or thigh bone, which is the largest bone in the body, presents a unique danger because of the risk that the bone could sever the femoral artery and the victim could quickly bleed to death. Some wilderness-first-aid courses offer instruction in treating a broken femur in the field. If you want to know how to deal with this type of injury, take a course. No matter how you deal with the broken-femur victim, he will need a rescue as soon as possible.

Similarly, a **dislocated shoulder** presents a unique, extremely painful, and serious medical problem in the backcountry. Some wilderness-first-aid courses will teach you how to reset a dislocated shoulder in the field; take a course if you want to learn how to do this. But bear in mind that there is a danger of causing further injury to the victim, and the victim will need rapid evacuation.

Altitude illness, or acute mountain sickness (AMS), takes a few different forms and can be mistaken for hypothermia, severe dehydration, or even the flu. At the least it causes discomfort, and at its worst can be fatal. Of particular concern are two conditions of advanced altitude sickness—**h**igh-**a**ltitude **p**ulmonary **e**dema, or HAPE, and **h**igh-**a**ltitude **c**erebral **e**dema, or HACE—both of which can lead quickly to death.

How well one adjusts to high altitudes depends on how much time is devoted to acclimatizing—slowly advancing to higher altitudes to allow the body to adjust to the reduced amount of oxygen drawn in each breath—and on each individual's biological capacity for acclimating, which cannot be predicted but can be learned through experience. No matter how diligent you are about acclimatizing, everyone has a limit on how high they can go before experiencing symptoms.

Level of fitness does not affect how well one adjusts to altitude. In fact, one theory holds that fit persons can suffer altitude illness sooner than less-fit hikers because the fit person tends to walk faster, with a more accelerated respiratory rate, which is suspected of contributing to altitude illness.

Avoidance is fairly simple: Gain altitude gradually in order to acclimatize. Walk slowly enough to maintain a comfortable rhythm of deep breathing, and consume plenty of fluids. Above roughly 8,000 or 10,000 feet, sleep no more than 1,000 feet higher each night than the night before, but each day walk to an altitude higher than your camp.

Symptoms can occur at 8,000 feet or lower in people not acclimatized, and include a painful headache, difficulty breathing, loss of appetite, nausea, and unnatural weariness. An advanced symptom is ataxia, or a loss of balance that resembles drunkenness. In addition, HAPE is characterized by extremely labored breathing and the sound of gurgling, and HACE by severe headache, possible hallucinations, and a rapidly deteriorating level of consciousness.

Treatment depends on the severity. Symptoms may wane and disappear by resting for several hours or a day at a particular altitude; otherwise, descend until feeling better. The drug acetazolamide, widely sold by prescription in the United States under the name Diamox, can reduce symptoms of altitude illness and facilitate acclimatization. Severe or unabated symptoms require descent. HAPE and HACE demand immediate evacuation of the victim to low altitude and hospitalization.

Bee stings result in no more than a sharp pain and localized swelling that heals within a day for many people. But a person allergic to bee venom can suffer a reaction known as **anaphylaxis,** which can be fatal if not treated. Avoidance is difficult because bees sometimes build nests in places where we cannot see them or don't see them until it's too late. (I've been stung by bees emerging from unseen ground nests as well as nests in backcountry outhouses—the latter circumstances being particularly unpleasant.)

Anyone with an allergy to any stinging insects such as wasps, yellow jackets, and bees should be aware of it and carry a bee-sting kit, or Anakit, including at least one epinephrine pen and antihistamine tablets.

Symptoms of anaphylaxis include rapidly reddening skin, itching, hives, and difficulty breathing; they may be mild at first but can advance to the point of cutting off the victim's airway, leading to death. Treatment of a person with difficulty breathing involves first giving the victim antihistamines if he is able to swallow, because antihistamines act longer than epinephrine and may alleviate the symptoms. If the antihistamines don't work, inject the epinephrine into a muscle—not a vein (read the instructions before going into the backcountry). Epinephrine is a short-duration treatment, though, and a second epi pen may be needed. Evacuate a victim whose symptoms persist.

Burns are caused in the backcountry by everything from spilled boiling water to lightning, and they can be minor or life-threatening. Avoidance is a combination of caution, awareness of risks (see Lightning section below), and luck. Symptoms depend on the extent and location of burns. With burns around the face and neck, watch for airway obstruction. Watch for symptoms of shock brought on by severe dehydration or fluid loss.

Treatment begins with removing the source of the burn, then putting the fire out. The latter includes understanding that burns can worsen even after the source of the burn has been removed; you have to thoroughly flush or cold-soak a burn and cool it. Remove a watch and jewelry from a burned area immediately, monitor vital signs, and ensure that a burn is not restricting circulation. Do not pop blisters. Apply a moist, cool dressing to a superficial burn, and a dry, sterile dressing to a burn that is leaking fluids. Evacuate anyone with blistered, leaking, or charred flesh the size of a quarter or larger. Keep the patient hydrated and guard against hypothermia.

Lightning strikes can occur randomly but also exhibit consistent patterns. Avoidance entails understanding where and when you are in danger. Thunderheads release the most electrical activity on their approach, especially within a mile. Calculate the distance of a thunderhead by counting the seconds between a flash of lightning and the ensuing rumble of thunder; five seconds equal one mile. Thunderheads move at roughly 20 to 25 mph, so a thunderhead four miles off will be within a mile of you in only about ten minutes.

Lightning strikes the highest object in an area—a tall tree, summit, or ridge crest—and its voltage will splash and flow downhill like water. Avoid close proximity to tall objects or high ground. Stay out of gullies and stream beds, overhangs and shallow caves, or even an open meadow where you are the highest object. If possible, get below treeline and find low ground among short trees, away from tall trees, cliffs, and water. Sit or squat on a pack or pad with your feet together to minimize injury from a ground current.

Symptoms often include unconsciousness, lack of respiration even though the heart may (or may not) still be beating, burns, and a host of potential trauma like broken bones. Treatment requires quick recognition of what has happened. With multiple victims, give priority to those who are unconscious and not breathing. Resuscitate a nonbreathing patient and monitor vital signs. Look for and treat burns, remembering that they are often small and superficial and that there is probably an entrance and exit wound. Lightning-strike victims are safe to touch—they do not carry stored electricity in their bodies.

Drowning is commonly caused by improper use or lack of a personal flotation device, a traumatic injury, a medical condition like hypothermia, fatigue or inability to swim, or becoming entrapped in moving water in a boating mishap. The best means of avoidance are always to wear a personal flotation device when boating and stay with a partner when swimming. Make wise decisions at river crossings (see chapter 6). Also, use a rescue line or other object to reach out to someone struggling in water, throw him anything that floats, or get to him in a boat rather than trying to swim to the victim. He may panic when you reach him and struggle with you, and you must never create a second victim—especially yourself.

Symptoms in the majority of victims include water in the lungs, unconsciousness, lack of respiration, possibly no pulse, and vomiting. Treatment begins with immediate CPR, even when there is water in the lungs. If the patient vomits, roll him onto his side, flush out his mouth, then roll him back and resume CPR. If your breaths do not cause his chest to rise and fall, the patient is probably in laryngospasm, which is the spasming of muscles in the throat as the brain's response to water entering the lungs; massage the windpipe area to relax those muscles and continue CPR. Humans, especially young children, can survive long immersions if aggressive CPR begins immediately and is continued until hospitalization.

Long-term Patient Care

In many backcountry accidents, the patient will remain in your care for hours or days. Monitor his condition, and remember to deal with his and your own needs. A conscious person will need to drink, may be able to eat, will probably have to go to the bathroom, and will be at various times hot or cold. Make him comfortable while you watch his condition.

Bear in mind problems that could arise when taking care of a patient for a long time, like infection of a dirty wound. Various backcountry ailments can precipitate or aggravate others. Dehydration often contributes to hypothermia or heat exhaustion and is exacerbated by high altitude or excessive exposure to sun. Severe dehydration and hypothermia cause disorientation, frequently leading to traumatic injury like a bad fall. Hypothermia leads to frostbite. Monitor your patient throughout the evacuation.

Remember this rule: It is always—always—better to let an injured person walk out on his own if possible than to try to carry him out. If you have to carry someone out, do not attempt it without adequate numbers of people. In rough mountain terrain, an adequate number might be around thirty rescuers per mile. Do not underestimate the difficulty of this operation. More often, you will stabilize the patient and send someone for help.

A makeshift litter, or stretcher, can be constructed using a pair of straight and stout branches and a tarp, tent rainfly, or similar large piece of cloth. Lay out the tarp on the ground. Place the two branches shoulder-width apart, centered on the tarp, so that the area of tarp between the branches is not more than one-third of the tarp. Fold the remaining one-third of the tarp on one side over both branches, then fold over the other side of the tarp. When you then lay the patient atop this rig, his weight should hold the tarp in place once you lift him.

Women's Issues

Menstruation need not keep a woman from venturing into the backcountry. You have to pack out any sanitary product, so tampons are a better choice than pads. My wife uses small tampons without applicators for backpacking, meaning much less extraneous packag-

the first-aid kit

A first-aid kit should be prepared with consideration to type of trip, the people on it—for instance, children and persons with medical conditions present special needs—and the destination. Pack everything into a thick, clear plastic zip-lock bag. And remember, simply carrying a first-aid kit does not make you safe; you have to know how to use what's in it.

First-aid-kit basics: two large cravats, two large gauze pads, four four-inch-by-four-inch gauze pads, several one-inch adhesive bandages (band-aids), one roll of one-inch athletic tape, a few safety pins, one six-inch Ace bandage, several alcohol wipes, a tube of povidone iodine ointment (for wound care), moleskin or Spenco Second Skin (for blisters), a knife or scissors, a paper and pencil, and a blank SOAP note form.

Other items might include: lip balm (which should be in your pocket anyway), sunblock, an Anakit (available by prescription), aspirin or an anti-inflammatory, and a SAM splint (a versatile and lightweight splinting device available at many drugstores). A snake-bite kit with antivenin for treatment of bites from poisonous snakes may be a wise addition in very remote desert areas, but at least one national park, Grand Canyon, recommends immediate evacuation of a snake-bite victim rather than treating the person with antivenin.

ing to carry out. After using them, wrap them in a piece of toilet paper and place them in doubled zip-lock bags in your pack. Never bury tampons—they take a long time to decompose, and animals dig them up. Bring ibuprofen for menstrual cramps.

Urinary tract infections tend to be more common in women due to the anatomy of a woman's urethra. In the backcountry, it's tempting as a woman not to use toilet paper after urination so that you don't have to pack out all the used toilet paper. Besides being smelly and uncomfortable, this leads to an increased chance of urinary tract infections, the symptoms of which are a burning sensation while urinating and increased frequency and urgency of urination. Use toilet paper when you urinate, especially if you are prone to urinary tract infections, and pack it out in doubled zip-lock bags. On a short trip, the used toilet paper won't take up much space.

Pregnancy does not have to spell an end to backcountry adventures. Carrying a heavy pack with a hip belt is a bad idea during pregnancy due to the pressure the belt places on your baby and your uterus. But it's OK to day-hike or go out overnight with a small pack that does not have a hip belt.

Don't exercise harder during pregnancy than you did before becoming pregnant. The exception to this rule is that if you were a couch potato before becoming pregnant, start a gentle walking routine or hiking on flat trails, gradually increasing your distances. Don't exert yourself to the point where you cannot carry on a conversation comfortably. Don't exercise in very hot weather. And don't venture too far from your doctor for prolonged periods of time either in the first trimester, when the risk of miscarriage is high, or in the third trimester, when the delivery date is approaching. Consult with your doctor about activity level during pregnancy.

Resources and Training

SOLO (Stonehearth Open Learning Opportunities), P.O. Box 3150, Conway, NH 03818; 888-SOLO-MED or 603-447-6711; www.stonehearth.com

Wilderness Medical Associates, RFD 2, Box 890, Bryant Pond, ME 04219; 800-742-2931 or 207-665-2707; www.wildmed.com

Wilderness Medicine Institute of the National Outdoor Leadership School (NOLS), P.O. Box 9, Pitkin, CO 81241; 970-641-3572; www.wildernessmed.com. National Outdoor Leadership School, 288 Main St., Lander, WY 82520; 307-332-1228 or 307-332-6973; fax 307-332-8811; www.lnt.org

chapter
eleven

WINTER IN THE BACKCOUNTRY

I **STEPPED LIGHTLY** on the unbroken snow, hoping by the force of will to make myself weightless. The crust held my heavy mountaineering boots afloat more than half the time. But on every third or fourth step, it would collapse with a sound like a truck rolling over a hill of potato chips, and I'd sink knee-deep. Pitching forward off-balance, I'd crash the other leg through the crust and plunge in up to that thigh. Sweating from the sudden burst of energy, I'd extract myself from the post holes and start again.

Glancing over at my friend Gerry, I saw he wasn't having any easier a time of it.

It had been my suggestion that we wouldn't need snowshoes on the Appalachian Trail in western Maine on the first weekend of spring. It hadn't snowed in at least a couple of weeks, so I figured what was on the ground would be as firm as a hardwood floor. But if that prognostication had missed wildly, we were certainly correct in anticipating a wintry and wilderness-like experience on such a remote stretch of the AT in Maine—where April, not March, comes in like a lion and goes out like a lamb.

Our perhaps overly ambitious plan had been to traverse a nearly fourteen-mile leg of the trail in two days, an itinerary we abandoned after we lost the first morning to cruising up and down lonely back roads and scrambling ten-foot-high roadside snowbanks just finding the trail.

With visions of floundering for days in deep drifts if we continued with our plan, we opted instead to pack in about a mile and camp for the night. Next day, we'd climb Old Blue Mountain and hike out the same way.

Far from population centers, that stretch of the AT may have seen no human visitors since October. There was not a boot print or snowshoe or ski track to be seen—a reminder that should something go wrong, there may be no one strolling along to find us for weeks.

Wind-driven snow smeared tree trunks, camouflaging the AT's white blazes. Some blazes were simply buried under drifts five and six feet deep. Countless blown-down trees obscured the way. We pushed and kicked through the thick canopy of branches pressing down overhead and the cooked-spaghetti tangle of blowdowns. We stopped frequently, scanning the woods until one of us sighted a blaze. When that failed, we'd backtrack to the last blaze in search of a trail corridor through the trees.

As we gained elevation, the arctic wind gathered fury. But the spring sun burned hot enough to redden skin and the wind disappeared and reappeared frequently with the shifting topography, making it difficult to find a comfortable clothing combination. Deciding that sweating was preferable to shivering in the wind, I kept my shell on.

Finally, at a ramp of ice, we snapped crampons onto our boots and crunched upward, above the highest trees, until the ground leveled out at the summit. Stinging gusts powerful enough to knock us off balance exploded randomly from the tide of air. Leaning into the wind, we strolled around to take in the views, shouting to hear one another above the brawling wind. To the north, the AT continued over Elephant and Bemis Mountains and the white-capped peaks of the Saddleback Range and Bigelow Mountain. To the south, the Mahoosuc Range thrust snowy backs into the sky.

Only the sun's warmth allowed us to last twenty minutes up there.

Then Gerry and I gave one another a brief nod, our signal that it was time to fight our way back down the mountain, retracing steps already erased by the wind in many places. We would pack up our camp and reach the road by midafternoon—covering barely five miles in nearly eight hours, and finishing the day physically whipped.

Winter transforms the backcountry into a new place, stunningly white and hypnotically silent. But extra care is needed to travel through the backcountry safely. This chapter will cover some fundamentals of winter backcountry travel.

Staying Warm and Dry

Traveling safely in the cold, for a day or several days, begins with a **solid foundation in three-season backcountry skills.** While remaining comfortable in deep cold certainly demands broader skills—and the colder it is, the more refined your skills have to be—on a basic level it entails meticulous adherence to the principals of three-season travel. Winter's harsher environment simply allows you much less wiggle room for error.

Pay even closer attention than in warmer months to slight changes in your comfort level, or the comfort of companions. Never delay taking whatever steps are necessary to avoid overheating or getting cold, even if that means stopping repeatedly to adjust your clothing. If your entire body feels cold, try several minutes of vigorous activity like walking uphill or skiing, or crawling into a sleeping bag. For cold feet or hands, try direct contact between the cold body part and warm flesh (an armpit, a companion's warm stomach). Hypothermia and frostbite are ever-present threats (see chapter 10).

The adequate consumption of **food and fluids** is critical to staying warm and keeping your energy up and your head clear. Your body's caloric needs increase in the cold, and you dehydrate quickly without realizing it, which can lead to hypothermia. Drink at least as much and as frequently as in warm weather, and eat more food more frequently than you would on a warm day (see chapters 4 and 5). A hot drink in an insulated water bottle warms a belly nicely on a cold day. Anytime you feel a chill, take a drink and eat something like a big chocolate bar. One of the benefits of winter is that no food goes bad—you can bring along anything you like.

Use wide-mouthed plastic water bottles, whose caps do not freeze easily. Insulate them with any of the bottle insulators available in stores, or even with an old wool sock. Pack them close to your body inside your pack, so your body heat helps prevent the water from freezing. Standing them upside-down will ensure that ice forms in the bottom and doesn't freeze the cap on.

You already know how to **layer clothing** to stay comfortable in changing temperatures and weather conditions (see chapter 3). The sure sign of a winter novice is someone who's overdressed or wearing any cotton, which should be banished from the winter backcountry wardrobe. Start out at the trailhead in just enough layers to be comfortable, but shed clothing as soon as you begin to feel a little

Winter travel opens up a new realm of experience. (Mt. Adams, NH)

perspiration. Find the right combination of exertion level and clothing layers to avoid perspiring heavily, because wet skin and clothing will not only make you cold; in winter they pose a serious risk. You may need to slow your pace—with heavier boots and clothing, and more stuff in your pack, moving in winter is usually more strenuous than in summer.

Anticipate and adjust before you start overheating or growing chilled. If you're about to start a steep climb, remove a layer before you begin sweating. Conversely, if you're about to emerge from the protection of trees onto an exposed, windy slope, put your shell layer on before stepping out into the wind. Any time you stop for even a few minutes, put on a warm hat and a jacket, because being immobile in temperatures below freezing cools your body within minutes.

Wear whatever clothing combination works for you. For example, a waterproof-breathable jacket might be all you need over a synthetic jersey while moving uphill in a light snow with no wind and a temperature in the twenties. Or with no precipitation or wind and a similarly mild temperature, you might be in shirt sleeves while your partner wears a light fleece jacket. But beware of environmental conditions that can lead to hypothermia and watch for early symptoms of it (see chapters 3 and 10).

Remember the adage, "If your feet are cold, put on a hat." Most body-heat lost is through your head. Carry an assortment of warm headwear like an earband, a balaclava, a neck gaiter, and a toasty wool or fleece hat for varied weather conditions.

Your extremities—**hands, fingers, feet, toes**—are particularly susceptible to cold and frostbite because of their distance from your heart and exposure to wind, snow, and cold ground. Except on days well above freezing, you will need warm winter or mountaineering boots (see chapter 2). Wear a thin synthetic liner sock under a heavy sock of wool and synthetic blend, and gaiters (preferably waterproof and breathable) to keep snow out of your boots and help keep your feet warm. In extreme cold, try using a vapor-barrier layer in your boot or socks, which is a nonbreathable and waterproof layer that traps moisture but keeps out cold; a simple plastic bag pulled over your foot before you put on your boot can work.

Layer your gloves and mittens, from a synthetic liner glove to a windproof and preferably waterproof-breathable shell mitten. Experiment with warm middle layers of gloves and/or mittens made of fleece or wool to see which combinations suit your needs, always making sure that the glove or mitten size will fit into your layering system. Always err on the side of having too many gloves and mittens rather than not enough.

Keep articles of clothing in handy places to make quick adjustments more easily in changing conditions. Carry gloves, mittens, hat, and earband in accessible pockets to swap on the move. Have your shell and/or fleece jacket on top inside your pack. It's also better to wear clothing that allows temperature adjustments, like a shell jacket or parka with armpit zippers, or pants with full-length side zippers, for ventilation. Middle layers of different weights—such as a lightweight fleece vest in combination with a heavier fleece jacket—allow flexibility for varying temperatures and conditions.

Clothing choices should reflect the greater risk of traveling the backcountry in winter as well as a knowledge of the environment you are entering. Dark, full-coverage sunglasses are almost always required to protect your eyes from the harsh glare of sunlight reflecting off

Backcountry travel in the winter requires warm clothing to avoid frostbite and hypothermia. (Mt. Lafayette, NH)

snow. Goggles are necessary in deep cold and strong winds to keep eyes from freezing shut. A waterproof-breathable jacket is virtually indispensable in winter, certainly above treeline or on a trip of more than one day. It should have a hood that extends far enough to shield your face. Your winter ensemble should include wind protection for your entire body, including a face mask if needed for extreme windchill. Take more extra layers than you expect to need, just in case.

Environmental Hazards

Besides what can sometimes be a constant struggle to stay warm, winter presents other hazards. One is the enhanced difficulty of **navigating and following a trail,** even on a route you've done in other seasons. Beginners are wise to stick to popular trails with a distinct ski, boot, or snowshoe track to follow. Many of the skills discussed in chapter 6 apply to winter as well.

As my story at the start of this chapter illustrates, following a remote trail can be difficult or even impossible. Storms blow trees down, and there are no trail crews removing that debris in winter. Blazes, cairns, and other trail markers get buried by deep snow. The trail corridor becomes hard to distinguish when you're walking atop several feet of snow, elevating you into the canopy of branches that would be high overhead in summer. You can't see the beaten treadway when the ground is covered with snow.

Watch closely for blazes or other trail markers, and if you go unusually far without seeing one, stop and look around. Backtrack if necessary to the last marker. When trail markers are hidden, look for the trail corridor through the trees, which is generally at least three or four feet wide and devoid of vegetation. When a trail is impossible to follow, or where one does not exist, good map and compass skills are necessary to plot your course (see chapter 6).

Anticipate potential route problems and prepare accordingly. Following a good trail or a route you know well can be faster on a firm surface of snow in winter—especially on skis—than it is in warmer months. But you might also be slowed by any number of factors, from the greater weight of your gear and clothing to soft snow. And days are short.

In pre-trip planning, find out what you can about the variables that can affect your trip, like snow condition and depth, whether a stream is sufficiently frozen to cross, whether an icy section of trail requires crampons, and whether a storm may have virtually obliterated a trail with blowdowns. If you know a region's climate and recent weather well, you can figure out some of this yourself, but land managers and local clubs are good sources of current information.

Terrain hazards are often hidden in winter, so you have to recognize when you're in an area that presents a certain hazard. In dense evergreen forests that receive lots of snow, so-called "spruce traps" are a serious danger, especially to anyone traveling alone. They are created when falling snow piles up atop the dense branches of saplings, burying the sapling but leaving air pockets beneath the snow surface. What looks like snow-covered ground when you're walking atop it will collapse beneath your feet, and you'll find yourself wallowing in powder with nothing firm underfoot, and possibly nothing to grab to pull yourself out. Either stick to the trail or tread carefully and watch for telltale crowns of evergreen needles poking up through the snow that may indicate a spruce trap. Space yourselves so no more than one person falls into a spruce trap.

Snow has an annoying predisposition to inconsistency. You may be walking easily on a solid crust one moment, post-holing to your thighs the next. Be careful, because post-holing abruptly with your weight lurching forward can result in an ankle or knee injury, or a hand injury when you reach out blindly to catch yourself. Similarly, a snow bridge over a creek or atop talus can be deceptively thin enough to break through, causing injury. Stay alert, recognizing when you may be on snow that's atop water or talus. If so, probe carefully ahead with a ski pole.

Skis and snowshoes distribute your weight over a greater surface area, reducing the chance of breaking through a snow bridge or falling into a spruce trap. Ski poles provide tremendous relief to your legs, knees, and lower back whether on skis or snowshoes.

Ice climbing, mountaineering, and backcountry skiing in steep terrain or on a glacier require technical equipment and knowledge in their use. Unless you have the proper equipment and training, avoid any terrain where avalanche is a risk. That broadly includes slopes pitched at an angle between 25° and 55°. Many people overestimate slope angle, so if you're at all unsure about avalanche risk, either consult with a management agency or choose another route.

Weather is a primary concern in winter. The advice offered in chapter 6 applies to winter as well, but remember that winter's cold

Winter weather can create obstacles, like the debris from this ice storm. (Mt. Hedgehog, NH)

Making camp and preparing food becomes much more difficult when temperatures drop. (Flagstaff Lake, ME)

makes bad weather that much more threatening. Don't extend yourself beyond your skill level, especially when the weather looks questionable.

The enhanced risks of backcountry travel in winter's cold logically dictate a higher level of preparedness for something going wrong. Base decisions about what safety gear to carry on where you are going and the implications of an injury that far from the nearest road. If help is hours away, you would have to keep an immobilized injured person warm, dry, well fed, and hydrated. Even on day trips, a party may want to divide among its members a space blanket, one sleeping bag and foam pad, and a stove and cook pot for melting snow, besides ample extra clothing.

Many of the principles covered in chapter 7 apply to winter camping as well, except that in winter the proper clothing and gear become even more critical (see above, and chapters 2 and 3), as does a greater diligence to actively taking whatever steps necessary to stay warm. A tent must be sturdy enough to stand up to strong winds and heavy snowfall, although you should regularly clear accumulating snow from any tent. Depending on the region and time of year, your sleeping bag should be rated at least down to 0° and perhaps to -20° or lower—remember, that bag is your last line of defense against the cold. Most butane-propane cartridge stoves will not burn in temperatures below freezing (see chapter 2), and a second stove is always a good idea on a winter camping trip.

These gear suggestions only scratch at the surface of what you need to know about sleeping outside in winter. There are many other little tricks and skills to learn, too many to cover in a book devoted to three-season backcountry travel. Learn from experienced winter campers. See also *Winter Camping* by Stephen Gorman, (AMC Books).

Most importantly, whenever heading into the backcountry in winter, make conservative decisions (see chapter 9). Winter foils the best-laid plans, so never assume you will accomplish what you set out to do (see Be Flexible section of chapter 1). Know when to change your objective and when to turn around and go home.

chapter
twelve

OUTDOOR ADVENTURE PHOTOGRAPHY

HAVING A PHOTOGRAPHIC RECORD *of the beautiful places we visit has always been a goal of backcountry travelers. But don't be intimidated by the term "outdoor adventure photography." It is, simply, shooting photos outdoors. Photography has always been, and always will be, the art of capturing a given moment of light. Its practitioners have been, and always will be, people who pursue photography at widely varying levels of expertise.*

Photographing the outdoors, and people engaged in physical activity outdoors, does present certain challenges, though, both in terms of the photographer's environment and the huge variations in light one can encounter. No book or single chapter can cover the subject completely—I studied photography for four years and have spent nearly two decades since then trying to improve my skills. My goal here is to provide beginners with some fundamentals and intermediate-level shutterbugs with tips on improving their photos.

Cameras, Lenses, Film

Two basic types of camera are most practical for backcountry use:

A **35mm SLR**, or single-lens reflex camera, enables high-quality photos with relatively lightweight equipment. Modern SLRs are capable of performing a variety of specialized shooting functions; yet anyone willing to spend a little time with one can master its use. They permit you manually to set the camera's shutter speed and f-stop for certain lighting situations or results, while having automatic-exposure settings that allow you to simply point and shoot. Amateurs with a real interest in photography who want to be able to shoot in virtually any light will prefer an SLR over a point-and-shoot. Autofocus is a common feature and worth the expense (see Lenses below). A built-in flash is a handy feature which can improve exposures in daylight as well as low light, although detachable flash units are usually more powerful and versatile (see time of day below).

Point-and-shoot cameras come in many kinds and are increasingly versatile. While some are as pricey as a good SLR, they are generally cheaper, lighter, smaller, and easier to use. But they do not offer the control over exposure and shutter speed, the lens versatility, or as many specialized shooting functions as an SLR. Most point-and-shoots have a built-in flash and a small zoom lens. This type of camera is designed for the person who wants decent photos without having to lug around a lot of stuff or spend much time learning how to use the camera.

Lenses come in two basic types: fixed focal-length lenses and zoom lenses. Zoom lenses are named for their ability to "zoom" in on a subject or pull back for a wider view with a twist of the lens barrel. Fixed lenses don't do that—they give you one perspective, one angle on and distance from the subject. Fixed lenses have three advantages over zooms: They are a little smaller and lighter, a bit sharper focusing, and more versatile in low-light situations—unless you get a very expensive zoom.

But zoom lens advantages outweigh their disadvantages for photographing outdoor activities because of their versatility in shooting a moving subject or a quickly changing scene. Many zooms are small and light enough for backcountry travel. While image sharpness varies among all lens models and is something to

Outdoor photography can add to your enjoyment of the backcountry. (Elm Mountains, CO)

compare when shopping, it is also affected by the photographer's skills, and minute quality differences between zooms and fixed lenses are in reality not easily noticed. In some low-light situations, the photographer can compensate for a zoom's inferior versatility by using a tripod or a flash.

For outdoor photography, if you own one zoom, get a wide-to-medium-length lens with a low end between 24mm and 35mm and a high end between 85mm and 120mm. For a second zoom, get a medium-to-long length of 80mm to 200mm or 300mm. Lenses that range wider than these examples often compromise too much sharpness and exposure versatility. In fixed–focal-length lenses, start with one wide-angle lens, like a 24mm or 28mm, and one medium-length lens, like a 105mm or 120mm. The exception to this advice is wildlife photography, for which lenses of 500mm or longer are ideal.

Auto-focus lenses, either fixed focal-length or zoom, vary in how quickly they can identify and lock on to the subject of your photo, and the importance of precision auto-focusing may be one of the most important factors in choosing a camera. Any reputable camera shop will let you load your own film into one or more of their cameras and field-test it outside their shop before deciding what to buy. Test the lens optics—how sharp an image it takes—by shooting a subject with fine details and sharp lines up close, exposing several frames of film at the full range of f-stops on the lens. Test the auto-focus by shooting a moving subject, like a friend on a bike moving across the frame as well as directly toward you, at various distances and focal lengths.

A brief word about **film**: Slide film provides higher quality than print film, especially professional slide film, which has a shorter shelf life than commercial film, should be kept refrigerated before use, and is usually purchased in bulk (see photo-magazine ads). Advanced photo system, or APS, film offers convenience while compromising quality.

Taking Photos

Poor photo **composition** is the most common mistake of amateurs. Think about what you want the photo to convey. To depict the grandeur and awesome scale of a place, place someone distant from you in the frame; she will look tiny compared to the surroundings. If the objective is to capture someone in action, fill up the frame—top to bottom, side to side—with the person. Don't be afraid of getting too close to your subject. Avoid dead space in a photo, that is, anything that does not enhance the image—such as too much blank sky or uninteresting ground. Don't stick your subject in the middle of a photo. Think of your photo as divided in thirds, and place a person in the right or left third in a horizontal. In composing a vertical scenic photo of distant mountains, shoot with a wide-angle lens, with a rock or wildflowers large in the foreground and bottom third of the image. To improve your own photo composition, look at good photos in books and magazines and see how they were composed.

Look for pictures that offer a unique perspective. (Symmetry Couloir in the Tetons, WY)

Exposure is the amount of light hitting the frame of film at the moment a photo is taken. It is determined by two factors, or camera settings: how large an opening the light passes through in your lens (the f-stop, or aperture setting), and how long the shutter is open (shutter speed). Any adjustment up or down in the shutter speed requires a corresponding adjustment to the f-stop to maintain a correct exposure, and vice-versa.

Use the aperture to manipulate **depth of field**—or the amount of your photo that will be in focus. To reduce depth of field, shoot with a medium-length or long lens (see above) at a low f-stop number (or large aperture opening). This effect is nice, for instance, to slightly blur mountains behind a backpacker who's in sharp focus. For maximum depth of field—for instance, to get everything in a scenic photo in focus—shoot at a higher f-stop.

Give priority to the shutter speed when shooting **a subject in motion.** Someone walking often can be frozen in motion at a speed of 1/125 of a second or faster; a runner will require at least 1/250. A moving subject also blurs more easily when it's close to the camera. Some blurring of the subject can create a desirable effect of implied motion: try shooting a cyclist at 1/60 of a second, or panning—moving your camera with the cyclist as you shoot at 1/15 or 1/30.

With an SLR, the general rule is never to shoot at a shutter speed lower than your lens focal length. For instance, if your zoom is at 28mm, with a steady hand you can shoot at 1/30 of a second without getting image blur from camera shake. When shooting with a 200mm lens, you need a shutter speed of 1/250, and so on.

The **time of day** is important when shooting outdoors. At midday, the overhead sun casts a flat, unattractive light over the land, and any shadows become exaggerated in photos. The most appealing light, for color and contrast, is when the sun is low, just after dawn and before sunset. Use a flash to provide "fill" light where it's needed, such as to reduce harsh contrast on a person in the foreground when the sun is high, or to brighten the foreground in low light.

For most outdoor photography, except in very low light or on gray days, I use a **polarizing filter,** which enhances color by

Use a human subject to add some perspective to a shot. (Adirondacks, NY)

reducing glare. Shooting perpendicular to the sun, rather than into or straight away from it, allows the polarizer to work most efficiently and gives you better contrast.

Lastly, **protect your camera gear.** Carry it in a pack that is at least water-resistant while allowing you immediate access to the camera. If there's any chance of it getting wet, tuck the camera away in doubled zip-lock plastic bags.

ABOUT THE AUTHOR

MICHAEL LANZA is a freelance outdoor writer and photographer. He regularly writes about outdoor destinations, reviews gear, and contributes feature stories and photos to *AMC Outdoors, Appalachia, Backpacker, Outdoor Explorer, Outside,* and *Walking*. He has written a guidebook to hiking trails in New England. He formerly served as interim editor of *AMC Outdoors*, syndicated a weekly outdoor column to 20 newspapers around New England, and cohosted a call-in program on the outdoors on New Hampshire Public Radio. A New England native, he earned a B.S. in photojournalism at Syracuse University and spent ten years as a newspaper reporter and editor.

He has hiked, backpacked, and climbed throughout New England, the Rocky Mountains from Colorado to Alberta, the desert Southwest, the Sierra, and the Northwest. Other favorite activities include road- and mountain-biking, nordic and backcountry skiing, snowshoeing, canoeing, and rafting.

He lives in Boise, Idaho, with his wife, Dr. Penny Beach, and plays as often as possible in Idaho's mountains and canyons.

ABOUT THE APPALACHIAN MOUNTAIN CLUB

SINCE 1876, the Appalachian Mountain Club has helped people experience the majesty and solitude of the Northeast outdoors. We offer outdoor skills workshops, guided trips, and lodging options for all levels of outdoor adventuring. Our conservation programs include trail maintenance, air and water quality research, and advocacy work to preserve the special outdoor places we love and enjoy for future generations.

Join the Adventure!

Take a hike, ride a bike, paddle a canoe. We believe that people who enjoy breathing fresh air, climbing mountains, splashing in streams, and walking on trails have more fun and take better care of the outdoors. Join the fun today. Call 617-523-0636 for membership information.

Outdoor Adventures

From beginner backpacking to advanced backcountry skiing, we teach outdoor skills workshops to suit your interest and experience.

If you prefer the company of others and skilled leaders, we also offer guided hiking and paddling trips. Our five outdoor education centers guarantee year-round adventures.

Huts, Lodges, and Visitor Centers

With accommodations throughout the Northeast, you don't have to travel to the ends of the earth to see nature's beauty and experience unique wilderness lodging. Accessible by car or on foot, our lodges and huts are perfect for families, couples, groups, and individuals.

Books and Maps

We can lead you to the best hiking, biking, skiing, and paddling destinations from Maine to North Carolina. With more than 50 books and maps published, we're your definitive resource for discovering wonderful outdoor places. For ordering information call 1-800-262-4455.

Check us out online at www.outdoors.org, where there's lots going on.

Appalachian Mountain Club
5 Joy Street
Boston, MA 02108-1490
617-523-0636

INDEX

A

ABC (Airway/Breathing/Circulation) procedure, 192
Accidents. *See* Emergencies/first aid
Altimeter, 121
Altitude, high, 8–9
   altitude sickness (acute mountain sickness), 206–7
Anaphylaxis, 207–8
Animals. *See* Wildlife
Appalachian Mountain Club (AMC), information about, 233–35

B

Backpack(s). *See* Pack(s)
Bears
   black, 165–66
   food, protecting your, 165–66
   grizzly (brown), 166, 168, 170
Bison, 172
Bivy bags, 53
Black flies, 173–74
Bleeding, 202–3
Blisters, 201–2
Boot(s), 38–40
   care of, 44
   fitting, 43
   lacing, for off-trail venturing, 135–36
   midsoles, 43
   outsoles, 42–43
   types of, 40–41

Boot(s) *cont.*
   waterproof-breathable liners, 42
Burns, 208
Bushwhacking. *See* Off-trail, venturing

C

Camera lenses, 225–27
Cameras, 225
Campfires
   Leave No Trace guidelines, 157
   regulations and restrictions, 155
   types of, 155–57
Camping
   availability of campsites, 9
   avoiding cold, 149–51
   introductory anecdote, 144–45
   low-impact, 152–55
   occupying your free time while, 151
   permits for, 14–15
   roughing it comfortably, 148–51
   selecting a site, 145–46, 148
   sharing the backcountry, 160–61
   waste, human, 158–60
Canyon hiking, 123, 125
Cat holes, 158–60
Cell phones, 142
Children
   food and, 107
   hiking and, 140
   water and, 97–98
Climate, 7–8
   clothing and, 84, 86

Index   235

Clothing
  boots, 38–44, 135–36
  buying, 80–81
  care of, 81–82
  climate and, 84, 86
  dressing for success, 69–70
  ethical choices, 83
  extra change of, 149
  fitting, 78–79
  gloves/mittens, 217–18
  hats, 217
  introductory anecdote, 67–68
  jackets, 79–80, 217
  keeping articles handy, 218
  layering, 70, 72–73, 215, 217–18
  off-trail, 133–34
  pants, 80
  sleeping bag, what to wear in a, 150
  socks, 72
  synthetics and wool versus cotton, 73–75
  technical outerwear, 75–76, 78–80
  waterproof outerwear, 75–76
  waterproof-breathable outerwear, 76, 78
  water-resistant/breathable outerwear, 78
  what and what not to take, 83–84
  winter, 215, 217–19
Compass, using a
  bearing, taking a, 120–21
  components, 118
  faceplate, 118–19
  declination, 118
  orienting your map, 119–20
  plotting a course, 120
Computers and other personal electronic devices, 143
Cookware, 64
Cotton versus synthetics and wool, 73–75
Courtesy, 141–42

D

Decision-making. *See* Leadership and decision-making

Deer, 172
Dehydrated fruits and vegetables, 106
Dislocations (injuries), 205–6
Distance, planning your, 7
Dogs, 143, 161
Drowning, 209

E

Elevation gain/loss, 9
Emergency(ies)/first aid
  ABC (Airway/Breathing/Circulation) procedure, 192
  altitude sickness (acute mountain sickness), 206–7
  anaphylaxis, 207–8
  bee stings, 207–8
  bleeding, 202–3
  blisters, 201–2
  burns, 208
  dislocations (injuries), 205–6
  drowning, 209
  femur, broken, 206
  first-aid kit, contents of, 211
  fractures, 205–6
  frostbite, 200
  head count, 191
  head injury, 193–94
  heat exhaustion, 196
  heatstroke, 196
  how much should you know?, 189–90
  hypothermia, 198, 200
  introductory anecdote, 186–87
  leadership and, 184, 190
  lightning, 208–9
  long-term patient care, 210
  lost/separated, what to do if you become, 125–26
  mechanism of injury, determining, 193
  menstruation, 210–11
  patient assessment, 191–95
  planning for, 23
  pregnancy, 212
  reacting to an, 190–91
Emergency(ies)/first aid

Emergency(ies)/first aid *cont.*
  response time and physical separation from civilization, 187–88
  SAMPLE (Symptoms/Allergies/ Medications/Past history/Last food and fluids/Events) history, 194–95
  shock, 203–4
  shoulder, dislocated, 206
  SOAP (Subject analysis/Objective analysis/ Assessment/Plan) note, 195
  soft-tissue injuries, 202–3
  spinal-cord injury, 193
  sprains, 204
  strains, 204–5
  strangers who need help, 184–85
  sunburn, 196, 198
  survey of the scene, 190–91
  urinary tract infections, 211–12
Equipment. *See* Gear
Ethics. *See also* Rules, playing by the
  clothing and, 83
  hiking and, 110–12
  human-animal encounters and, 164–65
  low-impact camping, 152–55

F

Fall, self-arresting a, 135
Feet, protecting, 217–18
Femur, broken, 206
Film, photographic, 227
Fingers, protecting, 217–18
First aid. *See* Emergency(ies)/first aid
Fitness preparation, 15–17
Flexibility, 24–25
Flora, nasty, 174–75
Food
  bears, protecting it from, 165–66
  children and, 107
  in cold temperatures, 107, 215
  dehydrated fruits and vegetables, 106
  introductory anecdote, 99–100
  for long-distance hiking, 101–2
  Minimalist School vs. Imaginative School, 105–6

Food *cont.*
  planning your meals, 100–101
  plants, edible wild, 107
  preparing meals, 102–3
  resupply of, 101–2
  what and what not to take, 103–7
Fractures, 205–6
Frostbite, 200

G

Gear. *See also* Clothing
  altimeter, 121
  compass, 118–21
  cookware, 64
  first-aid kit, 211
  GPS unit, 121–22
  introductory anecdote, 27
  maps, 5, 6, 116–20
  miscellaneous, list of, 64–66
  organizing and checking your, 17–19
  packs, 29, 31–35, 37–38, 136
  photographic, 225–27, 229, 231
  sleeping bags, 51–56, 148–51
  sleeping pads, 57–58
  stoves, 58–63, 150
  tents, 44–51, 149–51
  tips on buying, 30
  traveling with your, 21–23
  what and what not to take, 19–21
Gloves/mittens, 217–18
GPS unit, 121–22
Group size, 142, 161
Guidebooks, 5, 6

H

Hands, protecting, 217–18
Hats, 217
Head injury, 193–94
Heat exhaustion, 196
Heatstroke, 196
Hiking
  canyon, 123, 125
  children and, 140
  ethical choices, 110–12

Hiking *cont.*
  introductory anecdote, 108–10
  Leave No Trace guidelines, 111–12
  lost/separated, what to do if you become, 125–26
  long-distance, 11, 101–2
  navigating, 115–23, 125–26, 133, 137, 219–20
  at night, 137
  off-trail, venturing, 132–36
  older people and, 140
  river crossings, 127–32
  sharing the trail, 13–15, 141–43, 160–61
  solo, 137–40
  walking lightly, 113, 115
  weather and, 126–27
  in winter, 215, 217–20, 222–23
Human violence/other crimes, 175
Human waste, 158–60
Hypothermia, 198, 200

I

Injuries. *See* Emergency(ies)/first aid
Insects, 173–74

J

Jackets, 217
  features of, 79–80
  parka, jacket, or anorak?, 79

L

Layering
  first layer, 70, 72
  middle layers, 72–73
  outer layers, 73
  socks, 72
  in winter, 215, 217–18
Leadership and decision-making. *See also* Emergencies
  anticipating and heading off problems, 180–82
  flexibility, 24–25
  introductory anecdote, 176–78

Leadership and decision-making *cont.*
  knowing when to take charge, 182
  maintaining a positive attitude, 185
  thinking things through, 178–80
Leave No Trace
  campfire guidelines, 157
  group-size guidelines, 161
  hiking guidelines, 111–12
  how to contact the organization, 111
Lightning, 208–9
Long-distance hiking, 11
  food for, 101–2
Lost/separated, what to do if you become, 125–26

M

Map(s), 5, 6
  charting your course on a, 116–18
  orienting your, 119–20
Masses, avoiding the, 12–13
Menstruation, 210–11
Mittens/gloves, 217–18
Moose, 172
Mosquitoes, 173–74
Mountaineering, 134–35
Mountain lions, 170–71

N

Navigating
  altimeter, 121
  charting your course on a map, 116–18
  compass, using a, 118–21
  GPS unit, 121–22
  introductory anecdote, 115–26
  at night, 137
  off-trail, 133
  trails, indistinct and hard-to-follow, 122–23
  in winter, 219–20
Night hiking, 137
No-see-ums, 173–74

O

Off-trail, venturing
  clothing for, 133–34
  defined, 132
  first rule of, 133
  lacing your boots for, 135–36
  loading your pack for, 136
  mountaineering, 134–35
  navigating, 133
  scree, 134
  self-arresting a fall, 135
  snow, 134, 135
  talus, 134
Older people, hiking and, 140
Outerwear. *See* Clothing

P

Pack(s), 29–30
  care of, 38
  covers for, 38
  features of, 34–35
  fitting a, 32, 34
  frames for, 31
  loading and organizing a, 35, 37–38
  off-trail venturing, loading for, 136
  panel-loading, 31–32
  sizes of, by category, 33
  suspension systems for, 32
  top-loading, 32
Pants, 80
Permits, camping, 14–15
Photography, 224
  cameras, 225
  composition, 227
  depth of field, 229
  exposure, 229
  film, 227
  lenses, 225–27
  polarizing filter, 229, 231
  protecting your gear, 231
  subject in motion, 229
  time of day, 229
  tips for taking photos, 227, 229, 231
Planning a trip
  avoiding the masses, 12–13

Planning a trip *cont.*
  choosing a route, 3, 5–12
  emergencies, 23
  fitness preparation, 15–17
  flexibility, 24–25
  introductory anecdote, 1–3
  organizing and checking your gear, 17–19
  playing by the rules, 13–15, 141–42
  resources, 25–26, 212
  traveling with your gear, 21–23
  what and what not to take, 19–21
Plants
  edible wild, 107
  nasty, 174–75
Poison ivy, 174
Poison oak, 174
Poison sumac, 174
Pregnancy, 212

R

Rescues. *See* Emergencies/first aid
Resources
  backcountry-travel, 25–26
  emergency/first-aid, 212
Right-of-way, yielding the, 141
River crossings
  fording tips, 129–31
  guidelines for safe, 129
  introductory anecdote, 127–28
  tidal waters, 132
Roads, 11–12
Route, choosing a, 3, 5–12
Rules, playing by the, 13–15. *See also* Ethics
    campfires, 155–57
    camping permits, 14–15
    cell phones, 142
    computers and other personal electronic devices, 143
    courtesy, 141–42
    different users and, 141
    dogs, 143, 161
    group size, 142, 161
    Leave No Trace guidelines, 111–12, 157, 161

Rules *cont.*
    yielding the right-of-way, 141

S

SAMPLE (Symptoms/Allergies/ Medications/ Past history/Last food and fluids/Events) history, 194–95
Scorpions, 171–72
Scree, 134
Self-arresting a fall, 135
Separated/lost, what to do if you become, 125–26
Sharing the trail, 13–15, 141–42, 160–61
Shock, 203–4
Shoulder, dislocated, 206
Sleeping bag(s)
    bivy bags, 53
    care of, 55–56
    clothing to wear in a, 150
    down-fill, 52
    extra insulation for, 150–51
    fitting a, 55
    keeping it dry, 148–49
    mummy, 52–53
    shell of a, 53
    synthetic-fill, 51–52
    temperature ratings, 53, 55
    types of, 54
Sleeping pads
    care of, 58
    closed-cell foam, 57
    self-inflating mattresses, 57–58
Snakes, 171
Snow, 134, 135, 219–20, 222–23
SOAP (Subject analysis/Objective analysis/ Assessment/Plan) note, 195
Socks, 72
Soft-tissue injuries, 202–3
Solo hiking, 137–40
Spinal-cord injury, 193
Sprains, 204
Stove(s), 58–59
    boiling time of a, 61
    burn time of a, 61
    butane (canister), 59–60, 62

Stove(s) *cont.*
    care of, 62–63
    conserving fuel, 62
    tent, precautions when using in a, 150
    white-gas (liquid-fuel), 61, 63
Strains, 204–5
Sunburn, 196, 198
Supplies. *See* Food; Gear; Water
Synthetics and wool versus cotton, 73–75

T

Talus, 134
Technical outerwear. *See* Clothing
Tent(s), 44–45
    care of, 49–51
    color of, 48
    condensation in, 151
    cooking in, 150
    designs of, 45, 47
    entry to a, 47
    features, nice, 49
    free-standing, 45
    keeping it dry, 149–50
    poles, 47
    profile of a, 48
    setup, ease of, 48
    sizes of, 45
    types of, 46
    ventilation, 47–48
    vestibule of a, 48
    warmth of, 47–48
Terrain, 7, 220
Thorn-bearing plants, 174–75
Ticks, 174
Tides, 132
Toes, protecting, 217–18
Trails, indistinct and hard-to-follow, 122–23
Trip planning. *See* Planning a trip

U

Urinary tract infections, 211–12

V
Vandalism, 175

W
Water
    availability of sources, 9
    children and, 97–98
    how much to carry, 90–92
    how much to drink and when, 88–90
    introductory anecdote, 87–88
    treatment methods, 92–96
    water bottles vs. hydration systems, 96
Waste, human, 158–60
Weather, hiking and, 126–27
    winter, 220, 222–23
Wildlife, 10–11
    avoiding animal problems, 165–66, 168, 170–73
    bears, 165–66, 168, 170
    bison, 172
    deer, 172
    ethics of human-animal encounters, 164–65
    insects, 173–74
    introductory anecdote, 162–63
    miscellaneous smaller animals, 172–73
    moose, 172
    mountain lions, 170–71
    scorpions, 171–72
    snakes, 171
Winter in the backcountry
    clothing, 215, 217–19
    environmental hazards, 219–20, 222–23
    fluids, 215
    food, 215
    introductory anecdote, 213–14
    staying warm and dry, 215, 217–19
Wool and synthetics versus cotton, 73–75

NOTES

NOTES

NOTES